Precious Little Sleep

ALEXIS DUBIEF

PRECIOUS

LITTLE

SLEEP

The Complete Baby Sleep Guide
for Modern Parents

Second Edition

LOMHARA
PRESS

Precious Little Sleep
The Complete Baby Sleep Guide for Modern Parents
Alexis Dubief

© 2020 Alexis Dubief

Lomhara Press

ISBN 978-0-9975808-2-2 (paperback)
ISBN 978-0-9975808-3-9 (electronic)

Library of Congress Control Number: 2020942136

Cover and interior design by Peter Cocking
Illustrations by Daniel Bradford
Editing by Stephanie Fysh and Arlene Prunkl
Special contributions by Dr. Rebecca Ruid
Legal support by Robert Bertsche

A NOTE TO MY SLEEP-DEPRIVED READERS

I am not a medical professional, and I never have been. Rather, I am an experienced parent. I have worked with many families struggling with sleep issues, and have talked with countless medical professionals. I've also reviewed the hundreds of medical and scientific studies that are referenced in the footnotes—all so that you do not have to do so. (These journal articles are, however, useful tools in case you find yourself in need of literature to put you to sleep.) Even some of the literature out there is contradictory, particularly with regard to the unknown causes of sudden infant death syndrome (SIDS) and the benefits and risks of co-sleeping (which the American Academy of Pediatrics, some 60,000 pediatricians strong, considers an unmitigated hazard).

My goal in this book is to share with you my experience, understandings, and opinions. I cannot warrant or guarantee that following the information in this book will prevent your child from suffering medical injury. Nothing can replace the watchful eye of a loving parent or the expert advice of (and regular visits with) a skilled pediatrician.

My point is this: Nothing in this book should be construed as medical advice, which I am in no way qualified to dispense. No book can replace highly qualified medical care. The advice and strategies I outline may not be the right ones for your situation. Neither I nor my publisher shall be liable for any loss or damage allegedly arising from information provided in this book. When you have concerns about your child's health or sleep patterns, and in addressing your own child's particular sleep issues, you should always check with your pediatrician. That is because we all share one common commitment: that nothing is more important than the safety of your family.

To Yves, Duncan, and Brice.
You guys are better than unicorn magic.

Contents

Preface

~~~~~~~~~~~~~~~~~~

SLEEP IS LIKE air: you don't give it much thought until you can't get enough of it, then it's all you can think about.

It seems that sleep should happen naturally, like pooping. You might, therefore, reasonably assume that babies will simply fall asleep when they need to.

But they don't.

Newborns need a lot of coaching from us to fall asleep. It's easy to do "whatever works" to make that happen for the first few weeks because sleep is often scarce then, and hard to achieve. As those weeks stretch into months, however, the "whatever works" strategy will trap you with crap naps and bad nights.

Many people have experienced discrete periods of severe sleep deprivation—pulling an all-nighter for finals, going through basic training, taking a red-eye—but none of those prepare you for the relentless exhaustion that comes from months or years of parenting a non-sleeping child.

On top of the chronic sleep deprivation is massive stress—the feeling that you are failing your child, because they are *also* chronically sleep deprived. Nothing is more painful than watching your child, whom you adore, go through an entire fussy day of micronaps, or trying to coax an overtired child to sleep at bedtime . . . and then again at

11 p.m., 1 a.m., 2 a.m., etc., all while knowing that your child *needs* to sleep better but feeling lost as to how to help them do so.

A pervasive myth claims that sustained severe sleep deprivation is the price of parenting, one you should quietly endure because you love your children.

But the truth is that healthy sleep is not optional: it's *essential*—for our children and for us. Endless exhaustion is neither necessary nor beneficial. The drive to help your child sleep well is not selfish but rooted in the knowledge that sleep is best for *their* health and well-being.

My Promise to You

I've done my best to create a resource that will give you all the knowledge, tools, and strategies you need to establish healthy sleep for your family. Unfortunately, the realm of infant sleep information is often confusing and full of contradictory advice, making it seem enormously complicated.

But it isn't. It boils down to a half-dozen fundamental goals:

1. Ensuring safe sleep
2. Providing loads of soothing for younger babies
3. Sleeping at the right time
4. Establishing independent sleep
5. Closing the all-night restaurant
6. Being consistent

This book presents strategies that support these goals, and guidelines on how to apply those strategies based on your child's age and temperament and your parenting philosophy. If you follow the advice in this book, you can be confident that you're doing all you can to foster healthy sleep for your family.

How to Use This Book
. . . .

Parents are notoriously short on time for leisure reading. If you're a Level 6 Sleep Wizard, feel free to use the table of contents to skip to the relevant chapters for your situation.

However, most people should just go ahead and read the entire book. Now you're probably thinking, "What *is* this madness? I've been wearing the same underpants for a week, and if I don't have time to deal with *underpants*, I definitely don't have time to read even *half* a book." I hear you, I really do. Also, I'm totally not judging you about the underpants situation.

If reading the whole book is simply impossible and you're the parent of a newborn, focus on
• Chapter 1—Baby Sleep: Essentials
• Chapter 2—The Party That Is Newborn Sleep
• Chapter 5—Baby Sleep Power Tools

If you are the parent of a 4- to 6-month-old, try to carve out time for
• Chapter 1—Baby Sleep: Essentials
• Chapter 3—Bedtime Is the New Happy Hour
• Chapter 4—How Babies Sleep
• Chapter 5—Baby Sleep Power Tools
• Chapter 6—Teaching Baby to Sleep, Part 1: SWAP
• Chapter 7—Teaching Baby to Sleep, Part 2: SLIP
• Chapter 9—Eating and Not Sleeping
• Chapter 10—Becoming the Zen Nap Ninja Master

If your child is 6 to 12 months old, take a gander at
• Chapter 3—Bedtime Is the New Happy Hour
• Chapter 4—How Babies Sleep
• Chapter 6—Teaching Baby to Sleep, Part 1: SWAP
• Chapter 7—Teaching Baby to Sleep, Part 2: SLIP
• Chapter 9—Eating and Not Sleeping
• Chapter 10—Becoming the Zen Nap Ninja Master
• Chapter 11—Why, When, and How to Wean Off Your Sleep Power Tools

If your child is a toddler or preschooler, start with
• Chapter 4—How Babies Sleep
• Chapter 13—Older Kids, Siblings, and Twins

Chapter 12, (Un)common Sleep Setbacks, addresses less common issues, so dip in there if you've ruled out the more obvious causes of sleep struggles.

The appendix, Potential Medical Complications for Sleep, won't apply to 95% of you because the issues it presents are fairly rare. If, however, you suspect that your child is sleeping poorly due to something more than "because babies," the information there can form the basis for an informed conversation with your pediatrician.

This book combines what the scientific and medical communities understand about sleep and safety with things I've identified over my years of working with families. Science does not yet have answers to all of life's questions, so some of the recommendations here are based on personal observations. However, I've cited scientific references wherever possible so that you can identify what is based on research versus my own experience.

I have made my best effort to share with you all the knowledge I've gleaned from research, other parents, and my experience with loads of babies. I try to keep things light and to give you options you can match to your situation and parenting style. I'm not here to judge you or demand that you adhere to my framework, but instead to give you guideposts upon which to develop your baby's healthy sleep habits.

At times, helping our children sleep can seem like a monumental task. Something that will take months, require an enormous investment in gear, and is more than a little terrifying. Like hiking Kilimanjaro. I've been there too, at the base of the mountain, thinking, "This is a terrible idea."

And now I'm at the top, saying, "Hey buddy, come on up! It's not nearly as bad as you think it'll be. And the view from up here is spectacular!"

Introduction
My Journey in Baby Sleep
(a.k.a. Desperate, Confused,
and Failing on All Levels)

~~~~~~~~~~~~~~~

BEFORE I HAD children, I figured that billions of people have babies, so how hard can it really be?

Then I *had* a baby.

When Duncan was born, I had zero practical experience with babies. What was I going to do with this tiny creature? I was *lost*. Nursing, crying, swaddling . . . they had all seemed so *simple* in the baby class.

I full-on panicked.

Eventually, I calmed down and got a handle on the basics: how to change diapers without getting poop on myself, how to nurse a newborn (when you do something 18 hours a day, you get good at it pretty quickly), how to cut baby fingernails without cutting actual baby (note: I still don't know how to do this), how to feed the baby (apparently the way to feed him was *to do so endlessly*).

Except Duncan cried a *lot*. And when he wasn't crying, he was complaining . . . about being in the grocery store, being in the car, having his clothes changed, taking a bath, reading books, going out in the stroller, playing on the floor...The only time he wasn't crying or complaining was when he was nursing. So we did a lot of that.

He never slept. *Never*. It took 45 minutes of back-breaking labor to get him to take a 20-minute nap. Getting him to fall asleep at bedtime was a painful process that lasted longer than the Oscars. Worse, it was largely pointless, as he was up all night anyway, often for long, inconsolable stretches.

The books all suggested that this was normal, that some babies were just like this, and that if he was extra fussy, this was a sign that he just needed *more love*. I didn't love him enough?! Impossible! I adored him desperately.

But I didn't love the way he slept, by which I mean "barely" and "with great difficulty."

So I kept reading, tying myself in knots trying to reconcile the contradictory advice: nurse more, space out nursing, stick to a fixed schedule, don't let him get overtired, hold him constantly, help him learn to sleep without you, pacifiers are helpful, pacifiers are the devil.

This was the only way to get Duncan to take a nap. Look closely: that's not a smile, it's a grimace.

Nothing was working, and my sleep strategy amounted to "keep slogging through."

After months of crying and nursing and crying and not sleeping, I was diagnosed with low milk supply. While this diagnosis should have brought some relief, in practice it compounded the chaos by adding milk-inducing tea, drugs, and constant pumping to the list of things stressing me out.

This continued for months before my husband and I decided that the drugs, tea, and pumping weren't doing anything other than making me crazy. So we started to supplement with formula.

I live in Vermont, a mecca for all things hippie and natural. Whipping out a bottle of formula in public here isn't far off from teaching your toddler to smoke cigarettes. So on top of having failed at nursing, I now had to be that mom who bottle-feeds her baby.

In a desperate bid to keep nursing limping along, we combined nursing with formula delivered via a tiny feeding tube that I would sneak into Duncan's mouth while he nursed. On the rare occasion that we could sneak out to a playgroup (I do not have words for how desperate I was for adult contact), all the other moms would nurse their happy babies then chat about making zucchini bread while their kids took 2-hour naps. Meanwhile, I would get Duncan latched on while mixing formula with one hand, balancing the bottle on my shoulder (it had to be higher than him), getting the feeding tube into the bottle, and sneaking it into the corner of his mouth.

None of the other moms asked me what I was up to, but they averted their eyes the way you might if somebody was unexpectedly incontinent in public.

Even after we got the food situation sorted out, Duncan kept crying. And *not* sleeping.

I was assured repeatedly by our OB, lactation consultant, and pediatrician that this was normal. Physically, he was doing great. "Caring for a newborn is hard—you'll get through it!" they all said.

Really? Because nobody else at playgroup had babies who complained the whole time. The other women were launching successful Etsy shops selling hand-knitted hats that they made during their babies' luxurious naps. Duncan napped long enough for me to eat a cracker, sometimes two.

At 5 months, Duncan barely slept 8 hours at night, although it felt like a lot longer, what with all the waking up and crying.

I was completely failing at parenting. Duncan was miserable; I was miserable. I was committed to nursing, but I knew from the increasing amount of formula he consumed each day that I was losing the battle.

My husband and I were so exhausted, we could barely function. We lived on potato chips and canned soup. (It's amazing we didn't get scurvy.) We slept in shifts. I was desperate for weekends so my husband could share in the relentless baby soothing. He was grateful for work, which gave him a break from the chaos at home.

I hunted everywhere—books, magazines, websites, forums—for the golden ticket that would make it all better. Everything I read seemed to come down to putting Baby down drowsy but awake. How was everybody else managing this Herculean task? If I put Duncan on his back for even a nanosecond, he was screaming, and it would take a solid 20 minutes, and sometimes a warm bath, to get him calm again. If "put down awake" was the key to the kingdom, we were never, ever going to get in.

Some books suggested that nursing and co-sleeping were the answer. I was already desperation-nursing, so often that it was logistically impossible to nurse any more. Co-sleeping wasn't an option—not because I was opposed to the idea, but it didn't help. And it made me nervous.

I felt faded, like a transparent version of my old self, so faint that the sun could shine through me. I both cherished and resented Duncan. I fantasized about leaving him with my husband and going to a hotel. Just one day, alone. Heaven!

Instead, I did more research, scouring for clues to help Duncan sleep better and cry less. I was like Sherlock Holmes, if Sherlock Holmes was a ragged 36-year-old mom in unwashed yoga pants.

After months of desperate hunting, I came up with a new hypothesis: maybe Duncan had reflux. He didn't have the classic symptoms, but it would explain the crying and the non-sleeping. Our beloved pediatrician didn't buy it, but he was a nice enough guy to support my interest in a drug trial.

We started with medication... and it was *incredible*. No more screaming diaper changes. No more driving around at 2 a.m. because Duncan was inconsolable. Twenty-minute naps turned into 45-minute naps (short by many standards, but a *vast* improvement). Things weren't great, but "great" suddenly felt *achievable*. Maybe, someday in the future, things might be okay.

This was the start of our slow climb out of the deep, dark well. We still had a miserably sleep-deprived baby, but his tummy didn't hurt (much) anymore.

As Duncan felt better, things that were unimaginable before—having him fall asleep independently, extending naps—gradually became possible. Bedtime was no longer a prolonged mystery full of angst and tears. We were able to night wean.

Slowly, we started to *enjoy* parenting instead of simply surviving it, to see what those "I love babies" people were talking about.

But *oof*, what a year.

I had known that becoming a parent would be hard. I hadn't expected it to be *that* hard. The answers I had needed did exist, but none had been in a location or format that my sleep-deprived mush-brain could process. In my quest to answer basic questions like "How do I get my child to sleep longer than 20 minutes?" I'd become an amateur sleep scientist.

Surely, I thought, this shouldn't be so hard.

It was from that place, in 2011, that I started blogging. I wanted to share what I had learned with other tired parents, to perhaps spare them months of desperate searching.

Over the years, my readership grew from three, sometimes four people, to millions worldwide. That exposure created amazing opportunities, gave me access to leading experts, invaluable feedback and insights from thousands of parents, and eventually the opportunity to write this book.

Which brings us here. This book is everything I didn't know but wish I had known back in my early days of parenting. Time-tested and evidence-based tactics to tackle all the challenges, big and small, that stand between *your* family and healthy sleep.

1

Baby Sleep: Essentials

BABIES ARE FANTASTIC. They smell great, they're cuddly, and their toes are so squishy, it's a struggle not to grab the toes of random babies I pass on the street.

Babies who don't sleep, however, can be challenging. Non-sleeping babies are fussier and more likely to cry than babies who sleep well.[1] And when *they* aren't sleeping, *you* aren't sleeping.

About 40% of babies are "easy babies,"[2] which isn't fair, because the word *easy* suggests that an "easy" baby is like a magic kitten that frolics about, leaving a trail of rainbow gumdrops in its wake. Even easy babies require copious amounts of love, energy, and effort. You'll know if you're the lucky parent of one of these "easy" babies because you won't obsess about sleep. Why not? Because you won't *need* to. Easy babies are less fussy, cry less, and generally consolidate their sleep into long, predictable chunks with nothing more than a gentle nudge.

The remaining 60% of babies are more challenging, fussier, and may cry for non-obvious reasons. The term *fussy* seems so dainty when what it means is that babies rule the house as tyrants with crying fists of fury. They may need a lot of help to fall asleep, only to wake up 20 minutes later. They may wake up and stay awake at "this was cool back in college" hours of the night. They may take all your time and energy to the point that "brushed teeth" is the sole non-baby accomplishment of the day.

When a parent says, "I'm obsessed with sleep to the degree that my friends are starting to avoid me because I won't shut up about it," you can guess they've got a more challenging kiddo on their hands.

This book is for all parents, but especially those parents who have a challenging baby. Challenging babies make us work a little harder. See? Your baby is just helping you along your path of personal growth!

Ten Things You Should Know at the Start

Before we delve into the intricacies of baby sleep, let's get a few fundamental truths on the table at the outset so there are no misunderstandings later:

1. You are the best parent for your child. Sometimes parenting is hard and you might feel like a failure. You aren't. You are amazing! Nobody could do any better. This child is so lucky to have you as a parent.

2. You and your partner will get into one (possibly many) huge spats about your child and sleep. This is unavoidable. One night you'll be whisper-fighting at 3 a.m. about how to handle the crying baby. The next night you'll be convinced your partner is a total dolt (they aren't) who is pretending to sleep to avoid dealing with whatever is happening (they might be). Everybody gets grumbly when they're tired. Forgive each other. Someday you'll laugh about this.

3. Babies don't outgrow sleep issues; they grow into them. You might as well put on your big-girl/boy undies and deal with things today, because while they will outgrow those cute monkey jammies, they won't outgrow most sleep problems.

4. Corollary: sometimes babies don't sleep because they're babies. You may need to accept that, for today, this is as good as it's going to get. It's not always obvious if there is room for improvement or not, but I hope this book will help you make that determination.

5. Helping your child develop healthy sleep habits is one of the best things you can do for them. There's lots of noise around how to parent a child, and it's easy to feel overwhelmed by it all. But really, all that noise boils down to this: give your child all the love you have to give, read to them every day, play outside, and help them sleep. If you ignore everything else and do those things, you and your kid are going to be great.

6. Babies are a ton of fun. But if your whole day is spent obsessing about when, where, and how they will sleep (or not), it's hard to enjoy how much fun they are. We all get sucked into the vortex of sleep obsession, depression's slightly less terrible cousin. That vortex is a sign that it's time to make a change: it's sucking the energy out of you, and you're missing out on how great it is to watch a 9-month-old stick yogurt in their hair.

7. When you brought your baby home, a Sleep Fairy came home with you. Every baby has one, though parents are often too tired to notice their fairy flitting about. In any case, you can't count on Sleep Fairies to sort things out for you. They mean well, and they try, but Sleep Fairies are lazy and notoriously unreliable. This sleep stuff? It's all on you. Sorry about that.

8. Sometimes making a change means accepting that, in the short term, things may get worse. Try to be open to change even if it doesn't immediately go the way you hoped.

9. Sometimes, but not always, getting everybody to sleep requires a few tears. That's okay. Tears are just a sign that something isn't easy. Lots of things in life aren't easy, but few of them are as important as healthy sleep.

10. This book will help you come up with a plan to help your child sleep better. You need a plan. Not five plans, just one. I know you've got

nine baby sleep books, but for the next two weeks, let's be monogamous. Put on your detective hat, read this book, develop a plan, and execute it. If, after a few weeks, you find our relationship isn't working out, you're free to date around. But let's give it a fair shot first, okay?

Are You Ruining Your Child?

I'm going to assume that you've read all the fantastic literature that outlines how we're raising generations of chronically sleep-deprived kids and explains how sorting out your child's sleep issue is critical to avoid long-term issues of childhood obesity,[3] ADD, poor academic performance, behavioral problems, etc. All of this is entirely true, but I'm not going to freak you out about this stuff because you're probably plenty freaked out already.

You shouldn't be. Your child *won't* be chronically sleep deprived. The fact that you're reading this book indicates that you are a mindful parent who understands the importance of good sleep. You're more than capable of helping your young child get on a good sleep path or sorting out whatever is going on with your older baby or toddler. None of the stuff about chronically sleep-deprived kids will apply to *your* kid.

You and I both know that sleep is critical to you, your child, and your whole family. And that's all that needs to be said on the subject.

Sleep Safety

Many parents go nuts on Pinterest decorating their new baby's room, which is great. But when it comes to where your child sleeps, you basically want it to be dull, dark, and safe.

Dull. Babies are easily distracted by blinking lights, older siblings, you, etc. While a newborn might sleep fabulously in a travel crib in the living room while you practice the bagpipes nearby, eventually this arrangement is going to fail you. Anything in your baby's sleep environment that is not dull (toys that make noise or light up, mobiles) is counterproductive to your sleep goals.

Dark. Light reduces the body's ability to produce sleep-inducing hormones.[4] The ideal sleep space is very dark, with no more than a small nightlight for illumination. Room-darkening blinds can be helpful.

Safe. More than anything else, your child needs to sleep in a place that is safe. *Safe* means free from potential causes of injury (they can't fall out and bonk their head, or get tangled up in drapery cords) and, more importantly, *minimizes the risk of SIDS*, a.k.a. that thing you don't want to talk about because it's so scary but we're totally going to talk about it anyway.

Sudden infant death syndrome (SIDS) is the unexplained death of an infant under 12 months old. It is the bogeyman that terrifies parents at night. Although extremely rare, SIDS is the third most common cause of infant mortality (behind congenital defects and issues related to preterm birth),[5] resulting in 0.43 deaths per 1,000 live births (just under 1 in 2,000 babies) in the first year. The incidence of SIDS peaks between 2 and 3 months of age then tapers off dramatically after 6 months (although it can occur anytime within the first year).[6]

Although significant research has gone into the subject, and enormous gains have been made since the Back to Sleep Campaign (now called Safe to Sleep) launched in 1994,[7] scientists still don't have a clear understanding of why these deaths happen. There is, however, a general understanding that SIDS results from both environmental and biological factors.[8] Some of these—such as prematurity, being born male, and brain chemistry—are out of your control. So while doing all the right things vastly reduces your individual risk, it doesn't *eliminate* the risk. The loss of a child to SIDS is a terrible tragedy that can be made worse by the assumption that parents are at fault, even though they may have followed all the safe-sleep guidelines.

SIDS is technically different from accidental strangulation or asphyxiation (sometimes referred to as SUID, Sudden Unexpected Infant Death) but the bottom line is that you want to take all reasonable steps to avoid your child coming to harm.

Risk Factors for SIDS

According to the American Academy of Pediatrics,[9] the following have been identified as risk factors for SIDS:

- Being placed facedown for sleep (there is a similar risk for infants placed on their side, as this unstable position often results in baby sleeping facedown)

- Use of soft bedding (comforters, blankets, pillows, crib bumpers)

- Maternal smoking or drinking during pregnancy

- Exposure to secondhand smoke[10]

- Overheating while sleeping

- Poor or no prenatal care

- Co-sleeping , especially with infants younger than 4 months[11]

- Premature birth or having extremely low birth weight

Practical Steps to Reduce the Risk of SIDS

Based on known risks for SIDS (and SUID), the following guidelines are strongly recommended for all of Baby's first year:

1. Never put your baby on their belly or side to sleep. Always put Baby on her back to sleep,[12] and communicate clearly to other caregivers that they must do the same for the first year of sleep. Once Baby is flipping from back to front on her own, it's fine to allow her to continue sleeping that way. (Note: Many babies sleep better on their stomachs, and you may feel that it's okay "just this once" or because you have a monitoring device that claims to notify you if your child stops breathing. It is not. A good nap or fewer awakenings at night are not worth the increased risk. Don't count on technology to enable unsafe choices, because there is currently no compelling evidence that technology is reliable for this.)

2. Never use soft bedding where Baby sleeps. This includes pillows, blankets, sheepskins, stuffed animals, and crib bumpers, and this applies to both co-sleepers and crib-sleepers. If you're planning to co-sleep, all of the bedding will need to be removed from your bed.

3. Baby's sleeping surface should be firm. Don't put soft bedding underneath your baby—no quilts on the crib mattress, no rolled-up baby blankets under the sheet. Don't let Baby sleep propped on a nursing pillow, either.

4. Never sleep with your child on a chair or couch.[13] This happens more than you think: one parent takes Baby into the living room to enable the other to sleep and then accidentally falls asleep holding the child, or Mom sits in a chair to nurse and falls asleep there. This is an enormously risky sleep location.

5. Never allow your child to sleep with anything that could cover their face or head and thus lead to rebreathing exhaled air. This includes blankets of any sort, floppy toys or hats, loose swaddling, stuffed animals, and sleep positioners such as wedges.

6. Make sure Baby isn't too hot. A good guideline to follow is at most one more layer than you are wearing. If Baby has flushed cheeks, hot ears, or a sweaty neck, he is too hot. When in doubt, too cool is better than too warm.

7. Breastfeeding, especially exclusively, is enormously beneficial. There are many great reasons to breastfeed your baby, but add "reduced rate of SIDS" to the list.[14]

8. Have your child co-room with you for at least the first 6 months. Sleeping in your room may decrease Baby's risk of SIDS by as much as 50%.[15]

9. Give your baby a pacifier when they sleep.[16] It doesn't matter if it falls out after they fall asleep—the benefits seem to be specific to falling asleep with it in their mouth.

10. Keep your child's immunizations current.[17] While the causal factor isn't well understood, immunized babies are at lower risk for SIDS.

11. Ensure that your child's sleep environment is free of dangling cords or ropes. Drapery lines, electrical cords, camera cables, etc. pose a strangulation risk.

12. Don't use car seats for sleeping. Car seats are not safe sleep spaces, especially for very young or preterm infants.[18]

13. Check your crib or bassinet. Make sure it has not been recalled, that it was properly assembled, and that the mattress fits as it should. In the U.S. check with the Consumer Product Safety Commission.[19]

14. Talk to your pediatrician about your baby's safe sleep environment. Bring a picture. Ask for feedback.

Phew, what a relief to get that scary SIDS stuff out of the way! Now we can move on to fun topics, like squishy baby toes. Or squishy baby butts. So much great squishy.

What Safe Sleep Does and Does Not Look Like

Where Should Your Baby Sleep?
. . . .

Ideally, your baby will room-share (meaning sleep in your bedroom, not in your bed) for at least the first 6 months (the AAP recommends 12 months, but the evidence is strongest for the first 6 months). This has significant advantages:

- Babies who share a room with their parents have a significantly lower incidence of SIDS.[20] This is why the recommendation to co-room spans the age range when the probability of SIDS is highest.

- Newborns require a significant amount of night parenting. Having your infant nearby is simply convenient.

- Gently transitioning a 6-month-old to a new sleep location is a moderately straightforward affair. Convincing an opinionated 1-year-old to accept a change of scenery is like wrestling an enraged rhino.

The other decision is what safe-sleep surface you want your child to sleep on. I use the term *decision* to create the sense that you are in charge, but some of you will find that you're not, and that your infant will sleep in only one place. But let's assume for now that you get a vote . . .

The American Academy of Pediatrics (AAP) recommends all babies sleep in a crib, bassinet, or play yard that meets the safety standards of the Consumer Product Safety Commission (CPSC).[21] Combining co-rooming with crib-sleeping can be a challenge. Most cribs won't fit through a doorway, unless you're lucky enough to live in a Scottish castle. (If you *do* live in a Scottish castle, please let me know! I would love to visit.) Most parents aren't interested in assembling the crib in their bedroom only to have to disassemble and reassemble it in Baby's room 6 months later, largely because the process requires five able-bodied humans or perhaps one very talented octopus. Space limitations and your skills with power tools will determine how feasible co-rooming with a crib is for you.

This presents a bit of a conundrum. Talk about it with your pediatrician and, collectively, come up with a safe sleep space that enables you to comfortably co-room with your child *and* allows your child to actually sleep. There are many CPSC-approved bassinets and portable crib options that may fit more easily into your bedroom.

What about Co-sleeping?

Co-rooming is when your child sleeps in your room; co-sleeping is when your child sleeps in your bed. Sometimes co-sleeping happens all night. Other times babies sleep in the crib to start but join their parents in bed in the wee hours of the morning.

Parents sometimes consciously choose to co-sleep because it feels right for them to have their baby physically close at all times. This *proactive* co-sleeping is more likely to last the full night. Some co-sleeping families also co-sleep for naps.

Reactive co-sleeping occurs when parents did not plan or want to co-sleep but end up doing so out of desperation when their baby won't sleep any other way. Or they brought Baby into their bed for a feeding and fell asleep that way. Reactive co-sleepers tend to be less than thrilled about the whole experience but are too tired to kick up much of a fuss.

Proactive co-sleeping is a highly cultural phenomenon. Exclusively co-sleeping with infants or even older children is common in Asian countries: 59% of Japanese parents co-sleep with their babies.[22] In the United States, proactive co-sleeping is less common, with recent surveys putting it at 11% of families.[23]

The Co-sleeping Controversy

Co-sleeping has unfortunately become one of those polarizing parenting discussions. No matter what you choose, someone is bound to tell you, "You're doing it wrong."

A large attachment-parenting contingent suggests that co-sleeping is all but required to form a lasting emotional bond with your child. But there is absolutely no evidence that co-sleeping is necessary for parents to be emotionally responsive or to have a deeply connected relationship with their children. Sure, most mammals co-sleep, but they have no other option. When you spend the winter in a small hole in the dirt, co-sleeping is a matter of practical logistics and even survival. Animals also sleep in their own poop, but we aren't clamoring to replicate *that*.

That said, newborns require significant amounts of night parenting, and there are compelling reasons, both safety and logistical, to have your child share a *room* with you for at least the first 6–12 months.

Sharing a *bed*, however, has no bearing on your relationship with your child.

The AAP[24] has determined that co-sleeping is a SIDS hazard. A substantial body of evidence supports this position, and I would caution you not to casually ignore the well-reasoned position of over 60,000 pediatricians. This is not a random group of people who got lost on their way to a Phish concert: it is the largest organized body of licensed pediatric medical professionals in the world.

A well-researched meta-study on co-sleeping and SIDS confirmed the link between them, even in nonsmoking families. It also found that the extra benefits of exclusive breastfeeding did not outweigh the added risk of co-sleeping.[25] This is especially true for the first 3 to 4 months, when the risk of SIDS is highest.

You will see proponents of co-sleeping argue that the studies which form the basis for the AAP recommendation are flawed, or that they don't account for parental alcohol consumption or smoking. Or they'll point out that the incidence of SIDS is far lower in Asian countries despite a relatively high rate of co-sleeping (Hong Kong has one-quarter the rate of SIDS as the U.S., although this is likely due to a difference in the way infant deaths are classified).[26]

Science is always evolving, and we are always making decisions given imperfect information. Based on the information we have *today*, I would caution you not to ignore the AAP and its recommendation against co-sleeping, *especially* if you intend to co-sleep prior to 6 months of age.

Practical Considerations for Co-sleeping Families

If you and your pediatrician have made the mindful decision that co-sleeping is right for you, I have confidence that you will proactively minimize the potential hazards of your adult bed.

In addition to the safety recommendations listed previously, co-sleeping families need to consider the following:

- Co-sleep only if you are nonsmoking,[27] non-alcohol-drinking, and drug-free. Smoking parents should never co-sleep. Do not co-sleep if the mother smoked during pregnancy.[28]

- Do not co-sleep with siblings, pets, or adults who are not the parents.[29]

- Do not co-sleep if your child was born prematurely.

- Do not co-sleep with an infant younger than 4 months.

- Co-sleeping is not advised if either parent is excessively tired and difficult to rouse.

In addition, turn your bed into a safe sleep environment for an infant:

- Use a firm bed surface—no mattress toppers, air beds, or water beds.

- Do not use any pillows, blankets, or other thick bedding.

- Pull your bed away from any walls, and consider removing the headboard and footboard to reduce the risk of entrapment.

- Never leave a sleeping infant unsupervised in an adult bed—they roll out sooner than you might think.

- Strongly consider putting your mattress directly on the floor.

Safety Note. Make your bed safe for co-sleeping *even if you don't intend to ever co-sleep*. Regardless of what your intentions are at the outset, chances are good that at some point you will fall asleep with your baby in your bed. You may even be unaware it has happened, and you'll wake up in the morning next to a baby, wondering, "How did *you* get here?" It's better to assume this will happen and to proactively create a safe sleep environment than to be surprised when it happens and your baby is sleeping in an unsafe space.

It is entirely possible (albeit far more challenging) to establish healthy sleep habits while co-sleeping. Co-sleeping infants wake more frequently.[30] Children who co-sleep with their parents beyond infancy tend to get less sleep and also wake more frequently.[31] But co-sleeping and uninterrupted sleep *can* coexist, if you're willing to work at it, and if...

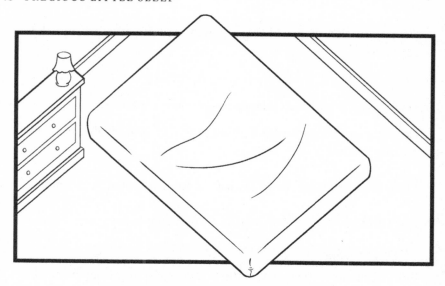

An Adult Bed Prepared for Infant Sleep

- All parties are unambiguously (or at least mostly) happy about the scenario. If you or your partner is resentfully co-sleeping, it's not working.

- All parties are able to happily sleep together. If Dad is sleeping in the guest room, it's not working.

- Everybody is actually sleeping. If one or more of the co-sleepers are sleeping poorly or not at all, it's not working.

- You have an exit strategy. If your exit strategy is to continue co-sleeping until your 7-year-old voluntarily chooses to sleep alone, great. If your plan is to transition your child to their own bed by their first birthday, also great ... as long as you have a workable plan to get them there. (Note: Gracefully convincing a toddler to move out of your bed is a challenge in the same way that learning Mandarin Chinese is a challenge.)

Many families default into reactive or desperation co-sleeping as a short-term fix to disrupted sleep. They're concerned about the safety risks. They don't want to do it. They want their own physical space, private time with their partner, or to be less accessible for nursing at night. They feel like this: "I'm not one of those moms who loves sleeping in weird positions with my precious minion clamped to my boob all night."

Yeah, me neither.

If you are co-sleeping out of desperation, *don't*. There are workable options to help you foster healthy and safe sleep habits without co-sleeping.

2

The Party That Is Newborn Sleep
(Hint: It's Not Really a Party)

BEFORE I HAD a baby, I had a pretty clear image of what life with a baby would be like. I figured it would be like a diaper commercial. I would be perfectly coiffed, gallivanting around with my cool mom friends in white capris and breezy espadrilles, carrying an adorable little baby who would happily chill out while I prepared healthy meals, folded laundry, or did postnatal yoga in the living room.

When I was 8, I thought I would grow up to be a professional horse jockey millionaire who married Erik Estrada. I'm not sure which of these expectations was more absurd.

My newborn baby looked *nothing* like the chubby cherub from the diaper commercials. Those commercials lied to me, is what I'm saying. If your experience was like mine, you came home from the hospital with a terrifyingly tiny, wrinkly, pinkish creature who cried a lot. You've probably heard the adage, "Most newborns cry 3 hours a day." You've also probably heard the old chestnut, "Newborns

New Parent Fantasy vs. Reality

sleep 18 hours a day." Or "Newborn babies eat, sleep, and poop." So apparently your newborn will sleep for 18 hours and cry or fuss for 2 to 3 hours,[1] which leaves babies with 3 whole hours for eating and pooping.

A first-time parent might look at that and think, "Well, it's a lot of crying and poop and such, but as long as they're sleeping 18 hours a day, I can handle just about anything for the rest. I made it through [insert: med school/special operations training/*Atlas Shrugged*]—I can handle a newborn."

Of course you can. And you will! But newborns are often surprisingly challenging, so let's break it down.

Things to Expect in the First 3 Months

Because we are book friends now (What, you didn't know? Yes, it's a thing, and I'll be by later to borrow a few things) I'm going to be honest with you. The first months are rough. You will feel all the emotions, frequently simultaneously. You will be filled with a love so incandescent, it burns. You will also find yourself routinely Googling "when do newborns get easier?" There will be days so jagged, you'll wonder what the people telling you to "cherish every minute" are talking about.

You are deep in the newborn forest. It's dark, lonely, and it can be hard to see a path forward. But you will find a way out. I promise.

It's also hard to clearly encapsulate what normal newborn sleep and behavior looks like because it's so variable. With that in mind, here are some things that are relatively common in newborn babies.

A Lot of Crying and Fussing

Newborn babies are hard. Okay, not all newborns—some are a snuggly loaf of bread that quietly hangs out with you all day. But most cry and fuss a lot. And most won't sleep 18 hours a day. Fourteen hours is more typical, with some newborns sleeping as little as 9.[2] On top of that, most newborns will have about ten fuss or cry episodes a day, which can make you feel like you are endlessly soothing a fussing or crying infant.

Of course, you *adore* your fussy new baby; the sun rises and sets with him. But in addition to caring for your baby, make sure you take care of *you*. Don't be shy to ask for help or to carve out opportunities for a bit of breathing space. Find a good friend who will care for your fussy peanut while you take a quiet walk. Sure, you could just power through, but parenting a high-needs baby will be a whole lot more fun if your gas tank isn't pegged on empty.

Crying peaks and sleep may be at its worst for the first 6 weeks,[3] but things should gradually improve from that point on.

Crying and fussing are, however, pretty standard newborn behavior, and are different from . . .

Colic and Extreme Fussiness

Roughly one-third of newborns are "extremely sensitive" (or "colicky," "high needs," "fussy," "persistent criers," etc.).[4] Really, though, colic is a catch-all term to describe "babies who cry a lot for mysterious reasons."

Sometimes colic is defined by the Rule of Three: a baby who cries or is fussy for more than 3 hours a day, 3 days a week, for 3 or more weeks in a row.[5] (This definition dates back about 60 years and persists because nobody has come up with anything better.) Colic crying tends to start at about 2 weeks and abates at 4 months. It is typically differentiated from standard baby crying by a few specifics:[6]

- It tends to occur in the late afternoon or evening.

- It is unpredictable—one moment Baby is content, the next moment screaming.

- Baby clenches up while crying (clenching their fists, pulling their legs up toward their tummy).

- Baby is virtually inconsolable; typical parental responses (nursing, warm baths, walks) don't fix things.

Caring for colicky newborns can be a backbreaking labor of love. Sometimes they need to be constantly rocked, held, or nursed, and even then, they still cry a lot. And colicky newborns sleep significantly less,[7] about two hours a day less than cheerier kiddos.

If you are the parent of a colicky baby, I would like to give you a hug. Know that the short-sleep issue is temporary and should resolve by 6 months. If it continues beyond 6 months, you've likely gotten caught up in some bad habits, which is understandable—colic throws everybody off their game. Just don't let Colic Survival Mode remain a way of life after colic subsides.

The Witching Hours

Most newborns are awake and miserable for an unfortunately long period in the evening, anywhere from 1 to 6 hours. This is known as the Witching Hours, and it generally falls between 5 and 11 p.m. Some lucky parents will find this to be a vaguely inconvenient hour or two during which Baby is a little fidgety. Others will have a baby who is red-faced screaming, won't eat, and won't sleep, and nothing seems to work, for hours. This is exactly when you're tired and hungry, and nobody can get any dinner together with all this crying going on.

Have faith; this is temporary, and generally abates by 8 weeks. But until then, here are some Witching Hours survival tips:

- Ask friends and family to come visit during the Witching Hours. I know you want to show off your little peanut in the best light possible, and nobody wants to dandle your fussy baby on their knee, but if somebody is willing to walk your fusspot about the neighborhood while you and your partner have a quiet meal, go for it.

- Change up the scenery. Move Baby from the bouncer to your lap to the baby bath then back to the bouncer. Go outside, go for a walk, come back in. Each "new" activity may work for only 10 minutes, so it's like a bad game of musical chairs. Don't be afraid to mix it up.

- Cluster-feed your baby. If Baby is happy feeding every 10 minutes, great! There is a time to try spacing out feedings to encourage Baby to "tank up" rather than snack. This is not that time.

- Run errands. Pushing an unhappy baby around the grocery store is no party. But going to the grocery store under any circumstance is no party, so you might as well double up.

- Go to bed when your baby goes to bed. This is likely to be the longest stretch of uninterrupted sleep you will get (2 to 4 hours for a baby only a few weeks old, 3 to 6 hours for a 1- to 3-month-old). This may not be a convenient time for you. You may feel like it's your only opportunity to shower, clean the house, or catch up on social media. But don't pass up on this chunk of sleep. A hundred years ago, people bathed twice a year. A few soap-free days won't kill you.

The Newborn Night Party

Many newborns will happily snooze the day away on your lap then contentedly stay wide awake in the middle of the night. The "sleep all day, party all night" behavior of newborns goes by various names, such as reverse cycling or, more commonly, day/night reversal. I refer to this natural and common phenomenon by the simple moniker "a bad time." While this erratic sleep pattern is as much fun getting a spider stuck in your hair, it's simply something you get through.

The Newborn Night Party happens for two reasons:

First, when Baby was happily ensconced in Mom's belly, you probably noticed that she became a circus acrobat the moment Mom lay down to sleep. (Note: this is not an indication of future career choices.)

During the day, Mom ran about, effectively rocking the unborn child to sleep. At night, when Mom went to bed, the rocking ceased, so Baby woke to play, often amusing herself by launching into parkour the minute Mom nodded off. This is one of the many reasons sleep is all but impossible during the third trimester (heartburn, the unceasing need to pee, and the uncomfortable feeling of your organs being squeezed into a clutch purse are also in the mix).

So before birth, it was *entirely normal* for your baby to be awake and partying at night. But what may have been a minor inconvenience while Baby was inside the belly quickly becomes a major inconvenience now that he's out.

Second, your newborn has not yet established a *circadian rhythm*, the hormonal mechanism that helps us regulate sleep so that we have the longest stretches of sleep when it's dark out and the longest stretches of awake time when it's bright. This developmental process typically happens by 2 to 4 months,[8] and you can't speed it up for love or money.

The "party all night" routine will feel rude and uncivilized, and you'll want to find a way to put an end to it as soon as possible. Parents are often advised to wake Baby more often during the day to teach that *day* is for play, *night* is for sleep. But waking a sleeping newborn just leaves you with a tired baby who wanted or needed to sleep and now is awake and unhappy about it. Further, it doesn't even resolve the night party issue . . . and *may* make it worse.

So what can you do? For starters, have faith that the developmental process will happen: your baby is going to get days and nights sorted out, and that night sleep will consolidate just fine with or without your help. Still, you *can* give it a nudge in the right direction by managing light exposure.

When your baby is awake at *night*, keep the lights dim, use white noise, and keep the activity level *low*. If your newborn night owl is awake for 3 hours, both you and Baby will get annoyed if you spend that whole time attempting to get her to fall back to sleep. Instead, try to soothe your baby to sleep for about 20 minutes. If it feels like an exercise in futility, concede defeat and try again 45 to 60 minutes later.

Conversely, when your baby is awake during the *day*, keep the activity and light levels *high*. Bright light exposure, especially in the morning, may help to establish a more reliable day/night pattern,[9] so go outside to play in the sun.

Over time, your long stretches of being awake at night *will* get shorter—not because of any mystical strategy on your part, but because as your newborn matures, so does their circadian rhythm.

A Note on the Newborn Night Party and Too Much Napping. If you have a particularly snoozy older newborn (2 months and up), it's easy to be concerned that your baby is up all night *because* they're sleeping too much during the day. This is *so* rare that I hesitate to mention it. The odds are overwhelming that this *does not describe your newborn*. Most newborns sleep so much during the day because their body is developing at a fantastic rate, their circadian rhythm is undeveloped, and they *need to sleep*. If, however, your older newborn is napping *vastly* more than suggested by the guidelines presented in this book *and* is resolutely waking up and staying awake for long periods in the middle of the night, you *may* want to consider gradually shortening their nap duration.

Baby Sleeps Only on You

There are few things in life more joyful than holding a newborn baby. They're tiny and squishy, and even though they don't really do anything, they're infinitely fascinating. When you're holding your child, your heart swells to such a size that, like the Grinch's, it feels too large to fit inside your tiny body. And babies thrive with physical contact, so holding your baby (or letting Grandma take a turn) is a loving and effective part of nurturing your newborn.

But often, newborns will either sleep *only* while being held or only sleep *well* while held. Your newborn could either take a stingy 20-minute nap in the crib or a luxurious 2-hour nap in your arms.

You can see that this presents a conundrum. We *want* to cuddle with babies because it is sheer joy. But babies who sleep only on Mom or Dad can be challenging:

- You never get a free moment because you always have a baby in your arms.

- It teaches Baby that "on you" is how we sleep, which is problematic as they get older. (More on this in Chapter 4, How Babies Sleep.)

- A newborn sleeping on you is fine—as long as you're awake. However, chairs and sofas are enormously unsafe sleep spaces for infants.[10] The risk of you falling asleep while cuddling your infant is high, so your child routinely sleeping this way is potentially hazardous.

So go ahead and enjoy some delicious newborn cuddle-naps periodically and while you're awake. But also use the tools and techniques discussed here to foster your newborn's ability to sleep without you present.

Newborn Sleep: What Is Normal?

Babies need sleep. A lot of it, in fact. The average newborn sleeps 14 to 18 hours a day.[11] This oft-cited fact creates the perception that babies are always sleeping. However, the reality is that they often sleep in itty-bitty chunks. And it may take every sliver of energy you have to get them to fall asleep in the first place, so while babies are actually asleep a lot, many parents feel like their entire life is devoted to helping them sleep. This often leads to the sense that their baby hates sleeping.

Trying to capture the range of "normal" for newborn sleep is like trying to paint the wind: you're going to fail, and you'll look silly trying.

Some babies will take 20-minute naps while others will take mammoth 2- to 3-hour ones. Some will sleep just 8 hours at night while others enjoy a leisurely 13-hour repose.

The truth is, babies vary enormously in the amount of sleep they get,[12] and that's just in the United States—there's even more variability when you look worldwide.[13] One study found that where average American 3-month-old babies sleep 13 hours a day, their Dutch counterparts sleep a whopping 15.[14]

Further complicating the issue, never at any point in all of history have the baby sleep experts agreed on how much sleep kids need, but they've all agreed: they aren't getting enough.[15]

But I digress.

The point is, pretty much anything a newborn can and will do in terms of sleep is "normal." But here are some themes that tend to pop up:

The First Two Weeks

For the first few weeks after birth, baby sleep can be as wobbly as a drunken leprechaun. Baby may sleep so much, you find yourself wondering what all of the fuss is about. Or she may never sleep longer than 45 minutes at a time, leaving you wondering how you can possibly make it through one more night.

However your baby has arrived on the scene, both Mom and Baby have gone through quite the ordeal. Your focus now is on keeping Baby safe, fed, and soothed. You're all adjusting to the newest family member, healing from birth, and figuring out basic functions like eating and pooping. Go with the flow.

Weeks 2–6

After the first two weeks, things start to lean slightly in the direction of "more predictable," but you are still firmly in the thick of it.

At least once a day your baby will sleep for a chunk of 4 hours or more. However, *when* that 4-hour chunk will happen is largely a mystery. You've undoubtedly been advised, "Sleep when the baby sleeps." This *is* great advice. Nonetheless, I'm working on a Magic 8 Ball that predicts when those 4-hour chunks will occur.

Those long(ish) chunks of sleep will not necessarily happen at night. In fact, at first they probably won't. They'll most likely occur between 9 a.m. and 2 p.m.—exactly when all your friends and family want to hold your baby so you can eat, sleep, and shower. Which, of course, you can't do because you've got to entertain the friends and family who are hanging out in your living room. Your newborn can, however, sleep just about anywhere. So use this opportunity to take your portable baby and enjoy outings with friends.

You will likely spend an enormous amount of time getting your baby to fall asleep. When you spend 4 hours a day bouncing a newborn on a yoga ball, you really start to wonder what your Sleep Fairy is doing with her time.

Your baby will also spend most of the day covered in various bodily fluids. Newborns are constantly spitting up, leaking through diapers, or having blowout poop that reaches all the way up their backs. Expect to change their clothes five to ten times a day.

At around 6 weeks, crying peaks and sleep is at its worst. This is not an easy time for parents. But don't despair—it's also temporary!

Weeks 6–12

Congratulations, you've successfully navigated the newborn sleep/cry blockade! You've just gotten over a huge hump; things will gradually get easier from here on out.

Your 6-week-old may still have an irregular schedule for naps and bedtime, but hopefully you're moving from the shock-and-awe "What just happened?!" phase of newborn parenting and starting to find your groove. Now that you've mastered baby feeding and soothing, this is a great time to become more intentional about how and when your baby sleeps.

It's still early, but you're heading into the zone (2 to 4 months) where establishing good sleep habits will keep you all healthy and sane, and will help you avoid future challenges. And I don't mean "challenges" as in cool, sassy adventures—I mean it in the sense of "things best avoided." Does this mean you can't have your older newborn sleep in a baby wrap while you go for a leisurely afternoon stroll? Of course not. They're still itty-bitty.

But the days of "newborn baby sleeps wherever and whenever" are ending. It's time to start using the tools discussed in this book to develop strategies for where and how your baby sleeps.

Helpful Newborn Sleep Guidelines

There is so much well-intended advice out there about what you should and shouldn't be doing with your baby that it can feel like you're drowning in it—which is a shame because all that advice boils down to just a few key things: feed your baby, hold your baby, love your baby, and consider the following guidelines while they're still a newborn:

Newborn Sleep Guideline #1:
Get awesome PJs.

Get really awesome footie pajamas. Preferably the kind with monkey faces on the feet. It's hard to get good toddler and big-kid pajamas with monkey faces on the feet, so you want to double down on these while they're little.

Newborn Sleep Guideline #2:
Don't sweat independent sleep.

Your child will, of course, need your help to master some crucial life skills, whether it's riding a bike, tying shoelaces, or pinning a corsage on his prom date without drawing blood. Falling asleep independently is a life skill that needs to be taught, but your newborn is unlikely to be ready to learn it. You don't need to worry about fostering healthy sleep habits 5 minutes after you arrive home from the hospital with your 7-pound petunia. Focus on more pressing concerns like feeding your newborn and keeping her safe.

A few lucky parents will be able to sing a quiet song, place their wide-awake monkey-footed-pajamaed newborn into the crib, smile warmly, and walk away while Baby quietly nods off to sleep for a delightful 2-hour nap. But for 98% of parents, the reality is that getting a newborn baby to fall asleep and *stay* asleep is a lot of work.

For now, go ahead and rock, cuddle, walk, and nurse or feed your baby to sleep. Relax and do what works—as long as whatever you're doing is safe, because...

Newborn Sleep Guideline #3:
Safety comes first.

Sometimes people are surprised by how challenging it can be to help a newborn sleep. Some may understand that babies should never be placed on their stomach to sleep, but their baby sleeps so much better that way. Or maybe the best way they've found to get Baby to take a nap is to hold her on their chest while they snooze in a recliner in the living room. And given what a struggle the whole sleep thing is, they start experimenting with sleeping scenarios that aren't safe. You can see why it would be tempting!

Please don't do this. Even if it works better, even if it feels like your baby likes it better. *Anything*, even a severely overtired baby, is better than increasing the risk of SIDS.

Newborn Sleep Guideline #4:
More soothing is better.

Newborn babies need a lot of soothing. For the first month or two, expect to spend a lot of time rocking, walking, holding, massaging, feeding, and bouncing your baby. Use every safe tool at your disposal, including pacifiers, swaddling, and white noise (more on these in Chapter 5, Baby Sleep Power Tools). These aren't "sleep crutches" or "bad habits," and you aren't spoiling your baby. You're giving your newborn what they need.

A brief note on sleep crutches

The world is filled with people warning you not to let your chunky muffin become "addicted" to sleep crutches (a.k.a. pacifiers, swaddling, nursing, etc.). Any reasonable person would flinch, thinking, "Well, I certainly don't want my child to become addicted to something, so best to avoid them altogether!"

This would be a mistake.

There is a time and a place for everything (except for kale—there is no good time for kale). When you are the parent of a newborn baby, the time to embrace so-called sleep crutches is *now*. They aren't crutches—they're happy-makers. Don't you want to make your baby happy? Do you want to be the parent who *withholds* happy-makers from their child?

Don't worry: we'll work through how and when to gently wean Baby off them. Nobody will be getting bullied because they're bringing their favorite pacifier to sleepover camp. If you have found something safe that helps your newborn cry less and sleep better, embrace it.

Newborn Sleep Guidelines #5:
Don't let Baby stay awake too long.

The oft-quoted phrase "Babies just eat, sleep, and poop" suggests that, like pooping, sleep will just sort of happen and is a natural thing that babies do.

If that were the case, I would not have bothered to write this book, and nobody would read it—just like nobody would read a book promising to help you teach your newborn to poop.

Babies do not reliably fall asleep when they're tired, nor do they always let you know when they need to sleep. Figuring out how and when to get your baby to sleep is *your* responsibility. This book will give you strategies to tackle both of these tasks. But unless you help your baby fall asleep within an age-appropriate amount of time, they *will* stay awake far longer than they should.

Thus endeth our deep dive into the world of newborns. From here on out we're talking about things that pertain to *all* kids, from birth on up!

3

Bedtime Is the
New Happy Hour

W HO CARES ABOUT bedtime? Going to bed is like brushing
your teeth: you do it because it's important, but you don't
want to read about it. Maybe I should replace this chapter
with a livelier topic. Like toenail clippings. Or drywall.

But bear with me: this is important. *When bedtime happens* and
what happens at bedtime will determine how the rest of the night will
go. If you've got all the dominoes of bedtime lined up, you've set up
your child, whether they're a newborn or a kindergartner, for the best
sleep possible. Conversely, if either the *when* or the *what* of bedtime
is mucked up, you can't sort things out at 2 a.m. You made your pro-
verbial bed when your child went *to* bed, and now you're *all* going to
sleep in it (or not, as the case may be).

This chapter is going to help you nail the *when*, and a substantial
portion of the remainder of this book will focus on the *what*.

When, of course, feels like *finally*. It takes a lot of energy to parent
a baby or a young child, and bedtime can seem like the finish line of

a marathon, possibly the *only* time all day you don't feel like you're sprinting. Bedtime is often followed by the longest stretch of uninterrupted sleep your child will have, so post-bedtime becomes your breathing space: time for adult conversation, to have your body all to yourself, "you" time.

Unless bedtime is a huge mess, in which case it goes more like this:

From birth she was a bad sleeper. I could never get her to sleep before 2 a.m. Like clockwork every night. —SUMMER

She goes to sleep at bedtime without a hitch. And then the fun begins. She wakes up every one to two hours after that. She's not hungry, just unhappy, and it takes 20 to 45 minutes of rocking to soothe her back to sleep. My back is killing me and I dread bedtime! —BETH

We never know when it's time for him to go to sleep at night. Sometimes he's rubbing his eyes and giving us sleepy signs at 6 p.m., but if we put him down too early he treats it like a nap. Other times he's wide awake at 9 p.m. wanting to play. We spend 3 hours a night trying to put him to sleep. —RACHAEL

I am afraid of bedtime. —STACEY

Do you *want* to be afraid of bedtime? *No, you do not.* So let's dig into this seemingly simple but crucial component of your child's sleep.

Demystifying Newborn Bedtime
. . . .

Newborn babies are a bit quirky when it comes to bedtime. Quirky sounds funky and cute, like your artsy friend who can pull off a severe bob and unironically wear Rubik's Cube earrings. However, when used in relation to bedtime, quirky means "challenging and inconsistent." The good news is that a wide range of behaviors are normal for newborns at bedtime, so whatever your newborn is doing is probably totally cool by newborn standards.

Side note: Newborns' standards of coolness are measured by the following criteria:

- Can it be sucked on? Yes/No

- Is it Mom or Dad? Yes/No

- Can it be pooped on? Yes/No

- Has it been pooped on? Yes/No

The following are all normal characteristics of a newborn bedtime:

Bedtime is late. Newborn babies often have a very late bedtime, frustratingly staying awake far past the point when you are actually enjoying their company. It can fall anywhere between 7 p.m. and midnight.

Baby may have one bedtime. Or five. Newborns don't have a well-developed circadian rhythm. Their sleep patterns can be inconsistent for the first few weeks. Your newborn may go to bed at 8:00 one night, 11:00 the next, and 7:00 the one after that.

Bedtime doesn't always happen when you want. Trying to get a non-sleeping baby to sleep can leave you both feeling exhausted and resentful. If you've been at it for about 30 minutes and it's not happening, it's time to graciously accept defeat. Move on to some other soothing activity (a warm bath, a stroller walk, bouncy-seat time) and try again later.

Bedtime may be a nap in disguise. Sometimes your newborn goes to bed easily, but just at the moment where you're going to kick back and ~~read Tolstoy, learn to macrame,~~ spud on the couch, Baby wakes up and *stays* awake. What just happened?! Your baby took a nap. For older babies, this may be a sign of a schedule problem. For newborns, it's because they're newborns.

Bedtime can still have a routine. Your newborn doesn't *require* a consistent routine, but it certainly won't hurt. Even a simple routine (diaper change, jammies, swaddling, and a song) helps establish a rhythm that will become more elaborate *and essential* as your child gets older.

Baby is largely dependent upon you to fall asleep. Newborns overwhelmingly need your help (nurse, feed, rock, cuddle, bounce) to fall asleep. Eventually, you need to teach your baby to sleep without you (see Chapters 6 and 7, Teaching Baby to Sleep, Parts 1 and 2). However, now is *not* the time to freak out about it. Very few newborns are able to fall asleep without *substantial assistance*. So while you are welcome to try putting yours down awake and have them fall asleep without you, don't feel like a failure if it's not working yet.

When Newborn's Bedtime Is Ridiculously Late

Sometimes your newborn baby will stay up college-student late. If your newborn goes to bed at 11 p.m., you have a normal baby. If your baby is still awake at 2 a.m., you have a problem. The most common causes of a baby who is awake when the bars close are:

• You're taking your baby to a bar. Please stop.

• Your baby is overtired. If your newborn baby has been awake since noon, he's likely so tired that it's now all but impossible for him to sleep.

• Your baby needs more soothing (more on this in Chapter 5, Baby Sleep Power Tools).

• Your newborn's sleep is shifted (more on this shortly).

Achieving Baby and Toddler Bedtime Victory
. . . .

Once your baby is no longer a newborn (by which I mean they're older than 3 months), you're no longer at the fickle whims of newborn mayhem. Bedtime is now an immensely powerful, important aspect of your child's sleep: it determines how easy or hard the rest of the night is going to be. This is good news, because 98% of what happens at bedtime is entirely at your discretion. Stop laughing—I'm totally serious.

Now that your kiddo is older, what *should* be happening at bedtime?

1. Bedtime happens at the same time each night.

Bedtime might fluctuate by 15 to 30 minutes (less is better), but it should no longer be a complete mystery. A consistent, predictable bedtime is one of the most powerful sleep cues you can establish. If you want your child to fall asleep easily every night (you do, right?), make bedtime happen at the same time every night.[1] This means managing the nap schedule every day so your child is ready for bed at a consistent time.

When we (both babies and adults) fall asleep at the same time every night, our body chemistry regulates itself around this consistency,

The Goddess of Consistency Forgives Nothing

creating a strong compulsion to sleep. This will bolster your child's ability to easily fall asleep at bedtime. Sure, you can blow off bedtime occasionally, but if you're routinely shuffling bedtime around, you risk the wrath of the Goddess of Consistency, who will smite you with her all-powerful smiting staff.

If you want to impress your friends, drop the phrase "sleep hygiene" into conversation while looking knowingly off into the distance (I do this often, which probably explains how few parties I get invited to). Because that's what we're talking about here: sleep hygiene. Good sleep hygiene = going to bed at the same time every night.[2] If you're letting your older kids stay up later on weekends, you're working against their circadian rhythm, and it can take *days* to re-establish it. The next weekend, you'd be essentially disrupting your kid's hormonal sleep regulation cycle just as it gets back on track.

Trust me. There's a wealth of research on this subject. It's one of the big reasons professionals with variable sleep schedules (airline pilots, swing-shift employees, doctors and nurses) have such a high incidence of sleep disorders.

2. Bedtime happens at the right time.

What is the right time for bedtime? Great question! The answer is "it varies," but if I had to put a stake in the ground, most kids between 3 months and 8 years of age should be going to bed around 7:30.

3. There is sufficient wake time before bedtime.

Making sure your child isn't awake too long is a prime responsibility for new parents. However, children need sufficient time being awake to accrue enough sleep pressure so they can successfully fall asleep and stay asleep at bedtime. Thus the period of time between the last nap of the day and bedtime is typically longer than any other stretch of wake time during the day.

A general guideline is that your child's wake time before bed should be 1.3 to 1.5 times longer than any other wake time of the day. However, asking sleep-deprived people to do math is inherently unfair, so here's a chart. While some babies fall outside the norm (there are definitely babies who need to go to bed by 6:30 or even 6:00), these numbers hold true for most.

Wake Time before Bedtime

Age	Hours Awake before Bedtime	Time Last Nap Ends (assuming 7:00 p.m. bedtime)	Average Bedtime	Total Hours Night Sleep
0–3 Months	1–4 (newborns are funky)	Variable	Variable to late: 8 p.m.– midnight	8–14
3–6 Months	2–3	4–6 p.m.	Shifting earlier: 7–9 p.m.	9–13
6–9 Months	3	4 p.m.	7–8 p.m.	9–12
9–12 Months	4	3 p.m.	7–8 p.m.	10–12
1–3 Years	4–6	3 p.m.	7–8 p.m.	10–12

You'll know you've found the right bedtime for your child when they fall asleep relatively easily. If your child is awake and farting about in bed for more than 20 minutes every night, bedtime might be too early. If you need to bounce your baby on the yoga ball for a solid hour every night, you have my sympathies. And also very muscular thighs. You are also probably starting bedtime too early. On the other hand, if your child is awake far longer than suggested in this table and is a fussy mess in the evening, bedtime may be too late.

Note: The "right time" for bedtime is almost always earlyish. Human beings have a sleep/wake cycle that is heavily influenced by daylight,[3] so it's no surprise that babies' and toddlers' bedtimes *and* wake times are closely aligned with dusk and dawn.

Most kids should sleep 10 to 12 hours at night[4] (11 is the average). While some can happily stay awake later *and* sleep later in the morning, most will wake up early regardless of when they go to bed; 6:30 a.m. is typical. If this is true for your kiddo, a bedtime far later than 7:30 p.m. makes it impossible to get 11 hours of sleep. For most kids, a too-late bedtime results in too little night sleep.

As your baby turns into a kid,* there will be many pressures to push bedtime back: swim lessons, barbecues, the logistics of getting home from work... It's hard to keep bedtime early. Like trying to get back into your pre-pregnancy jeans, this is a challenge, but worth the effort.

4. You are "defending" bedtime against late naps.

Bedtime is your shining castle, and you need to dig a moat of nap-free time around it to keep it safe. Late-afternoon or evening naps, even 5- to 10-minute car or boob naps, can throw off bedtime. This may mean you can't go anywhere in the car or stroller after 4 p.m. because that 5-minute nap on the way to the park can sabotage bedtime—a challenge for parents driving babies home from daycare in the evening.

5. You have a consistent routine.

It's time to get serious about routine. A consistent and soothing bedtime routine provides a cue to your child that it's time to sleep. Your routine should include activities that are enjoyed by all and that you can do without fail every night for the next 3 years or more. "Boob or bottle, bath, books, bed" is a classic.

6. Baby is falling asleep in the same place each night.

Baby's sleep space doesn't have to be the same place they nap, but it does need to be the same place night after night. You want to avoid situations where Baby sometimes sleeps with you, sometimes sleeps in a bassinet in your room, and sometimes sleeps in their crib. The Goddess of Consistency will reward your efforts.

7. Baby sleeps in only one place each night.

Sometimes babies start the night in one place and move to a second one later. Usually the scenario for this is that Mom or Dad triumphantly puts Baby to sleep in a crib but Baby starts waking up with increasing frequency until the tired parents concede defeat and pull

---

* This happens sometime between their first and fifth birthday. You never actually notice it happening—one day you'll be looking at baby pictures and you'll glance at your gangly child sprinting around the house with sharp elbows and an evil glint in their eye and you will realize that while you were busy living life, your baby turned into a kid, and you won't be sure how you feel about it.

Baby into bed with them to try to curtail the nighttime shenanigans. Don't feel bad if this sounds familiar—this is often how reactive co-sleeping occurs. However, your goal is to help your child establish a strong "this is where I sleep" association, which means working toward having them sleep in the crib all night. Also, studies suggest that older children who switch beds during the night get less sleep than those who remain in one place throughout.[5]

A Brief Note on Bedtime Routines

People often ask if their bedtime routine is okay, to which I respond, "It is if you like it!" A great bedtime routine is full of calming activities (massage, songs, interpretative dance...) that you all enjoy. Baby baths are popular because naked babies are adorable and most babies love water play. I also recommend books, because a good book makes everything better. The only firm requirement is that you're consistent. Additionally, it's best to...

- Move from high-light and high-energy activities toward increasingly low-light, low-energy activities. If you want to have a giant tickle party as part of your bedtime routine, it should happen before you segue into massage and quiet singing. Outside play on a sunny day and anything involving screens (cellphones, TV, etc.) are not recommended during the hour before bedtime.

- Move increasingly toward the bedroom. You don't want a routine where you go upstairs for bath, then back down for a bottle, then back up to read in the bedroom. Ideally, your activities move you progressively toward the bedroom and become increasingly dark and quiet.

Common Bedtime Problems and How to Fix Them

Bedtime Is Too Late

Late bedtime is a common challenge, one that manifests with bedtime battles, frequent night waking, and a too-early start to the day. "Bedtime is too late" could also be phrased "Baby is awake too long before bedtime," resulting in a kid who is overtired. Overtired kids have a hard time falling asleep and staying asleep. If your child is awake far longer than indicated in the chart earlier in this chapter, chances are their bedtime is too late.

The solution is to move bedtime earlier by 15 minutes a day until either you are close to the wake time suggested here or your child is no longer easily falling asleep at bedtime. If your child previously fell asleep without issue and is now struggling, you may have overshot and bedtime is now too early.

Bedtime Is Extremely Late

Sometimes babies go to bed very late at night (this can happen with older babies/kids as well, but it's more common for newborns). Your baby might be up until 1 a.m. and then (not including night feedings) sleep until noon the next day—Baby is getting a healthy 11 hours of sleep at night, but the timing of "night" isn't lining up with the rest of civilization. Or possibly the shift is less extreme—say, a baby who goes to bed at 9:30 p.m. and sleeps till 8:30 a.m., but you need to get Baby up at 7:00 a.m. to get to daycare, so the effective result of the later bedtime is an overall reduction in sleep. In either scenario, moving bedtime earlier would benefit everyone.

You can accomplish this by waking your baby up 15 minutes earlier each morning. At the same time, shift everything *else* in the day, so that concurrently all naps and bedtime move up by 15 minutes.

While this is happening, it's helpful to keep the lights dim from your target bedtime until the actual bedtime: if your goal is an 8:00 p.m. bedtime and your child currently goes to bed at 11:00 p.m., keep things dim and chill between 8:00 and 11:00. Similarly, try to expose your child to bright outdoor light as soon as they wake up in the morning. This light exposure will bolster your efforts to slide bedtime up by encouraging your child's circadian rhythm to shift earlier.

If your baby is getting less than 10 to 12 hours of sleep *and* has a very late bedtime, keep the time they wake up in the morning the same but gradually move bedtime earlier by 15 minutes a day.

Let's take an extreme example and assume your baby is up until 1 in the morning and then sleeps till noon and your goal is to move Baby's night to 7:30 and waking time to 6:30. Start by waking her up

15 minutes earlier each morning: 11:45 a.m., 11:30, 11:15, etc. Expose her to bright outdoor light as soon as possible after she wakes up. At the same time, shift all naps and bedtime up by 15 minutes per day, so bedtime is 12:45 a.m., 12:30, 12:15, etc. Keep Baby indoors with medium or low light exposure from 7:30 p.m. till bedtime. In this scenario, it would take about 3 weeks to hit your goal of a 7:30 bedtime.

People often resist this strategy. They're exhausted from being up with a baby till the wee hours of the morning, and they've read a bunch of general sleep advice advocating "Never wake a sleeping baby," or "Sleep begets sleep." But trust me—waking your baby up earlier, gradually, is definitely the answer. It can take days or weeks to get to your target bedtime, but when you finally get a few hours of child-free time in the evening, you'll be glad you did it.

Some parents resist this gradual process because it takes too long. They figure, "We're just going to skip all that falderal and put her to bed at 7:30 instead!" This is a risky plan because going to bed before your body is ready is challenging. We're wired for alertness just before bedtime,[6] so making massive shifts by going to bed *earlier* pushes you into the zone where you're fighting biology. Some flexible children will roll with your rapid approach, but slow and steady is a more reliable technique.

Bedtime Is Inconsistent

Sometimes kids have a wildly inconsistent bedtime. With newborns, it's often better to let bedtime float like a dragonfly based on how naps went that day (long, short, or nonexistent).

For kids older than 3 months, locking in on a consistent bedtime is a crucial component of sleep. Variable bedtimes can make it harder for kids (and all people, frankly!) to fall asleep and stay asleep.[7] Also, studies of older children indicate that inconsistent bedtimes are associated with a higher rate of behavioral problems.[8]

So if your goal is to help your child sleep better at night (and it is, right?), take a long, hard look at your schedule and see what adjustments can be made so bedtime happens as close to the same time as possible every day of the week. Then lock it down.

Bedtime Is Too Early

Sometimes kids go to bed too early. Wait, wasn't I just ranting on about how most kids have a "bedtime is too late" issue? Man, I need to cut back on my writing aids (by which I mean mojitos). But bear with me.

It can be challenging to figure out the best bedtime for your child, and clearly I'm encouraging you to maintain a reasonably early bedtime—you don't want to push bedtime back unless it's clear that your bedtime is *actually* too early. So how do you know?

Here are some strong indicators:

• Your child consistently struggles to fall asleep at bedtime. Ideally, babies and older kids fall asleep within 20 minutes of going to bed.

• Your child is routinely awake and unable to fall back to sleep for long periods of time in the middle of the night. (This alone is not a compelling symptom however, there are other possible causes of middle-of-the-night waking—see Chapter 4, How Babies Sleep.)

• Bedtime is not preceded by a significantly long stretch of awake time. (See the chart earlier in this chapter.)

• Your child has a healthy amount of sleep (10 to 12 hours at night) but wakes up too early (4 or 5 a.m.). If you're hoping to get Baby to sleep until a more reasonable 6 a.m., pushing bedtime back an hour might be the answer.

If you're experiencing a combination of these issues, you may want to experiment with gradually pushing bedtime later by 15 minutes a day. Start small and let things settle in for a few days before assessing the results. If there is no improvement after 7 nights, go back to your original, earlier bedtime.

Bedtime Sucks

Once your child is no longer a newborn, bedtime should be your favorite time of day... literally. Kids in jammies are fantastic, second only to naked bathtub babies, which are inarguably the greatest thing that has ever existed in all of history. Cuddling and reading to or with your kids is the best. And having a few brief hours of kid-free time afterward so you can reconnect with your life outside of parenting, have an uninterrupted conversation with your partner, or read a book is essential to your very survival.

Bedtime can, of course, suck for many reasons:

- It takes ages to soothe your baby to sleep.

- You need to go back into your child's room 5,000 times before they actually fall asleep.

- Your child is up so late that you're going to bed 5 minutes after they do.

- Bedtime is one unendurable stretch of limit-testing cries for more [water/hugs/kisses/books/trips to the potty/blanket adjustments].

It's time to figure out *why* bedtime sucks and develop a solid plan to improve it. That plan will vary depending on your child's age and the specific source of bedtime suckage, and you may feel too tapped out to deal with it. But the first step is going to be tackling the wooly mammoth in the room, which is the subject of the next chapter.

I've received many fantastic emails from parents who colorfully describe their bedtime woes, but none captured it so well as this one: "That nugget on the right? That fat little cutie? Let's just say that our bedtime routine currently consists of prayers, holy water, and a few 'The power of Christ compels you!'"

4

How Babies Sleep
(a.k.a. The Chapter You're Tempted to Skip Over Because It Sounds Tedious but You Shouldn't Because It's Fundamental to the Whole Enchilada.)

HERE ARE SO many mysterious things happening with your baby during the first year that it can sometimes feel like they're an unknowable creature that has escaped from Dumbledore's closet. One of the most unfathomable issues is *why* aren't they sleeping? It could be:

- a sleep regression
- a growth spurt
- teething
- vaccinations

- constipation
- overtiredness
- not being tired enough
- because you blew off the nap this morning
- because it's Tuesday
- too cold
- too hot
- illness
- your partner did it
- garbage truck noise
- poop

So you call up your good friend Google and start trying to suss out why your baby isn't sleeping, and Google tells you it's due to some or all of the reasons listed above. This launches you down a rabbit hole of doubt that generally ends up somewhere dark, lonely, and smelling of cabbage.

Pro tip: Kids almost never wake up due to wet diapers. Parents have an instinct to change diapers in the middle of the night to avoid potential waking due to wet diapers. My advice is to avoid any nighttime diaper tomfoolery if at all possible. Unless Baby has pooped or pee is leaking through, a diaper is not waking up your kiddo. We are lucky enough to live in an age of unbelievable technology, which includes diapers able to contain *enormous* amounts of pee. Take advantage of it.

Figuring out why your child isn't sleeping can be confusing (the world is chock-full of bad sleep advice), but it gets a whole lot easier if you have a solid understanding of the fundamentals of how sleep works.

What's Going On Under the Hood

To figure out how to successfully foster your child's sleep skills, you should first understand how babies sleep. Specifically, it's helpful to understand the following four concepts:

How Babies Sleep

Sleep has two key stages—REM and non-REM (REM stands for "rapid eye movement," also referred to as "active sleep")—and the amount of time you spend in each stage changes as you age. Babies spend about 50% of the time in active (REM) sleep,[1] which by early adulthood has decreased to 20–25%.[2] Active sleep is a relatively light phase commonly associated with movement—grunting, twitching, making funny faces, etc. The large amount of time spent in REM sleep is why babies are such noisy sleepers (and thus make bad roommates) and partially explains why they wake so frequently. Also, the amount of time spent in active sleep increases toward morning, which is one of the reasons babies wake more frequently as the night progresses.

A sleep cycle is made up of both REM and non-REM sleep. Adults have a mature sleep cycle of about 90 to 110 minutes, while a baby will cycle through the sleep stages about every 50 minutes. Adult sleep is also characterized by long, uninterrupted chunks of sleep: although you cycle through light-sleep phases, you don't fully wake during them but rather transition back into deeper sleep.

Babies, however, have much shorter and lighter sleep cycles than adults, which leads to a natural pattern of waking up anywhere from two to eight times a night.[3] Sometimes they may need your help or a quick meal to fall back asleep. Sometimes they just scuttle about a bit and fall back to sleep independently (you are probably unaware of these arousals). But I promise you that between bedtime and morning, your baby wakes frequently—probably more often than you realize.

The Process of Sleep

We have many circadian rhythms (the term *circadian* is derived from Latin, meaning "approximately one day"),[4] but the one most relevant to our purposes is the sleep/wake rhythm. It is because of the sleep circadian rhythm that adults have a long, uninterrupted stretch of sleep at night and are able to stay awake for a long, uninterrupted stretch during the day. We are born, however, with an immature sleep circadian rhythm, resulting in sleep being somewhat randomly distributed around the clock for the first few weeks; a more mature consolidation of day/night sleep occurs between 1 and 2 months.[5]

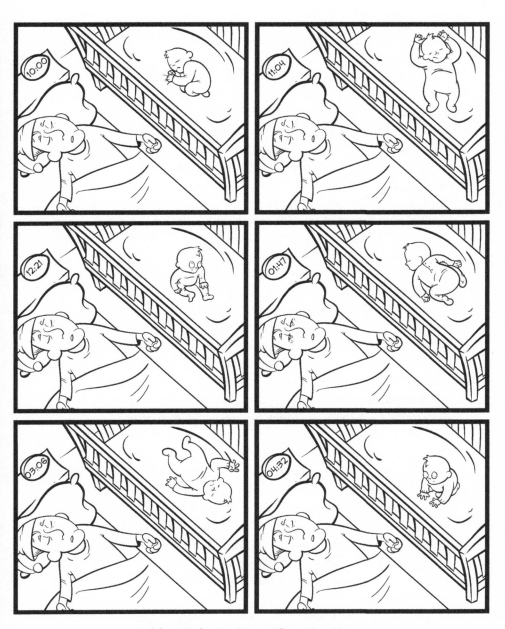

Babies Wake Up More Than You Know

When you have a mature sleep circadian rhythm[6] *and* you go to bed at the same time every night, your biology (including the hormone melatonin) regulates itself to promote sleep.[7] This is some powerful sleep juju.

Sleep is further propelled by the sleep drive.[8] (The technical term is *homeostatic sleep drive*—impress your friends!) Sleep drive is the pressure to sleep that increases the longer you're awake. For adults, our sleep drive builds up throughout the day, peaking just before bedtime, when the pressure from this accumulated sleep drive combines with our circadian rhythm to compel us to sleep. Sleep drive dissipates as we sleep, becoming weaker as we get closer to morning, then rebuilds when we're awake during the day.

The circadian rhythm is relatively puny during the day,[9] so nap sleep is largely regulated by accrued sleep drive. I like to visualize sleep drive as a limp balloon. While your child is awake, the balloon slowly fills with air. If you put your child down for a nap too early and their sleep balloon is sad and saggy: *no nap*. Wait too long, and your balloon overinflates and pops: *no nap*. The balloon also deflates easily—fall asleep for 10 minutes on the ride home and the balloon deflates: *no nap*.

The circadian rhythm and sleep drive combine their Wonder Twins powers at bedtime, making the compulsion to sleep then the strongest of the day. This compulsion gradually erodes as your child sleeps, which is why you'll find your child waking more frequently and struggling to fall back to sleep as they progress toward morning.

Object Permanence

Object permanence[10] is a fantastic new skill your child will eventually acquire (slightly less cool than giggling, but far cooler than the ability to reach into their own diaper for a handful of poo). Object permanence means that infants remember things exist even if they can't immediately see or touch them. Until it develops, out of sight is out of mind. Object permanence is why babies find a game of peek-a-boo such a hoot, and why they will hunt for a toy you've shown them and then hidden under a blanket.

It is also closely linked with stranger anxiety and separation anxiety, which occur because now your child actually remembers that you exist when you aren't physically present. For the first time, they are capable of missing you—which is really sweet but hard to enjoy when they burst into tears the second you leave the room. (Say goodbye to your ability to go to the bathroom alone!)

Scientists used to believe that object permanence didn't develop until babies were 8 months old, but recent research suggests that babies as young as 3.5 months are aware that objects exist after they've been removed from view.[11]

While the scientific community continues to debate the age at which you can reliably play "Where did Mr. Froggy go," anecdotal experience suggests that object permanence tends to become an issue for your child's sleep at about 6 months (give or take a month or two).

Object permanence affects sleep because your child falls asleep *with* you (rocking, feeding, nursing, cuddling) and wakes up later only to find you *missing*. Due to their mad object permanence skills, they can now remember that you *were* there, and now, mysteriously (from their perspective), you aren't! In fact, *any* change in their environment between falling asleep and waking can be problematic, including:

- Mom or Dad are missing (there when they fall asleep, gone when they wake up)

- location changes (they fall asleep on you, wake up in their crib)

- devices that run on timers and shut off (white-noise machines, mobiles, musical devices, etc.)

- things that can fall out (I'm looking at you, pacifier!)

Babies who have not yet developed object permanence can be happily rocked, bounced, or nursed to sleep. They'll wake at night to be fed or rocked back to sleep, but they're not waking because you've disappeared—they're waking because their circadian rhythm hasn't clicked in yet or because, as newborns, they need a lot of help to cycle through light arousals at night. But for a time, putting your baby down 100% asleep will seem like a winning strategy because it is winning.

Once your baby develops object permanence, however, they remember that something has changed since the time they fell asleep—typically, *you've gone missing*. Where previously they fell back to sleep on their own from a light-sleep phase, now they wake themselves fully... because you were there, and now you aren't. Worse, they're generally pretty upset about it. Instead of waking and looking for a quick bite to eat or a cuddle, they're grumpy and difficult to soothe. In their own baby way, they're yelling, "Hey! Where did you go! Dude, not cool!" When this happens, the best-case scenario is that your child will wake occasionally to check on you. Worst case, sleep will totally hit the skids.

If you continue to surprise your baby by changing the circumstances after they fall asleep, you'll find yourself with a baby who starts fighting sleep. They become hyper-vigilant[12] at bedtime because they know you're trying to sneak out. The baby who used to cuddle and laugh with you at bedtime is now agitated and anxious. Falling asleep can take hours because the biological pressure to sleep is warring with their desire to keep an eye on you.

Imagine if you went to sleep in your own room only to later wake up in your neighbor's bed. Assuming your neighbor isn't Tom Hardy or Emma Stone, you would rightly be pretty upset about the mysterious change of scenery. You would immediately become fully awake, and even after you tromped back home, sleep would be all but impossible. The mystical teleportation into your neighbor's house would make it challenging to fall asleep the next night as well, because you would lie there worrying about it happening again. Which is a great segue into...

Sleep Associations

All people have sleep associations—activities, locations, or items that are closely associated with sleep. My sleep associations involve my husband's presence, being in a bed, and reading before I turn out the lights. Remove any one of those, and I struggle to fall asleep. This is why I guilt-trip my husband about how I never get enough sleep when he travels for work (it has nothing to do with staying up ridiculously late binge-watching trashy TV, obviously).

Human beings lock in on sleep associations and then need those associations whenever they're falling asleep (or at least sleep better with them). They also may need them when they cycle through light

Waking Up in a Strange Place: Less Fun Than You Think

sleep during the night. Adults, however, have a mature sleep rhythm with less REM sleep, so while I have a sleep association of "reading in bed," I don't wake up at 2 a.m. needing to read some more in order to continue sleeping. #thingsmyhusbandisgratefulfor

Babies don't sleep like adults.

Your child's sleep associations are those activities and objects that occur *near to or at* bedtime—your wonderful bedtime routine, their sleep place, any Baby Sleep Power Tools (see Chapter 5) you're using, white noise, lovies, etc.

This is an important but often misunderstood distinction. Most people are convinced the goal is to have their child fall asleep without direct parental involvement. While that may be true for some babies, activities that happen *near to* sleep can result in sleep associations even if the child is *awake* at the end of that activity.

Sleep associations cause problems when they're *not persistent through the night*. If your child associates sleep with particular things that *are* persistent throughout the night—being swaddled, nightlights, lovies, being in the crib—then you've got great, sustainable sleep associations. Every time your child wakes at night, they'll find their sleep associations present and unchanged, and will readily and independently fall back to sleep.

Negative sleep associations, on the other hand, include:

- falling asleep with a pacifier, which falls out of the mouth during sleep

- falling asleep nursing or eating, waking later without the bottle or nipple in their mouth

- falling asleep cuddling with you, waking up alone later

- falling asleep being bounced on a yoga ball, waking in their own bed

- falling asleep with music or a mobile playing, waking in silence

A common example of a problematic sleep association is rocking a child while singing a few bedtime songs. Baby falls asleep and is placed gently into the crib, but later wakes throughout the night and is unable to go back to sleep unless a parent rocks her. Similarly, a child who is nursed at bedtime then goes awake into the crib, where he falls asleep independently, may wake at night and resolutely not go back to sleep unless nursed.

You may have noticed that this looks a lot like an object permanence problem, because they're related. If your child associates sleep with some non-persistent item, location, person, or activity, when they wake up (as babies frequently do), they won't be able to successfully fall back to sleep independently. You'll know this has happened to you because you'll try to help your child fall back to sleep in other ways and absolutely nothing but [insert non-persistent sleep association here] will do.

How Baby Sleep Goes Off the Rails

Blah blibbity blah brain stuff blorgle sleep blah. Even to me, this sleep stuff is pretty dry. But the bottom line is this:

- Baby sleep is different from adult sleep.

- Babies wake up a ton at night, and these wakings become more frequent as you move closer to morning.

- The longest stretch of uninterrupted sleep occurs just after bedtime.

- It is normal for babies to move and make a lot of noise when they sleep.

- When you have an appropriate and consistent bedtime, the biological compulsion to sleep is powerful.

- The compulsion to sleep declines the longer you sleep until *poof!* it's gone and you wake for the day.

- The drive for sleep at naptime is relatively puny and subject to wake time (too long/too short) issues.

- The inability to fall asleep independently at bedtime leads to frequent and persistent night waking.

- Surprises are great at birthday parties, but terrible after bedtime.

Not falling asleep independently at naps and/or bedtime is the root cause of 99.8% of all chronic baby and toddler sleep problems. (The remaining 0.2% are due to failed Sleep Fairy intervention. Sleep Fairies are just the worst.) Hopefully, understanding how sleep works will save you many tears, sleepless nights, and unnecessary hours with

Google. How sleep works is the answer to most of the sleep questions you will have, will see on the internet, or will hear bandied about at your playgroup. It is the key to gently weaning your child off night feedings, lengthening naps, and fostering long stretches of uninterrupted sleep at night. And it will make your hair grow thicker and more lustrous (okay, I'm making the last part up).

Lack of independent sleep can cause problems in many ways, but consider this common scenario:

A loving new mom nurses her newborn baby to sleep at bedtime then sneaks Baby into the crib. This newborn wakes up once or twice to eat at night, but it's manageable, and after hearing horror stories from friends, both parents are thrilled at how well things are going. On nights Baby wakes only once, they start whispering excitedly about the possibility of gently weaning off that feeding, with the goal of landing in the Shangri La of truly sleeping through the night.

A few months go by, and instead of fewer feedings, *more* feedings are popping up, like malevolent mushrooms. Often those feedings are happening barely an hour after the last.

Finally, Mom, quite reasonably, deduces that Baby can't *possibly* be hungry. "She just ate!" So she sends in her partner to help Baby go back to sleep. "Maybe she pooped? *You* go check."

Well, despite all Dad's best efforts at rocking, bouncing, singing, and massaging, Baby is just not having it. And rightly so—none of those activities, no matter how lovely, are associated with sleep. *Nursing is.* So Dad feels like a failure. He assumes he lacks some essential baby-soothing skill, concedes defeat, and requests that Mom go deal with it. Mom resents Dad for not trying hard enough or for feigning incompetence so he can go back to sleep (don't blame Mom for this—she's super tired and cranky), but goes in to nurse because "Fine, whatever, give me the baby, you big oaf." (Both partners probably feel the other is being unreasonable in this scenario.) Mom nurses kiddo, who, *boom*, falls back to sleep. Everybody goes back to bed for an hour... and the cycle repeats.

As the weeks go by, Baby starts to demand longer periods of nighttime nursing or cuddling to fall asleep. What used to be 2- or 3-minute nursing sessions at 2 a.m. are now epic 20-minute boob-a-thons throughout the night. Mom and Dad scramble for answers. Is this a growth spurt? Diminished milk supply? Bedtime too late? The internet is full of answers, and they try them all, but nothing seems to make a difference.

At the same time, bedtime, previously a brief affair, is turning into a drum solo at a Grateful Dead concert—long and complicated. Baby still falls asleep easily while nursing, but her eyes pop open the second her butt hits the crib, forcing the parents to restart a new 20-minute nursing-and-rocking session. Maybe the crib is cold? The mattress is too firm? Should they medicate for teething? When was the last time the pediatrician checked for ear infections?

They reminisce, somewhat bitterly, about the days when she woke up only once to eat. "Remember that time 3 months ago when we slept? That was awesome."

Bedtime evolves into a dreaded process that can trudge on for ages. The constant waking at night is taking a toll on everybody. In desperation, they turn to co-sleeping, which makes them both nervous. But Baby is happy if she's nursing, and they're both too exhausted to fight about it any longer. Now that Mom is so accessible, though, the "night-feeding" sessions expand so that Baby is basically clamped onto Mom all night long—which would be fine if Mom was happily sleeping this way, but she's not. Her back hurts, and she's feeling trapped. She worries about safety.

Dad is sympathetic, but he's getting baby-kicked in the kidneys so often that it makes sense for him to sleep on the couch, which he does, although he feels guilty about it. Mom agrees to the couch plan: "We shouldn't both be exhausted." But she can't help feeling a bit abandoned too.

Baby is now a healthy, happy 9-month-old whom they adore completely, but there is an edge of resentment about the sleep situation.

She's eating more solids, though, so that should help, right? She won't be this fixated on nursing *forever*—when they wean, things will get better. Babies are young for *such* a little while. Mom and Dad just need to dig deep and push through. The world is full of stories of babies who miraculously started sleeping through the night. Maybe she's not ready, but she will be soon. Maybe?

However, in the context of our conversation on how babies sleep, we can see what is *really* happening here:

- Baby isn't falling asleep independently and has a sleep association that is some combination of Mom, cuddling, and nursing.

- When Baby wakes up (as babies do), she can't fall back to sleep without those associations present (Dad, therefore, was doomed to fail).

- They also have an object permanence issue: Baby falls asleep in Mom's arms but wakes up in the crib. That unsettling experience makes it harder for Baby to fall asleep—she fights sleep, turning bedtime into a long slog.

- The demand to nurse becomes more frequent because, as Baby matures, she's trying to recreate her sleep association at every sleep cycle, so that she can happily resume sleep.

- Because there is confusion about why the night waking is happening, the parents are unable to resolve it. Instead, they take action to adapt to it (by not sleeping, sleeping separately, unwillingly co-sleeping, and becoming a human pacifier). So sleep deteriorates until . . .

- All members of the family (well, at least Mom and Baby) have significantly disrupted sleep, Mom and Dad are no longer able to sleep together, and bedtime is dreaded and tedious.

This story is a common one, but sleep issues aren't specific to nursing. Other parents are up all night bouncing babies on yoga balls, patting baby butts, feeding bottles, reinserting pacifiers, rocking, cuddling, etc. Sleep issues aren't unique to night sleep, either: the same pattern can be even more pronounced for naps.

The common denominator, however, is a child who hasn't learned how to fall asleep independently.

Things aren't always this severe. Babies are like snowflakes—they ~~fall from the sky~~ ~~melt on your tongue~~ are unique. Some can be nursed to sleep at bedtime and will wake up only twice a night. Others will sleep reasonably well until midnight but then wake hourly till dawn. The pattern of sleep disruption varies, but the fact that *sleep is disrupted* is consistent.

There is a solution: *your child needs to learn to fall asleep without you.*

Sleep myth #1,024

"They'll stop waking up when they're ready."

In contrast to everything we've just discussed about how babies sleep and why falling asleep independently is crucial, persistent parenting mythology says that babies will simply sleep better when they're ready.

This may be the most insidious sleep myth of all time, because it suggests that *you* are an overly zealous ogre, and your attempts to get your child to sleep better are actually pushing them to do something they're not developmentally ready to do. Which makes you a pretty selfish and terrible person.

But here's the reality. Yes, newborns have tummies the size of a marshmallow, and no, they can't store up much glycogen in their body, so of course they need to eat frequently to fuel their rapid growth and development. And yes, newborns are born with fractured sleep and it takes some time for that to morph into a more reasonable day/night, wake/sleep cycle.

But when your 6-month-old baby is waking up four to eight times a night and requires your intervention to fall back to sleep, it's not because they're "not ready." "Waiting it out" won't do anything other than turn you into the parent of an 18-month-old toddler who is waking up four to eight times a night.

You are *not* a garbage person. You are *fantastic and smart*, and you've realized that parenting a baby is not an event in the Hardship Olympics. You have the ability to improve the quality of your baby's and, by association, your own sleep outcomes. And doing so is unambiguously better for all involved.

Teaching Baby to Fall Asleep
. . . .

Sleeping isn't an inherent skill—it has to be learned. You've been teaching Baby to fall asleep since the minute he was born, probably through some combination of nursing, feeding, patting, cuddling, and rocking. When babies are younger than about 2–3 months, these methods are effective and totally reasonable. Very few newborns will fall asleep without considerable assistance from you, so failing to do these things results in a baby who doesn't sleep.

These activities form the foundation of how you've taught your baby to sleep. From your baby's perspective, feeding, cuddling, patting, rocking, or whatever else you've done forms the basis of "how we fall asleep." Remove one or all of these elements, and your child will complain, immediately and with great gusto. So, wisely, you continue with the feeding, cuddling, rocking, etc.

But as your child gets older, these activities will begin to fail you. What this failure looks like will vary based on the individual child, but it will typically include some combination of the following:

- Naps become or stay short. If your child was taking short naps, they will remain firmly in the Short Nap Camp. If she was taking long naps, those naps will shorten to 20 to 45 minutes.

- Falling asleep at bedtime will take longer, or you will need to make multiple attempts.

- Any attempts to put Baby down before she is so deeply asleep that she's a limp piece of bacon draped across your arms will result in screaming.

- Baby will routinely wake up about an hour after bedtime, and resettling will be enormously difficult.

- Baby will have an uninterrupted chunk of sleep earlier in the night and then will start waking at progressively frequent intervals as it gets closer to morning.

- Morning wakeup will shift up from annoyingly early to "now you're just being rude" early.

- Any attempts to ignore night wakings will result in copious tears. Any response on your part other than "whatever you did at bedtime" will be flatly refused.

Helping your child fall asleep and stay asleep is not easy. Helping your child learn to fall asleep independently can be harder than waxing your own back hair. It is also worth the effort.

Life after Independent Sleep
. . . .

Understanding how sleep works is crucial. The good news is that once independent sleep is established, things can improve rapidly, often looking a lot like this:

He grumbles for barely a minute before going right to sleep. It's amazing! He still wakes up and sits a few times each night but lies down and falls back to sleep almost immediately. Surely, this is what heaven feels like! Freedom to have grown-up time with my husband at night! —ELLEN

After falling asleep on his own, my child slept for a record 8 hours straight last night! —KATHY

Nursing her every 45 minutes and having a cranky baby made us both feel desperate and helpless. Now that she's putting herself to sleep, my child is more rested and alert. —SARAH

I was rocking and nursing my baby to sleep and he was a crappy napper, but I shrugged that off because he was sleeping 11 hours straight at night. That was until he began waking up at 10:30 p.m., 12:30 a.m., 2:30 a.m., and 5:00 a.m. We stopped nursing to sleep and guess what? Now he plays in his crib for a few minutes and sleeps until 3:30 a.m.! —LIBBY

My daughter slept through from 6 weeks to 5 months—then, object permanence hit. We thought it was teething. The last 3 months we have been up three to five times a night for either a few minutes or hours, waiting for her to "finish teething" and magically sleep again. I realized I was in denial and had to make a change. We taught our daughter to fall asleep independently and she stays asleep for 11 hours! —KATE

My son started waking almost every hour, and after two nights of that I was all, "No, thank you!" We realized he needed to learn how to fall asleep on his own and we made that our priority. He's now 8 months and sleep hasn't been an issue (for the most part—ugh, teething) in a long time. —RACHEL

Wanna join these guys on Team Independent Sleep? Yeah, you do. Luckily, you've got a number of viable tools and strategies to aid you in your quest. And these are outlined for you in detail in the following *three* chapters.

5

Baby Sleep Power Tools

HERE'S A QUIZ for you (everyone loves quizzes, right?). First, read these quotes from actual parents:

- *My little dude will not sleep anywhere but in my arms. And when he hits the 45-minute mark, he wants a boob plugged immediately. That's it. I've been reduced to arms + boob.*

- *My son will be 4 weeks old tomorrow. He will sleep at most 10 to 60 minutes in his crib. We can't keep going like this.*

- *Our baby is 8 weeks old and hates sleeping. Our pediatrician laughs it off and says she has FOMO (fear of missing out). I laugh in the office and then promptly cry the second I put her in the car. My husband and I haven't eaten a meal or slept in the same bed together since she was born. We take turns trying to soothe her endlessly.*

- *We have been trying to put our baby down drowsy but awake, but he just ends up crying hysterically the moment he is put in his crib and will carry on and on until he is picked up. We spend anywhere from an hour and a half to 3 hours trying to get him to sleep at night. The only thing that works—but it takes forever—is bouncing on an exercise ball with a bottle and white noise. We'll do this until he is totally passed out, but the moment we lay him down, he wakes up and starts crying and we start the process over. This is not the postpartum exercise program I was hoping for.*

· *I may be close to my wits' end. My 11-week-old son will not give me a moment's peace. He will not be calm or sleep if he isn't being held. Within 30 seconds of being put down he starts screaming and shadow-boxing the air like invisible demons are after him. He cries so intensely that he becomes soaked with sweat. When he does fall asleep, I put him down and then he wakes up within 5 to 15 minutes, screaming. We can't wear the same pair of underwear for unlimited amounts of days, and there are only so many mushrooms and small animals I can forage from the backyard before I need to go grocery shopping, so I need him to sleep or be calm with someone else so I can do things. Right now, he's so cozy and adorable snuggled in my arms, but I know the second I put him in his sleeper he's going to be back to battling the invisible zombie hordes. It's exhausting for us both.*

So, quiz time.

What is the common theme here?

Okay, yes, there is a faint air of desperation throughout, but that's not the theme I'm looking for.

It's this: how hard it is to help babies *fall* and *stay* asleep. And when we can't get our babies to *fall* asleep and *stay* asleep, we fall back on tactics that are exhausting, unsafe, unsustainable, and that make the transition to independent sleep enormously challenging.

Pretty depressing, eh? Well, before you curl up in that blanket fort, fear not—you've got some powerful tools to help you in your quest to foster healthy sleep for your child.

What Is and Isn't a Good Sleep Power Tool

You can't make your baby sleep (or eat or poop, for that matter). Which, I guess, means this whole book is pointless. If you can't make your baby sleep, why waste your precious free time reading about something you have no control over? Why did you even buy this stupid book? This is the worst book ever, and it's going into the recycle bin as soon as—

Hold the phone. I said you can't *make* your baby sleep, but I never said you are entirely powerless. There are many things that you can *and should* do to *encourage* your child to sleep, and while ultimately the "falling fully asleep" part is outside of your purview, you've got tremendous influence in the matter.

There are many ways to help your child fall sleep, but some are relatively effective while others cause more problems than they solve. The Sleep Power Tools are about encouraging sleep in ways you won't come to regret months down the road.

A Sleep Power Tool is a technique that will safely and significantly encourage your baby to fall asleep and stay asleep. To be included in the list of Sleep Power Tools, a technique has to adhere to *all* of the following criteria:

- It significantly elevates the degree of soothing, and thus increases the odds of a baby falling and staying asleep. You can't make a baby sleep, but you can make it really challenging to stay awake.

- It successfully functions (more or less) for the duration of the time your child is sleeping. Thus, anything on a timer is, by definition, not eligible, because timers turn off.

- It works without your involvement. Most parents find that the car is an excellent Sleep Power Tool: hop in the car, Baby sleeps. However, until self-driving cars become a thing, the car is eliminated from consideration.

- It is not you. Parents are the Kings and Queens of Sleep Power Tools,* as most babies will happily sleep while being held by you, while lying on you, and/or while clamped onto your boob. Unfortunately, this configuration is often unsafe and uncomfortable, so this chapter will give you some workable alternatives.

· It is something you can gently wean off in the future. So you can use that tool without worrying that you'll be stuck with it like a bad tattoo.

Not all Sleep Power Tools will work for all ages. Most are specific to newborn babies. Others are useful for many years. Not all tools work for all children. But typically there is an optimal combination of tools, usually identified through trial and error, which will maximize the sleep for your child. "Maximize" doesn't guarantee you the duration of sleep you might hope for, but if the Sleep Power Tools are used correctly, you're doing all you can to help your child sleep. Some kids will sleep a lot, others less, based on their individual biological needs and temperament, but that is beyond your control.

* "You" as Sleep Power Tool

Newborns often sleep best on you. This gives you enormous flexibility in the early months to meet friends for coffee or watch trashy TV. In fact, I strongly encourage you to do so because holding a sleeping infant is "what if Hogwarts was a real school and you could go there" great.

My goal here is not to vilify having a baby sleep on you. Cuddling to sleep or nursing to sleep may be the *only* thing that works for particularly high-needs newborns. Nor am I suggesting that you must eternally forgo the gentle joys of a sleeping infant in your arms.

There are, however, some really important reasons why you, the parent, who is the best of all Baby Sleep Power Tools, *are not listed here*. Having your child sleep on you is like a salted-caramel cupcake: it's fantastic, but if you eat them all the time, it's going to lead to troubles, including:

· teaching Baby that "on you" or "with you" is the only way to sleep, which is categorically unsustainable over the long haul

· making convincing an older baby who has spent their whole life sleeping on you to sleep elsewhere a massive challenge, which is how parents get stuck as the permanent human mattress

· creating an unfeasible sleep/nap arrangement if you have older children (what mischief will your older kids get into while you're napping with your beloved minion clamped on your boob?)

- unsafe sleep situations—an infant on your lap on the couch while you're awake is fine; an infant on your lap on the couch when you fall asleep is not

- the absence of an elegant transition strategy to get to independent sleep

So please enjoy the fantastic sleep mojo that is cuddling, especially when your child is a newborn. But be mindful that our goal is to gradually foster safe, sustainable, and independent sleep, which, for most people, will require establishing sleep that doesn't involve you.

Power Tool #1: White Noise

White noise is the most effective, easiest to implement, and least expensive sleep aid for babies. It is also the sleep aid parents frequently don't use, or don't use correctly. I've had parents tell me they don't want to use white noise because they are afraid their baby will become addicted. Or they don't want to have to invest in a $70 machine. Or they think they are using white noise, but it's so quiet it couldn't drown out the fluttering of a butterfly.

Which is a shame, because white noise is one of the easiest things you can use to help you and your baby sleep better. Why?

- White noise reduces stress in babies. What do babies get stressed about? Just about everything. They're stressed when they're overtired; they're stressed because their world is more stimulating than they're ready to handle; they're overwhelmed by lights, faces, and excitement. White noise creates a safe space for them by blocking out that stimulation.[1]

- White noise helps babies sleep. In fact, white noise helps babies both fall asleep more easily and stay asleep longer.[2] Babies have what are called "sleep arousals," usually about every 20 to 45 minutes, when they cycle into a light-sleep phase (for more on this, see Chapter 4, How Babies Sleep). Some babies are unable to fall back into deep sleep after the arousal, so naptime is over. White noise helps babies gently navigate these arousals to get longer, more restorative naps. It also helps block out the noise of life (older siblings, doorbells, garbage trucks . . .) that can interfere with sleep.

- White noise helps babies cry less. Did you know people universally make shushing sounds to babies? Because shushing (which is just home-made white noise) helps calm babies! But the key to using white noise to help calm a crying baby is that it needs to be louder than the crying.[3] Holding a screaming baby while shushing at the volume of a spring rain shower is useless—your baby can't hear the shushing over their own crying. You need to shush loudly (sounds a bit ridiculous, I know!). Also, you may need to shush for a while, but sustaining loud shushing can be a challenge. If you're starting to feel dizzy or see stars, it's time to outsource your shushing to a device, whether that's your phone, old radio, or a white-noise machine.

- White noise may reduce the risk of SIDS. A relatively famous study (famous if you read a lot about baby sleep, that is—honestly, you should be a little proud if you haven't heard of it) suggested that babies had a reduction in the risk of SIDS if they had a fan in their room.[4] Nobody knows why the fan helps—it could be by circulating the air so Baby is not rebreathing the same air they just exhaled, but it may have to do with the white noise the fan makes. We do know that white noise reduces active sleep, which is the sleep state during which SIDS is most likely to occur.[5]

- White noise will help you sleep. Ideally, most of us will have our newborns sleeping in the same room with us for the first 6 months, but babies are terrible roommates. They grunt, gurgle, fart, kick, snort, and grumble. It's almost impossible to sleep through even the smallest whimper, especially when they're a few inches away. White noise will help mask these small sounds so you can sleep better.

- White noise is easy to wean off. When your baby is older (generally after their first birthday), you can wean off white noise by gradually reducing the volume. Boom, done.

How to Use White Noise

Although it's fine to use a fancy white noise generator, you don't need to buy one. Many people use free white noise apps on their phone or tablet. And if parting with your phone whenever your child is sleeping doesn't suit you, any old boom box or clock radio set to static will work. Some air purifiers or humidifiers also make enough noise.

Turn the volume up to roughly 50 decibels—about the level of somebody taking a shower if you are standing in the bathroom. It shouldn't be uncomfortably loud—if it bothers *you*, it's probably too loud. As a comparison, normal human conversation is about 60 decibels.[6] Leave the white noise on whenever your baby should be sleeping, and make sure it won't turn off.[7] Any CD or other device that stops won't work, or, more accurately, it *will* work . . . *until it turns off.*

Generally, white noise is only to be used while your baby is asleep. You want your child exposed to the stimulation of speech, music, and life when they're awake. White-noise can then become a powerful sleep cue.

Is White Noise Safe? Notes on the Rat Study

In 2003, researchers at the University of California published a study[8] in which baby rats were raised in a sound-deprivation chamber—exposed to loud, unceasing white noise for the entirety of their ratty childhoods. Understandably, those baby rats grew up weird, and now everybody is afraid that white noise will damage their child. However, there is no evidence to suggest that the use of moderate white noise when Baby is sleeping will harm your child, and there is a good deal of evidence that suggests it may even be beneficial. As with everything, talk with your pediatrician to come to a conclusion you feel comfortable with.

Power Tool #2: Swaddling
. . . .

Swaddling is one of the oldest soothing techniques known to humankind. It helps babies sleep better and is almost irresistibly cute. Beyond the adorable "burrito baby" factor, there are some compelling reasons to swaddle your baby:

Less crying

One study found that swaddling resulted in a 28% reduction in crying.[9] This is especially true over the first 2 months, when babies are particularly fussy and difficult to soothe.[10]

Better sleep

Your newborn baby will sleep better and longer if you put them to sleep while swaddled.[11] Swaddling prevents newborns from startling themselves awake with random arm movements (newborn arms are notoriously flappy,[12] and babies will wake themselves by inadvertently batting themselves in the face).[13]

Reduction in SIDS?

Does swaddling reduce the incidence of SIDS? Support for the idea that swaddling reduces SIDS includes the following:

- Some studies show a decreased risk of SIDS associated with babies sleeping swaddled on their backs.[14]

- Parents who swaddle their babies are far more likely to put them on their backs to sleep.[15]

- Although swaddled babies sleep better, they are more arousable when exposed to noise (lack of arousability has been linked to SIDS).[16]

- A retrospective 8-year study looking at SIDS and infants who were swaddled found no significant risks while being swaddled and sleeping on their backs.[17]

- Sleeping swaddled hinders Baby's ability to flip over onto his stomach,[18] the position most associated with an increased risk of SIDS.

- Swaddling also makes it hard for newborns to inadvertently cover their heads or face with bedding.[19]

Seems simple, right? But it's not. The American Academy of Pediatrics doesn't feel there is compelling evidence that swaddling reduces the risk of SIDS.[20] Further, in 2007, a *Journal of Pediatrics* review of research on swaddling highlighted the benefits of swaddling but also pointed out what has been consistently demonstrated: swaddled babies who are placed facedown or who flip onto their tummies are at a dramatically higher risk of SIDS than unswaddled babies,[21] further confirmed by a more recent meta-analysis.[22] Some experts therefore suggest that parents stop swaddling after 2 months, when babies may begin flipping over.[23]

You're tired, though, and slogging through academic research gives most people a headache. Let's break down the key points you need to know:

- Swaddling helps babies sleep better.

- Swaddling is safe as long as your baby is on her back. Thus, as long as your child isn't flipping over from back to tummy, swaddling is fine.

Listen—I'm not secretly a swaddle-blanket salesperson. I don't have a horse in the baby-swaddling race. But if you're struggling with newborn sleep, swaddling almost always helps.

How to Swaddle Your Newborn Baby

Baby swaddling is a lot like origami: there are many ways to do it, and the right method is the one you most prefer. You have successfully swaddled your baby when their arms don't pop out afterward.

Swaddling a baby with their arms straight down at their sides is the most efficient—it's harder to break out when your arms are straight than when they're bent. But some babies prefer to be swaddled with their arms bent, so feel free to experiment.

In either scenario, the key to successful swaddling is that the arms are flush with the body and the swaddling blanket is relatively snug—snug enough that Baby can't wiggle about, but loose enough that you can comfortably get two fingers in there. (This rule also applies to fitting a bra, FYI.)

The focus of swaddling should be the upper body—the benefits of swaddling stem from keeping the arms largely immobile and close to the body. There is no benefit in swaddling Baby's lower body. In fact, there is a chance that tightly swaddling the legs could lead to Baby developing hip dysplasia.[24] Your baby's legs and hips should be able to move freely while swaddled.

Most people master the fundamentals of swaddling fairly quickly. However, your Baby Houdini might break free while swaddled. Don't worry—this happens to the best of us. Babies are small and squirmy, you're tired, it's dark out. It's like wrapping a Christmas present, only the present is an angry puppy and you're all out of tape.

My own baby origami skills have been wanting, so I generally resort to swaddle blankets with Velcro,[25] which are not necessarily better or more effective, simply less error prone when you're in a dark room at 3 a.m. Most Velcro options include a sack that helps keep baby's legs warm but doesn't constrain leg or hip movement.

Babies will typically fuss or even cry when being swaddled (also true for diaper and clothing changes). This negative response to the *process* of being swaddled does not mean that Baby doesn't *like* swaddling or won't sleep better *while* swaddled. Don't let the complaining fool you. You're laying the foundation for less crying and longer, more continuous sleep.

Swaddle Safety

Swaddling is great, but you do need to be mindful of a few safety concerns:

- Never put a swaddled baby on their tummy. This has been mentioned before, but it's worth repeating. Sleeping facedown while swaddled increases your child's risk of SIDS by at least 12 times, which is far riskier than sleeping facedown unswaddled.

- Make sure other caregivers are 100% clear on this rule. There have been instances of daycare providers putting swaddled babies to sleep on their tummies, which has led to the AAP and other child advocacy groups coming out against swaddling at daycare[26]—not because swaddling is bad, but because lack of awareness was resulting in too many swaddled babies being placed facedown to sleep. Make sure all people in charge of your child's care understand the safe-sleep rules.

- When your child can flip over onto their tummy, you are done with swaddling. Full stop. As soon as you see signs that your child is close to flipping (pushing themselves up onto their side is a strong indicator), you're done with swaddling.

- Don't let Baby overheat. You don't want your baby to be too hot, swaddled or not. In the summer, your swaddled baby may need to be naked underneath the swaddle. Or you may want to experiment with muslin blankets, which are more breathable than cotton or fleece.

Power Tool #3: The Pacifier

The pacifier is one of those Baby Sleep Power Tools that people tend to shy away from, fearing their baby will become addicted to it and will end up a social pariah when they show up at the senior prom with their adult-sized binkie pinned to their lapel.

I too used to poop on pacifiers (not literally—please, I'm not a heathen!). It can be hard to get your baby to take a pacifier to begin with. You have to try out a whole slew of them to find the magic one that works for *your* baby, then you have to make sure you always have some handy (pacifiers seem to get lost even more often than car keys), and despite your best efforts, they're always falling on the floor in public restrooms. Then there is the fear that pacifier use will hinder your nursing efforts (although the myth of "nipple confusion" has been largely debunked). And eventually, you have to figure out a way to get your baby to give up their beloved paci, which is harder than getting them to give up a cupcake. Note: Getting a child to give up a cupcake is notoriously difficult.

So for a long time I figured, yeah, babies have a powerful urge to suck and seem to love pacifiers. But is it worth it?

In a word, *yes*. Can pacifiers cause sleep problems later? Possibly. But there are some compelling reasons to consider the pacifier as part of your newborn sleep Power Tool arsenal, for many reasons:

- Sucking on a pacifier while falling asleep has been shown to significantly reduce the incidence of SIDS.[27] (Note: You don't need to put it back if it falls out—the benefit comes from having it when falling asleep.)

- Pacifiers are enormously soothing for babies and, when combined with other soothing techniques (notably, swaddling and white noise), can significantly improve sleep[28] and reduce crying.[29]

- Introducing pacifiers after breastfeeding has been successfully established can meet Baby's need to suck[30] while giving Mom's boobs a much-deserved break (and your partner a chance to step in). Despite previous beliefs about pacifier use undermining breast-feeding efforts, current research suggests that pacifier use doesn't negatively impact breastfeeding[31] and may even help nursing moms be more successful.[32]

Why Pacifiers Get a Bad Rap

"But I've heard all these horror stories about babies who are using pac-ifiers and are up all night needing the pacifier popped back in! What about the thousands of Pacifier Moms bemoaning their pacifier prob-lems, huh??" And there *are* some legitimate concerns associated with pacifier use:

Pacifiers sometimes cause tooth problems for older children.
If your child is over 2 (some of this applies to kids over 2; all of it applies to kids over 4), they're at higher risk for tooth decay[33] and maloc-clusion[34] (a fancy term for having crooked teeth and needing braces, which will run you at least $3,000 to fix,[35] so that's a pretty compel-ling argument to ditch the paci before your child's second birthday).

Also, I can all but guarantee that your 4-year-old pacifier-loving child will get teased on the playground. It's not cool, but it totally hap-pens. So all in all, many good reasons to wean off the paci before 2 ... but not good reasons to keep your newborn baby from enjoying a nice pacifier while they're little.

Pacifiers sometimes cause sleep problems.
If your baby can fall asleep only with the paci in their mouth, you may find yourself becoming a professional Pacifier Reinsertion Specialist,

called upon to provide your services every hour all night (or nap) long. Pacifier Reinsertion Specialist is a crappy job with no pay, long hours, and no chance of professional advancement (though it does help fill the job gap on your résumé). And some babies will happily fall asleep using the paci at bedtime then demand to nurse constantly because while the paci was "good enough" earlier in the night, as Baby's sleep drive wears off, only boob or bottle will do.

But not *all* babies will require your reinsertion services or demand to nurse or eat constantly. Some babies won't care that the paci has fallen out. Some babies will quickly figure out that they can replace their own paci. And some babies will simply outgrow their love of the paci before problems materialize.

In short, you've got a significant amount of time, especially during the fussy newborn months, when the pacifier provides *enormous* safety and sleep benefits. And the "problems" associated with pacifier use may never be an issue for your baby, and not for months or even years to come.

If you're struggling to get your newborn baby to fall asleep and stay asleep *today*, consider adding the pacifier to your sleep routine. Later, you can choose weaning off the pacifier if or when it becomes a problem.

Getting Baby to Take the Pacifier

Babies often struggle against things (diaper changes, swaddling, pacifiers) that are essential or helpful to their health and happiness. Lots of babies will show the same amount of interest in pacifiers that I show in vehicular maintenance (read: none). But you should try, hard.

- Buy four or five different kinds of pacifiers. Worst-case scenario, baby rejects them all and they become cake decorations for a friend's baby shower.

- Offer the pacifier when your baby is not starving. A starving baby will justifiably get angry when a milkless nipple is shoved in their mouth.

- Offer the pacifier at different times of day. Baby wasn't interested this morning? Try again later. Try tomorrow.

- Experiment with the "pull-out" technique. Place the pacifier into Baby's mouth and then gently flick at the paci as though you're trying to pop it out. Babies' natural response is to suck harder. This does two important things. First, it keeps your baby from instantly spitting out the pacifier and may help them get used to it and even (gasp!) come to enjoy it. Second, it strengthens your baby's suck muscles so that they become better at keeping the pacifier in their mouth, even while sleeping (and thus not need your reinsertion services).

- Try putting a little breast milk or formula on the tip—but no honey, because infant botulism is a real thing.[36]

- If you're nursing, have somebody other than Mom try. Sad but true: somebody who is not Mom will have the best luck with most things.

Ultimately, some babies just won't take the paci despite all your best efforts. If nothing works, okay. You tried. C'est la vie. It's a good tool, but not the only tool you've got.

Power Tool #4: Sleep Schedule Management

"Sleep schedule management" is a phrase with all the sex appeal of an overcooked brussels sprout. But this Baby Sleep Power Tool is foundational to the effectiveness of all the others because if you're trying to help your baby sleep and they're overtired or *not tired enough*, it's going to go poorly. Most of the Power Tools focus on *how* your child falls asleep—this last is about *when*.

Most babies will not simply nod off when they need to. In fact, most will happily (or fussily) stay awake for ages, far past the point when their little bodies need to fall asleep. When awake too long, babies become crabby and difficult to soothe. Even worse, being awake too long can impact sleep hormone and stress hormone production,[37] making it *even harder* to sleep.

Similarly, if babies haven't been awake long *enough*, they won't be sufficiently tired to fall sleep and will justifiably get pissed off at you when you try to put them down for a nap. So, as covered in the previous chapter (How Babies Sleep), the timing of sleep is critical.

Wake Times, Naptimes, and Bedtime

Age	Number of Naps	Duration of Naps	Time between Naps	Time Awake before Bed*	Bedtime	Hours of Night Sleep	Total Hours of Sleep per Day
Birth–6 Weeks	4–8	15 min.–4 hrs.	45 min.–1 hr.	1–4 hrs. (newborns are funky)	Variable but often late: 9–11 p.m.	8–14	14–18
6 Weeks–3 Months	3–5	30 min.–2 hrs	1 hr.–1 hr., 45 mins.	1–2 hrs.	Variable but often late: 8–11 p.m.	8–13	11–15
3–6 Months	3	1–2 hrs.	abt. 2 hrs.	2–3 hrs.	7–9 p.m.	9–12	12–14
6–9 Months	3	1–2 hrs.	2–3 hrs.	abt. 3 hrs.	6:30–8:30 p.m.	9–12	12–14
9–12 Months	2–3	1–2 hrs.	abt. 3 hrs.	4 hrs.	6:30–8:00 p.m.	10–12	12–14
12–18 Months	1–2	1–2 hrs.	3 hrs.	4–5 hrs.	7–8 p.m.	10–12	12–14
18 Months–3 Years	1	1–2 hrs.	–	4–6 hrs.	7–8 p.m.	10–12	11–14

*Babies can typically stay awake progressively longer as the day goes on. For example, a 3-month-old who can only stay awake comfortably for an hour between their morning wake-up and first nap may be perfectly happy staying awake for almost two hours between naps 2 and 3 and for a full two hours or more between their last nap and bedtime.

You'll want, if at all possible, to manage the sleep schedule such that your child is not awake too long or not long enough. Which raises the question: How do you know when it's time for your child to sleep?

If you're *really lucky*, they'll tell you.

Signs That Your Child Is Tired

Some babies remain perfectly happy regardless of how long they've been awake. Others seem just fine until they melt down suddenly, like a slushie in the sun. But some babies give really great signals that they're tired. Your baby might be tired when she:

- starts fussing
- cries for no apparent reason
- loses interest in toys or activities
- must be held
- stops making eye contact
- moves her arms or legs more jerkily
- seems interested in food but won't eat when the food is offered
- rubs her eyes
- blinks in slow motion
- yawns

Tired toddlers and preschoolers become more tantrumy or physical (hitting, grabbing, throwing). Older children or teenagers often don't show outward signs of being overtired, a fact that can mask underlying fatigue (which can have significant consequences).[38]

The challenge with "sleepy signs" is that babies are often unreliable about giving them. Or by the time they exhibit them, they're already *over*tired. So keep one eye on your child and the other eye on the clock. While your child may or may not tell you it's time for sleep, the clock will remain your steadfast friend.

How long your child can comfortably stay awake will depend on their temperament, their age, and, it can seem, the phase of the moon, but this chart should give you a strong starting point. If the amount of time your child is awake is vastly under or over the times suggested here, chances are you're trying to get them to sleep too early or too late. (Nap schedules are discussed in greater detail in Chapter 10, Becoming the Zen Nap Ninja Master.)

Sleep Power Tools Summary: Putting It All Together

When it comes to Sleep Power Tools, few babies need all of them, but all babies will need some. A handful of lucky ones need almost none. However, chances are this is not your baby. (People with easy unicorn rainbow babies generally aren't reading books on baby sleep. They're too busy making handcrafted scrapbooks of Baby's first year during jumbo naps. Don't hate them, but do ask if they can make you a handcrafted baby book since they're making them anyway.)

While there are no hard rules, these are the Power Tools that are likely best for your baby based on your child's personality and age.

White noise
When: The first year
Which babies: All
Use white noise whenever your baby sleeps, throughout the entire first year. Even if your baby has been sleeping without white noise, if they're under a year old, it's not too late to start.

Swaddling
When: Birth to 2–4 months
Which babies: All
Almost all babies will sleep better when swaddled. If your baby is under 2 months of age and you haven't been swaddling, it's not too late to start. For many babies, sleeping while swaddled in a dark room with white noise will provide all the soothing they need.

Pacifier
When: First 4–6 months (although some will continue to use the pacifier successfully until they are 2)
Which babies: All

Newborns need a lot of soothing throughout the day, not just when they're sleeping, so you might find yourself using the pacifier for sleep and also for general fussiness, car trips, Witching Hours, etc. As your baby gets older (after 6 to 8 weeks), try to make the pacifier unique to sleeping. (Don't worry if you still need to use it on rough days—when baby is sick or just cranky.)

Managing the sleep schedule

When: For all eternity (although it's most important for the first few years)

Which babies: All

Some babies are more flexible about blowing a nap, stretching the nap schedule, or generally being inconsistent about sleep. But these babies are anomalies—don't count on yours being this flexible. And even if Baby seems perfectly content to float erratically along, an elastic approach to the sleep schedule will almost always undermine your sleep goals. Ignoring the schedule on occasion is reasonable and necessary because life happens, but routinely blowing it is all but guaranteed to lead to sleep chicanery.

Baby Sleep Power Tools by Age

Age	White Noise	Swaddle	Pacifier	Schedule
0–3 Months	×	×	×	×
3–6 Months	×	×	×	×
6–9 Months	×			×
9–12 Months	×			×

What about Lighting?

I didn't include darkness as one of the Power Tools, but you could argue that I should have.

You'll probably find that newborn babies are capable of sleeping in brightly lit and noisy spaces, creating the impression that babies are flexible and that a dark sleep space is unnecessary. But the truth is, the whole "sleep in bright light" thing works only for newborns.

As babies age, their body develops a more mature circadian rhythm. Recent research has illuminated (ha, see what I did there?) the fact that light exposure near or during sleep can have a significant negative effect on our ability to sleep.[39]

Thus, your newborn is welcome to nap in a bassinet in the living room if that suits your purposes. But after about the first few months, sleeping in darkness is strongly encouraged.

What about Lovies?

A lovey is a small, safe transitional object that babies cuddle with as they're falling asleep. The challenge is that there is no commonly accepted definition for what exactly a lovey is. To some, a lovey is a small square of soft fabric. To others it's a life-sized stuffed panda.

The AAP SIDS position statement says that there should be nothing soft in your child's crib until after their first birthday.[40] This would preclude the use of a lovey.

While younger babies are unlikely to care about a lovey, older babies and toddlers love to grab, rub, chew, smell, or suck on soft things. If your child is one or older, a small (ideally breathable fabric) lovey is probably safe. Discuss it with (or even better, show it to) your pediatrician before introducing it for sleep.

Allies in Independent Sleep

One of the fundamental themes of this book is fostering independent sleep for your child. Hopefully, I've convinced you to embrace some if not most of the Sleep Power Tools, as these are stalwart allies in your quest to gently teach your child to sleep. Hopefully, you've also noticed that most of the Power Tools are used primarily within the first 3 to 6 months. You've probably concluded that this time frame, with your Power Tool allies firmly by your side, is most conducive to gradually coaxing your child to fall asleep independently.

This isn't to say that fostering independent sleep is impossible after 6 months, but your child will have aged out of many of the Power Tools at that point. And in the quest for sleep, the more allies you have, the better.

Teaching Baby to Sleep, Part 1: SWAP
(Sleep With Assistance Plan)

F I GAVE you some eggs, vanilla, and a vat of hot water, could you make a flan? If I tossed in some chocolate, could you make a souf-flé? No?*

Because as wonderful as it is to have great tools to work with, you also need to have a great *plan*. The next two chapters focus on specif-ically that: identifying and implementing the best plan to teach your child how to fall asleep independently.

For people who haven't yet had a baby, this seems achievable. "How hard can it be?" I hear them say. "You put them in their crib, they play with their toes and coo until they fall asleep." Then you have one, and your dream of putting Baby down awake seems as unat-tainable as qualifying for the Olympics. In fact, if you choose a less popular event (we're talking curling here, right?), it would be *easier* to

---

*If you *are* the sort who can whip up fab desserts with three ingredients and no recipe, I would very much like to invite you to come hang in my kitchen.

qualify for the Olympics than to put Baby down in the crib and have them actually fall asleep in there. In fact, maybe we should just put our efforts into making it into the Olympics. Surely if you were to manage a gold medal you would get high-paying sponsors and could use your Olympic celebrity earnings to afford a full-time sleep nanny who could continue rocking, cuddling, feeding, or patting your baby until they go to college, and all of this would be more readily achievable than teaching your baby to fall asleep without you.

However, if making the Olympic curling team seems like an unrealistic solution, let's develop an alternative strategy...

The Easiest Time to Teach Baby to Sleep

Yes, there is an "easiest time." Note I did not say easy, just easiest. The rule of thumb is "younger is better." While wine gets better with age, sleep training does not.

The easiest time to work on teaching babies to fall asleep on their own is when they are about 2 to 4 months old. If you are the parent of a 2- to 4-month-old, you may be thinking, "You are a HUGE LIAR!" And for some babies, it's *never* easy. Maybe you prefer the phrase "less horrible time"? But I can promise you that it doesn't get any easier as they get older.

Babies are born without a well-developed circadian rhythm, which is why they essentially nap 24 hours a day. The circadian rhythm (along with sleep drive) is an essential component of falling asleep at bedtime, so you want to wait for that to develop before moving forward with SWAPs. It tends to happen at around 2 months, and there are some key signs to look for:

- The time at which your baby falls asleep at night becomes more predictable (within a 30-minute window).

- Bedtime is followed by the longest stretch of uninterrupted sleep for the day.

- Your baby falls asleep fairly quickly at bedtime (i.e., it used to take 45 minutes of vigorous bouncing on a yoga ball but now happens within 10–15 minutes of rocking).

Why is this the best time to teach your baby to sleep?

- They're young enough that you can still safely and effectively use any or all of the Power Tools. And trust me, when you're trying to gently convince a nurse-to-sleep 4-month-old to sleep without nursing, those tools are essential. Removing nursing from sleep is like having somebody take your diamond tennis bracelet and hand you a pink plastic tiara. The Power Tools are like somebody taking your plastic tiara and handing you a cozy duvet and a nice cup of tea.

- Your younger baby is still learning how to fall asleep and thus is far more malleable than an 11-month-old, who is firmly convinced that there is only one way to fall asleep.

- Sleep association issues can start to cause noticeable problems as early as 2–3 months. Even younger babies sleep better when they do so independently.

- Some fairly predictable sleep setbacks occur between 4 and 9 months (sleep regressions, teething, separation anxiety, etc.—see Chapter 12, (Un)Common Sleep Setbacks). Starting early ensures that you've established a strong foundation for good sleep before hitting those potential snags.

- Experience suggests it is vastly more likely that families will adhere to safe sleep guidelines when they're actually sleeping. Establishing healthy sleep hygiene as soon as possible benefits the family on every level.

Perhaps a more useful way to consider the issue of "when" is to simply say, "now." Because unless you just gave birth yesterday, this month is going to be easier than next month. Barring extenuating circumstances (baby is sick, you're in the midst of an ill-advised 3-week camping trip), the ideal time to start chipping away at this is today.

Teaching Baby to Sleep: The Fundamentals

The #1 question I get asked is "What's up with your hair?" The #2 question is "How do I teach my baby to fall asleep?" Parents all over the world are hoping for a magic solution so secret that no baby book ever mentions it for fear of diluting its potency by having too many people know about it. I will share that solution with you. It is, however, sadly magic-free.

Teaching your child to fall asleep independently is a lot like convincing them to eat vegetables. You don't put a giant broccoli salad in front of a 4-year-old and expect them to dive in. You sneak a little veggie into the mix here and there until, over time, you end up with a child who consumes enough vegetables to avoid getting rickets.

Consider the fact that you've *been* teaching your child how to sleep since the day they were born. You've used techniques like rocking, cuddling, and nursing or feeding. Because that's how you've always done it, it's the only way your child knows how to sleep. Teaching your child to sleep independently means introducing *new* techniques and sleep associations that lead to better-quality sleep *because those new things are persistent* throughout the night.

This means falling asleep in a different way. And guess what? Doing something differently is *harder* than doing it the way you're *used* to doing it.

We're going to discuss a number of techniques to foster independent sleep that are aligned with your child's temperament, personal preferences, and age. However, any effort to teach your baby to sleep should be based on a solid foundation that includes the following:

- Start with bedtime. There is a huge biological compulsion to sleep at bedtime, so this will almost always be an easier journey than mastering independent sleep at naptime. Is bedtime magic? It is at my house. It's the only time of day when two adults can hear themselves speak at normal conversational volume. It's also your best starting point.

- Have a consistent, age-appropriate bedtime (see Chapter 3, Bedtime Is the New Happy Hour). If your child has been falling asleep at the same time every night, it's almost impossible for them to not sleep at this time. This is how you stack the sleep deck in your favor.

- Have a consistent bedtime routine. It doesn't have to be long—20 to 30 minutes is fine—but it does have to be a series of calming activities that you can commit to doing every night.

- Make sure that the bedroom is dark. Blackout blinds are almost always required. Darkness is a powerful sleep cue and will help induce sleep. Nightlights are fine.

If you've mastered the basics, you're ready (and you are, right?) to start teaching your baby independent sleep.

Six Sleep With Assistance Plans (SWAPs) to Help Baby Learn to Sleep without You

Experience has shown that while there may be "one ring to rule them all," there is no "one way to teach babies to sleep." Babies are individuals with unique temperaments and their own sleep associations. With enough commitment and consistency, any method will work, but things go more smoothly when you start with a strategy that is the best fit for you and your child.

To this end, here are six Sleep With Assistance Plans, or SWAPs. As a category, SWAPs (generally) involve a gradual approach, require a substantial degree of parental involvement, and take a bit longer to implement (as compared to the methods outlined in Chapter 7, Teaching Your Baby to Sleep, Part 2).

I've coined the term SWAP because everybody else has coined *their* own baby sleep term and I was feeling left out. And also because it's a good umbrella term to encapsulate the range of strategies that gradually encourage independent sleep.

Many infant sleep philosophies focus on "gentle" methods, but "gradual" is a more accurate term. Gentle is often assumed to mean "no cry," and for most of us, "no cry" is an unrealistic target. When you deviate from the norm, most babies will squawk, fuss, or even scream boisterously. Some will cry loudly and with great gusto even as you're actively trying to soothe them. The term "gentle" also creates a dichotomy where everything else defaults to "harsh," which is both unfair and inaccurate.

A few tears don't mean that you're unloving or that you're doing the wrong thing. Tears mean you're frustrating your child, and that's *absolutely okay*. Part of your job is to give your child the space to muddle through hard things as they develop new skills. This is neither the first nor the last time your child will struggle to overcome a challenge. Don't let angry or upset feelings derail you. Change is hard, and all human beings resist it. Have faith in your kiddos—they're capable of wondrous things.

The SWAPs focus primarily on *gradually* making small changes to how your child falls asleep. The upside to using a SWAP is that many can be highly successful with younger babies. Also, many parents have deeply held philosophies that make being present or taking a more gradual approach appealing. And while I use the word *gradually* a lot in this chapter, for some adaptable babies, a SWAP can work within days. If you are just beginning to consider options to help your child learn to sleep independently, I would encourage you to start with a SWAP.

The downside of SWAPs is that it *may* take weeks before things improve. This, as you can imagine, requires that you remain committed to persistent implementation of your plan the whole time. As the days pass, you may come to fear that it's all a huge exercise in futility. The bedtime routine that previously wrapped up in a neat 15 minutes is now a 94-minute cycle of frustration. It's easy to get derailed and slip up and go back to the old way "just one time." But that one time can unravel all the headway you've made. I don't share this to dissuade you, simply to give you some perspective as you decide if a SWAP is really the right strategy for you.

Without further ado, here are the SWAPs for your consideration. Please peruse the full list and pick the *one* (there can be only one!) that you feel most ready to commit to for *at least* 5 days.

More Soothing

Who This Is Best For: Babies under 4 months; older high-needs and/or reflux babies

As discussed in Chapter 5, Baby Sleep Power Tools, younger babies need a lot of soothing to settle into sleep. Especially for newborns, the default source of soothing is *you*: babies sleep on your lap, while you babywear, during nursing, in your arms... All of which is great if it works for you. However, often it doesn't. Sleeping on you can lead to unsafe sleep situations. Sometimes you need your body free so you can [work/care for older children/take care of your own needs].

Having a baby who won't sleep longer than 20 minutes if they're not on your lap becomes a problem.

Similarly, kids with reflux or colic, or who are just generally high-needs (because some babies are like that), will need more soothing far longer than you might expect.

Here are some signs you have a baby who needs more soothing:

· They take persistently short naps.
· They struggle to fall asleep.
· They wake at night substantially more often than could be reasonably explained by hunger.
· They only sleep on you.

The solution is often to provide more soothing. And how do we do that? You guessed it—the Baby Sleep Power Tools.

People often skip this step due to the mistaken belief that "independent sleep" is the same as "no Power Tools." Or they view it as a step backward—"But we stopped swaddling at 6 weeks!" The place we're all working to move toward is the one where your child is capable of falling asleep on their own at naps and bedtime, creating the basis for them to sleep solidly through the night, with minimal tears (yours or theirs) in the process. The goal is not *no* sleep tools—it's the *right* sleep tools.

If you aren't already using these and your child is under 4 months, consider using or reintroducing:

· white noise
· a dark room to sleep in
· swaddling (provided they are not showing signs of flipping in either direction)

If you're already using those tools and sleep is still elusive, kick it up a notch with:
· a pacifier*

---

* As noted previously, pacifiers are powerful soothing tools that can *sometimes* be problematic. The issues with pacifiers are largely specific to older babies, so they can still be a safe and effective method to provide soothing to younger babies. If, however, the pacifier is actually *causing* sleep problems, then move on to "Weaning off Sucking," below.

If you are successfully swaddling your child and putting them down awake in their crib with the white noise playing and walking out the door while they fall asleep, winner winner chicken dinner! If not, add a second SWAP to your plan.

Fuss It Out (FIO)

Who This Is Best For: Most babies older than 2 months

Use all the great Power Tools that are age-appropriate for your child. Soothe your child until they are calm and drowsy. Put them in the crib while they're still awake. Walk away.

Set a timer for 15 or even 20 minutes. Wait for the full time allotment before returning to your baby—15 minutes can seem like an eternity, but it's not, so no cheating. Regardless of how improbable it may seem that Baby will actually fall asleep, *wait*. Baby may fuss and grumble. Baby may sound as though he's furious with you. (Note: He's probably furious with you.) Give him space, see what he does with it.

If your baby falls asleep, *shazam!* You've done it. This doesn't mean you're done and sleep will be one big puppy party from here on out, but you've taken a *huge* step toward independent sleep.

This is your new bedtime routine. You may have some hiccups along the way and need to go in and help your child periodically, but for the most part you've successfully found a way to help your child sleep without you.

But what happens if the timer goes off and your child is *not* asleep? Now you've got a decision to make, depending on the circumstances:

1. Baby is calm but awake. If baby is happy, you're happy. Leave well enough alone and see what develops.

2. Baby is fussy or grumbly but not screaming. For the sake of your experiment, fussy is okay for now. Give it some more time and see what develops.

3. Baby is screaming as though to wake the dead. You're probably thinking you should rush in, because the last thing anybody needs is a house full of recently awakened dead people. And probably you should. But before you do, consider this small caveat: some babies actually will scream and scream and scream and then

boom!—sleep. For these babies, there is no gradual decrease in screaming to indicate sleep is imminent. It's like flipping a switch: SCREAM then SLEEP. If this is your child, they could be one minute away from sleep. Unfortunately, we don't currently have a litmus test to know if your child is one minute or 1 hour from sleep, so determining the best course of action at this juncture requires some guesstimation. Perhaps you wait a few more minutes just to see what develops; perhaps you consider this a failed experiment and go back to your usual method of soothing your baby to sleep. Listen to your gut instinct.

If your FIO experiment does not result in sleep today, that's fine. Wait a day, or even a week, and try again. Your baby is developing at an incredible rate, so what doesn't work today may be a rousing success next week. Keep experimenting.

"Wait," you say. "Isn't this just Cry It Out (more on this in Chapter 7) with a better name?"

No, it's not. Cry It Out is not an experiment; it's a committed decision. Fuss It Out is simply giving your child a brief window of time to see what they can do if you give them some practice space. While it won't work for all babies, many will actually fall asleep quickly and easily once their parents remove themselves from the process. (Yes, sometimes our involvement *is actually the problem*.) And, unlike Cry It Out, FIO has a set, relatively short time limit. If it's not working, we end the experiment and go back to our regularly scheduled method.

The Double Take

Who This Is Best For: Younger (under 4 months) babies, but can be attempted with kids of all ages

Soothe your child *fully to sleep* using whatever method works best for you, and place them in their bed. Once they are there, wake them *just slightly*. Then allow them to fall back into a deep sleep *in* their bed.

Your instinct is to flinch away from the suggestion that you undo all your hard work by waking them back up, but this technique helps your baby identify that they are, in fact, in their bed, so that when they wake later in the night, they're not surprised to find themselves there.

The key here is to remove any unsustainable sleep associations *before* waking them back up. If your child falls asleep with the pacifier, remove the pacifier before waking them up. If your child falls asleep while being held or nursed, make sure to put them down or pop them off first.

Sometimes it's physically hard to do—waking a sleeping baby is like making good gluten-free bread: easy in theory, challenging in practice. You may need to unzip their PJs, tickle their tummy, or make razzberries on their toes.

How awake do they need to be? Somewhere between "eyes barely flutter open" and "discussing the latest issue of *The New Yorker*." People generally err on the side of "not awake enough" because they're afraid of mucking things up. You'll know you've achieved "awake enough" when your baby grumbles about your rude behavior. Another sign that they're "awake enough" will be a reduction in night waking.

Caveat: This is a great technique to experiment with, but it may not resolve all sleep-association challenges. Remember, sleep associations are formed by activities that occur at *or near to* the time your child falls asleep. Waking up slightly at the conclusion of a 20-minute rocking session may remove the rock = sleep association . . . or it may not. If you've successfully implemented the Double Take with your child for a number of nights with no subsequent improvement in sleep, then it's not working, and it's time to move on to a different technique.

Gradual Weaning

Who This Is Best For: Younger (2- to 6-month-old) babies on up

As the name suggests, gradual weaning is simply taking baby steps to progressively do less of whatever it is that you're currently doing to help your child fall asleep. There are many approaches to gradual weaning, but they all boil down to the concept expressed by this haiku:

Gradually do less
Tears and complaints may ensue
Press on regardless

"Yes, but *how* do I put my baby down awake without [rocking/nursing/sleeping on my chest/her pacifier]?" People are looking for a

What Type of Baby Do You Have?

	Motion Junkies	Suckers (bottle, nursing, pacifier)	Cuddlers (co-sleepers, nursing)
How They Fall Asleep	Being held while you walk, rocking, bouncing on an exercise ball, during babywearing.	Nursing, feeding, sucking a pacifier. Might enjoy their own fingers or thumb sucking (although generally this isn't a problem).	Must. Be. Held. Sleeps on or near you, on your chest, on your lap, or while being worn. Refuses to fall asleep if not in direct physical contact with you. Generally prefers one parent over the other.
Level of Weaning Difficulty*	Low*	High	Medium

* This is a relative scale. They're all hard to gently wean off.

stepwise process to follow because they're tired and afraid of making mistakes, and I understand that "just do less of what you're doing" isn't particularly helpful.

So let's break it down by looking at whatever your baby is really into. Broadly speaking, most babies fall into one of three categories, although your baby may be in more than one.

Gradual Weaning for Motion Junkies

Who This Is Best For: Younger babies (2- to 4-month-olds)

Option #1: Jiggle the crib

Continue rocking or bouncing your little one until they are drowsy or almost asleep. Put them into the crib and then jiggle the crib until they fall asleep. Please note: Jiggling is just as the name suggests—light jiggling. This is not a violent motion, but simply replicating (as much as possible) the bouncy motion your child enjoys.

At first you may need to rock or jiggle the crib for a long time, so don't get frustrated if your little one is still squawking at you after 20 or 30 minutes. This is new, and jiggling in the crib is not nearly as much fun as bouncing on the yoga ball with you. Use your bedtime words or continue to shush while doing this. If you can, try to avoid direct eye contact, as that can be very stimulating for babies.

On subsequent nights, provide less and less crib jiggling. So if on night #1 it took your baby 35 minutes to fall asleep, try to stop jiggling at 30 minutes, then 25, 20, etc., until the jiggling is no longer necessary. Your child may fuss, cry, or scream while you do this. That doesn't matter. What matters is that the process ends with them falling asleep *in the crib*.

With this method you are still present, so you haven't entirely kicked your independent sleep problem—your child is falling asleep with you there and will be upset when they wake up later to find you mysteriously *missing*. But ideally, after 3 or 4 nights you're simply putting baby in the crib (no jiggling) and walking out the door. At this point you should see a dramatic reduction in night waking.

Option #2: Pat transition

Babies who are older (6 months or more) are challenging because they want to put everything you own into their mouth, and your keys and cellphone are always coated with drool. They also tend to express their disapproval with your "sleep in the crib" plan by standing up. Jiggling the crib while your 8-month-old baby is standing in it is not going to lead to sleep.

If this is happening to you, you can modify Option #1 by lightly placing your hand on your child's back or tummy (depending on whether they are independently flipping themselves over or remaining on their back) and gently patting them like a drum. This provides a soothing trifecta because:

1. You are present.
2. You're making direct physical contact.
3. The patting helps to recreate the sensation of motion that your motion junkie enjoys.

It has an additional benefit in that you can use this method to coax your baby to stay lying down while you help them learn to fall asleep in the crib.

As with Option #1, you may have to stand there patting your baby for a long time. If you are short and reaching into the bowels of the crib for an hour is going to throw your back out, this may not be the best option for you. But if you can stick it out, gradually reduce the amount of patting by at least 5 minutes a night. Eventually you'll be able to lay Baby gently into the crib and have her fall asleep without direct physical contact with you.

Initially, Baby is still falling asleep with you present and will likely continue to wake during the night (again, you haven't quite cleared the "independent sleep" hurdle because you are present and patting as they fall asleep). However, your goal is to progressively reduce the amount of patting at bedtime to "none" so you can leave the room *before* your child falls asleep, at which point the night waking should significantly diminish.

Gradual Weaning for Suckers

Who This Is Best For: Babies under 4 months

Helping a baby who loves to suck learn to sleep *sans* sucking is a challenge because sucking is a binary function: you either *are* or *are not* sucking. Some babies are so into sucking, they cling to their [pacifier/bottle/boob] like it's the last hot wing at the Super Bowl party.

If your baby is that much of a sucker, then I would like to talk to them about a time-share in Atlantic City. Oh wait, not that kind of sucker...

Option #1: The pull-out method

[Insert inappropriate joke here.] Let your baby suck (boob, bottle, or paci) until they are calm and drowsy, then pop them off and put them in their bed. If they are relatively calm—quiet to mild fussing—leave them alone. If they get upset, reinsert boob, bottle, or paci (ideally while they remain in their bed, although this may not be feasible for nursing moms) until they are once again calm and drowsy, but pop them off *before they fall asleep* and put them back in bed. Repeat until you achieve success.

The Pull-Out Method can be challenging (and sometimes painful!) for nursing moms. If your baby is fighting this process to the point that your breasts are getting sore from the abuse, stop. It's not worth creating nipple lesions that could lead to infection. The Pull-Out Method does work well for many babies, though, and I don't want to dissuade you from trying it for your little sucker. I do want to arm you with the knowledge that babies frequently get pretty pissed at you while you're doing this. This "pissiness" is not specific to the method but is a normal human response to change. The amount of time between "popping off boob" and "returning to put back on boob" may leave just enough time to give your partner the side-eye and say, "We are being punished for sins in a previous life."

Many parents observe that their child is either sucking or FURI-OUS, so popping them off while quiet is a near impossibility. As this goes on, you may be tempted to concede defeat and let your child fall asleep while sucking. This would be a mistake. It's critical that you pop them off *before* they fall asleep. If you work at this for 45 minutes then let them suck until they're fully asleep, you've wasted that 45 minutes. So let them suck until they are calm and drowsy then pop them off. Repeat as necessary.

The first night may be a challenge, but subsequent nights should get significantly easier. Eventually, sucking should become vastly reduced or, ideally, fully removed from your bedtime routine. When this happens, the last bottle or nursing session of the day should get shuffled to an earlier part of the routine, ideally 15 to 20 minutes before your child falls asleep. The previous routine (e.g., bath, PJs, books, boob, bed) is now modified to reflect a significant gap between sucking and sleep (e.g., boob, bath, PJs, books, bed).

This is a critical but often skipped step. Yes, it's wonderful that your baby has successfully figured out how to fall asleep without sucking. But sucking *near* bedtime can fully sabotage your efforts by maintaining the existing suck = sleep association. So do a well-deserved victory lap, but don't forget to remove sucking from the final steps of your routine.

Option #2: The anything-but method

Separate the last nurse, bottle, or paci from bedtime by 20 minutes. Help your baby fall asleep without sucking using any of the following that you feel are most appropriate for your child:

- A lovey to hold or chew on (if your child is old enough). Ideally this smells like Mom, so wear it tucked into your bra for a few days.

- Rubbing their back or belly or patting them like a drum.

- Shushing or quietly repeating phrases like "Time for sleep, bub."

- Cuddling.

This may seem like a lateral move because it is a lateral move. Your baby is still not falling asleep without you. They are, however, falling asleep without sucking. And as mentioned earlier, sucking, due to its binary nature, is the hardest thing to gently wean off. The Anything-But Method is a transition from a suck = sleep association to a something else = sleep association where "something else" is something we can more easily or gradually wean off. Some people resist this idea because they want to skip jumping over 472 sleep hurdles and just get the job done. Which is totally fine: if hurdles aren't your thing, feel free to skip ahead to Chapter 7, Teaching Baby to Sleep, Part 2: SLIP. But any gradual approach to independent sleep is, unfortunately, going to require a hurdle or two.

Most often, you've now turned your sucker into a cuddler (and babies who love to nurse to sleep are de facto cuddlers anyway), so we can start gently weaning out of *that* using the next SWAP.

Gradual Weaning for Cuddlers

Who This Is Best For: Babies up to 6 months

Teaching your baby to sleep without your body can be challenging. Parental cuddles are the gold standard of baby soothing. Convincing your child to fall asleep without your cuddles is like asking them to move out of the Taj Mahal. What can you offer them that will make moving out of the Taj Mahal sound like a good idea? Nothing, that's what.

This transition takes a bit of time and coaxing, but it can be done. The crib is the safest space for your child, and this method can help your baby learn to sleep in one.

Every time your child falls asleep on or with you, you're teaching your child that *your body* is an essential element of sleep. You need to gradually teach them that your body is not, in fact, essential, and you can do this by gradually making itty-bitty adjustments to the way your child falls asleep.

Pro tip: If your baby is really into *one* parent (as is often the case for nursing moms), you may want to temporarily remove *that* parent from the scene during the bedtime routine. Your baby may get pissed at you because Mom is their favorite lovey. Now you're stealing lovies from a baby (next you'll be kicking puppies, you monster!). But babies will accept change more readily from the parent who is *not* their human lovey.

Step 1

If necessary, teach your child to fall asleep while lying down. Often, babies are worn to sleep (in wraps, for example) then either stay worn for the duration of sleep or are snuck into their crib once asleep. These babies have a sleep association that involves cuddling, motion, and being upright. If this describes your child, start by getting them used to the idea of sleeping motionless on their back.

If your baby is less than 2 months old, it may be helpful to start by swaddling. Babies who are carried or worn to sleep are often used to and enjoy the feeling of confinement, and swaddling can replicate that sensation.

At your normal bedtime or naptime, go through the same consistent sleep routine you typically do (hopefully, this is more involved than just "babywearing"). Help your baby to fall asleep: pat their back, rub their belly, sing quietly... The goal here is not independent sleep (yet)—it's sleeping motionless while lying down. You are present and touching your child but they are not sleeping on you or cuddled up next to you. Ideally your child is in the crib/bassinet and you are present and touching them but they're falling asleep in their own sleep space.

Step 2

Gradually reduce your engagement with your child as they fall asleep. Each night, do less of whatever you do—singing, talking, patting, etc.—either by shortening the duration (from 20 minutes, say, to 15) or by decreasing the intensity (so that butt-patting morphs into a hand gently laid on Baby's back).

Continue for several days until, after your bedtime routine, you are simply present but not actively engaging. You might sit quietly in a chair nearby.

Step 3

Fade out your presence at bedtime. Each night move the chair two feet farther from the crib and two feet closer to the door.

After a few days, you should have moved yourself out of the room. Put Baby down awake in the crib and walk out the door (or, more commonly, sprint out the door with the velocity of an unladen swallow). Your child is falling asleep independently in their own crib. Mission accomplished!

What This Looks Like for Co-sleepers

Co-sleeping parents can feel stuck between a baby who either sleeps on you or is furiously upset. Ideally the goal is to move your child into the crib as quickly as possible. Some parents may find that moving directly to the crib is too abrupt a change and that a more gradual approach is required. Here's what this might look like through a series of nights:

1. Baby is used to sleeping snuggled tight next to your body, so you put a small space—an inch or two—between you. Kiddo is not keen about this and continues to shift over every time you move. So you use your hand to gently weigh her down and maintain the space. She's not happy about this, and lets you know, but you persist even though the bedtime routine now takes 45 minutes. You are convinced this will never work and dinner is getting cold downstairs and why did you ever listen to this stupid book? Eventually, it does work. But your partner ate all the dumplings and watched your favorite show while you were stuck upstairs. This sucks.

Gradual Weaning for Cuddlers

2. You expand the space between you to 6 inches. Baby is barking her displeasure about this, but you're firm yet loving. You hold your hand gently on her belly while singing quietly, and after 20 minutes she falls asleep. Your partner is given explicit orders not to watch TV until you return. You mean it, you are not kidding. If you are stuck in bedtime purgatory, he should be too.

3. Tonight there is a one-foot gap between you and Baby and it takes her only 8 minutes to fall asleep. However, you're still there, singing with your hand on her belly, and she's still waking frequently at night. Is this working? Probably not. You are all doomed.

4. Tonight the gap between you and Baby is as long as your arm. Your hand is still on her belly at bedtime, but you sing or use your words for only 3 minutes then pretend to sleep . . . which is hard, because she's chewing on your knuckles, but you stick with it. You give an Oscar-caliber sleep performance. Incredibly, it works.

5. You are definitely creating space at bedtime, which is great, but now it's time to remove your hand from her body, and that does not go well. She crawls over to you a few times, forcing you to place her back on "her side" of the bed. But you continue to sing or use your words, and within 5 minutes she's asleep.

6. You put Baby down, lie nearby, sing a few songs, and she falls asleep. You are clearly the Great Maharaja of Baby Sleep and you can't believe you ever doubted yourself, as you obviously have exceptional baby sleep skills. Is there a baby sleep competition you should sign up for? Maybe this is a new career!

7. Feeling sassy, you decide to put Baby in the crib next to your bed, which has previously been used exclusively for laundry storage. Because you are the Maharaja of Baby Sleep, you are confident this will be a breeze. Baby has other plans. You're back to singing with your hand on her belly. Bedtime takes 30 minutes and your partner ate the last slice of pie.

8. Your partner is under strict instructions to neither eat nor to watch anything cool while you are upstairs. In fact, he should bake a pie

for you to compensate for last night. You are committed to the crib plan, but Baby isn't keen. Amazingly, it takes only 10 minutes of singing with your hand on her belly to get her to fall asleep. What is this feeling you have? Is it . . . hope? Is that what hope feels like?

9. You put Baby in the crib and sing for 5 minutes. No touching. She falls asleep. It's a miracle! You and your partner celebrate with some much-deserved homemade pie.

Evaluating Your SWAP Progress

Sometimes, things will go poorly and you will be convinced that you're doomed. Your knee-jerk reaction will be to go back to whatever you are trying to gradually wean off because "at least that works." It's easy to get stuck with "it's not great but we can live with it." It takes real courage to move in a new direction. Change is scary, and your negligent Sleep Fairy will whisper, "This isn't working—go back to the old way!" Sleep Fairies are terrible. Also, they'll eat the last of your ice cream but leave the empty container in the freezer.

As with any experiment, some things will work and some won't. Some days will go more smoothly than others. If you've identified a SWAP that feels like the best fit for you, commit to it for 5 to 7 days. *This is key.* Mastering a new skill takes time and commitment. Nobody bats a home run when they first step to the plate, but it doesn't mean you don't have a home run *in* you. Just keep swinging.

Here are some signs that you *are* on the right track:

- Bedtime is an enjoyable activity that all participants look forward to.

- Your child is sleeping longer or with fewer interruptions.

- Your child sleeps in the same location all night long.

- You're feeling confident enough to start working on a similar strategy for naps. Or, if you're already working on naps, naps are getting longer or your child falls asleep at naptime more easily.

- You are currently at or moving toward a solid age-appropriate night-sleep/feeding schedule.

If, however, you have fully and consistently committed to your SWAP for about a week and some or all of these things are not true for you, it may be time to re-evaluate the plan. Your plan may not be working for any number of reasons:

- It's not the right strategy for your baby. All babies are different.

- You're not being consistent. The Goddess of Consistency is an unforgiving wench. You want to be constantly moving in one direction. Even a small step backward can derail your efforts.

- You got stalled. You started on your plan to change things up at bedtime but got scared. (If so, you're in good company—this is really common.) Instead of continuing down the path to change, you made some smaller changes and then . . . stopped. Now you're stuck in the Valley of No Progress. It's hot in there, and there are lots of spiders. It's okay to pause to catch your breath, but you don't want to hang around there. Because spiders.

- Travel, illness, regression, or a growth spurt blew up on you. It happens. Reset the clock and start again.

If it's been 3 to 5 days and you are overwhelmingly convinced that your SWAP is a crushing failure, there are generally two possibilities:

1. You're doing it wrong. Yes, I said it. Generally, the issue is either not trying hard enough or dabbling. After a long slog of a day, you don't want to arm-wrestle with baby sleep issues at bedtime because your reservoir of emotional energy is empty. So instead of digging in, you fall back into old habits. Everybody does this. You're forgiven. But now you know: it's not going to work without commitment—inconvenient, scary, sometimes stressful commitment.

2. This isn't the right technique for you. You made a solid go of it, but it didn't work out. Hit the pause button, take a few days, and reconsider your approach. Maybe it's time for a new plan.

It goes without saying (but I will say it anyway just so we're all on the same page) that this stuff is REALLY, REALLY hard. And momentum is working against you—you've been doing things one way for ages, and babies don't like change. They also don't fall asleep easily. That combines with teething, sleep regressions, travel, daycare, illness, etc. to make teaching Baby to sleep feel like a Sisyphean task. It's easy to give up.

But don't. You *can* do this.

And one way or another, you *will*.

Still Up All Night?

Once your child is falling asleep without your direct assistance, you should immediately see at least a 50% reduction in night waking. Some kiddos will go from frequent night waking to sleeping through the night within a few days. Others will keep waking frequently and demanding tons of assistance to fall back to sleep. Often the pattern looks something like this:

1. Bedtime is a relatively smooth affair where Baby is falling asleep independently.

2. There is a longer stretch of sleep in the beginning of the night but things get progressively worse as the night goes on.

3. There may be brief periods (10 to 20 minutes) of grumbling here and there.

4. You try to coax Baby back to sleep with various techniques, but only one works reliably.

5. It takes increasingly more involved intervention to get Baby to fall back to sleep toward morning.

You did what you were supposed to do at bedtime, so why are you stuck in Crap Sleep Purgatory? There's a niggling issue tripping you up, and it's probably one of these:

• You're [rocking/cuddling/nursing/feeding] Baby until they're mostly asleep. People often ask, "How awake is 'awake enough'?" The answer is, if you're still seeing the pattern above, it's not awake enough.

- You're nursing or feeding at bedtime. If the last step in your bedtime routine is a nice nursing session or a bottle, you're likely inadvertently reinforcing the eat = sleep association. Switch up your routine so that there is about a 20-minute gap between the last bottle or nursing session and bedtime.

- You put Baby down awake in the crib with a pacifier. I hate to be a buzzkill, but if your older baby is falling asleep with a pacifier, they haven't entirely learned how to fall asleep yet. Even if the pacifier falls out before they actually fall asleep, using the pacifier at bedtime can sustain Baby's suck = sleep association. You'll know you have this issue if your pacifier-loving baby requires you to reinsert the paci all night long, or they fall asleep happily with the pacifier but then fight your gentle night-weaning attempts with the ferocity of an angry Viking.

- You're hanging around until Baby falls asleep. Your child has developed a "you're there" = sleep association and now wakes up in the night unable to fall back to sleep because you're no longer there. Hanging around is a great transitional step toward independent sleep—the key word being transitional. Eventually you must leave the room before they're asleep.

- A timed device shuts off. As a general rule, if it works on a timer (mobile, music, sleepy sheep, stars projected onto the ceiling), you don't want it. Unless it's a coffee maker that automatically makes a fresh pot at 6 a.m., because those are awesome.

When SWAPs Are an Epic Failure

What if you've tried your best but your efforts at implementing a SWAP have been a huge mess and bedtime is a frustrating, drawn-out process for all involved? Then your SWAP is not working for you. Full stop.

SWAPs won't work for all children. Some kids respond to your efforts to make gradual change by fighting *harder* and *longer* to keep things as they are. Change is hard, and your child may say, "Stick to the *old* plan, Mom, STICK TO THE OLD PLAN!" Your attempt to implement a SWAP may have turned bedtime into an endless gladiatorial battle, and those never end well. It doesn't mean you are failing or that you have a bad kiddo. It's just not the right approach. SWAPs aren't for everybody.

It may simply be that a SWAP is not a good fit for your child. That's okay. You can consider...

7

Teaching Baby to Sleep, Part 2: SLIP
(Sleep Learning Independence Plan)

THE PREVIOUS CHAPTER focused on gradual strategies to foster independent sleep, known collectively as SWAPs. SWAP strategies are often highly effective, and I encourage you to start there. But SWAPs don't work for everybody. SWAPs may not work for you if:

- sleep is so disastrous that "chip away at it gradually" is not a viable option

- your physical and emotional reserves are on empty (let's be honest—the SWAPs require you to have some gas in the tank)

- you've tried one or more SWAPs without success

Another option is sleep training *without* parental assistance. This is known by many names (cry it out or CIO, Ferberizing, etc.), but fundamentally it comes down to putting your child in a safe sleep space—generally a crib—at bedtime and letting them figure out how to fall asleep on their own. Predictably, this involves some tears, because change is hard and tears mark the struggle to do something new.

A brief note on cry vs. no-cry sleep strategies

Many parents have the impression that while sleep is important, it's not nearly as important as sparing our children from upset feelings or frustrations, that helping them sleep is great as long as the child *never complains about it*, that strict adherence to no-cry sleep surpasses all other considerations: family health, safety, adequate sleep for the child, maternal well-being...

But the reality is that many kids will *need* to cry a bit as they figure out how to fall asleep, even when parents use "no-cry" strategies. Many of these strategies, even the SWAPs discussed in this book, involve some degree of crying or fussing *while a parent is present or periodically returning*. So while the labels "cry it out" and "no-cry" have become pervasive, they're neither accurate nor helpful.

The question is not "Are we open to a few tears as part of this process?" It is "Based on where we are in regards to sleep, our child's temperament, and what we've learned from previous attempts, which strategy will be the most effective strategy for our child?"

A strategy is effective when:

1. We (as parents) have a high likelihood of implementing it successfully.

2. It's a good fit for our child based on age, temperament, etc.

3. It results in significant positive change within a reasonable time frame.

Ideally, we're evaluating sleep strategies based on how effective they are at establishing healthy sleep for the family. The strategies may involve more crying or less. They may take weeks or just a few days. There is no wrong or right, just what works best for your child.

Unfortunately, the dichotomy between cry vs. no-cry has led to substantial misinformation, confusion, and parent shaming around sleep training methods. Further, there are many frustratingly persistent myths about it.

Sleep Training Myths

· ·

1. People resort to sleep training because they are lazy, ignorant, or selfish.

People use this approach because, although they've worked diligently to help their child learn to fall asleep using other methods, those methods are not working. And because, they are thoughtful people who understand how important sleep is to human beings, they've made the rational choice to cease doing what isn't working.

2. It will break the bond of love or trust between you and your child.

Are you responsive to meeting your child's needs every day? Have you been doing this since birth? Will you continue to do so in the future? Of course! Sleep training occurs for a few hours over the course of a few days. Compared to the months and years you will spend with your child, it doesn't even register. The research the anti-sleep training contingent likes to reference on this topic is focused on hideously abused and neglected children in truly tragic circumstances.[1] That is not even remotely what we are talking about here.

3. It will damage your child.

There is no evidence that a few nights of crying will harm your child in any way. Some day in the near future, when it's time to leave the sandbox, your child will cry for 30 minutes and you won't pause to wonder if you're damaging your child (nor should you). There is, however, ample evidence that chronic sleep deprivation leads to bad outcomes for all members of the family, including your child.

4. It is something you will have to redo on a regular basis.

When it comes to sleep, all kids have bleeps and blurps. This is not specific to sleep training—it's part and parcel of having children. Illness, travel, the arrival of a new sibling, because they feel like it . . . There will be rough sleep days in your future, but that's independent of how you teach your child to fall asleep.

5. Sleep training lasts forever.

Some parents will say things like "We've been doing CIO for months" when what they really mean is "We've been putting our child down awake at bedtime for months" or "Baby grumbles for a few minutes at bedtime." This has created the perception that sleep training takes an eternity. The truth is that, done correctly, it's a relatively brief affair.

6. You don't need to train your child to sleep—they'll figure it out when they're ready.

On a long enough timeline, your child will learn to fall asleep without you. Never in all of history has a child gone to college still requiring their mom to nurse them to sleep.

But how many years of sleepless nights and bedtime battles are you willing to wade through? Sleep associations, both good and bad, are incredibly persistent. Kids quickly grow out of their pajamas. They grow out of their interest in chewing on toys. They do not just grow out of unsustainable sleep associations.

7. It is unnecessary because plenty of gradual sleep-training methods will work just as well.

Some more gradual methods will work great for some babies. But they most definitely do not work for all babies.

8. No-cry sleep training involves zero tears.

This may be true, on occasion, for some lucky parents. But rarely. Babies' reaction to "no-cry" sleep may range from fussing to screaming, but very few will not cry at all.

9. You cannot do sleep training and subscribe to attachment-parenting (AP) philosophies.

Attachment parenting has, unfortunately, become a bit of a predicament for families. Somewhere along the line, AP became synonymous with co-sleeping, breastfeeding, babywearing, baby-led weaning, using only locally sourced organic produce, and a whole host of other lifestyle choices. Deviating from this set of choices suggests that you are not an AP parent.

Which is ridiculous. We are *all* attachment parents. We are deeply attached to our children, as they are to us. Secure attachment occurs when parents are reliably tuned in to and meeting their baby's needs.[2]

How you choose to be sensitive and emotionally available to your child is, of course, entirely up to you. Some people enjoy nursing, babywearing, etc., which is fabulous, as they've found methods of parenting that work for their family. You can also be entirely sensitive and emotionally available while using formula or expressed breast milk, having your child sleep in a crib, etc. *All of these* are entirely valid parenting and lifestyle choices. The bonds between parent and child are forged *when* you are emotionally and consistently responsive to their needs, not by *how* you respond.

Similarly, AP and sleep training are not contrary ideologies. Sleep is a basic human need[3]—a need that, when met, enables your child to grow and thrive, and a need that, when met for parents, lets them be emotionally available to their children. If you decided to use sleep training, you have come to the rational conclusion that it's the best way to meet *your* child's need for sleep. And having a well-rested child (in addition to being well rested yourself) will further enable you to have the emotional reserves to be available and sensitive for your child throughout the day.

10. It is a cure-all for baby sleep woes.

Sadly, no, sleep training is not a baby sleep Swiss Army knife. It has a very specific purpose: to break out of unsustainable sleep associations and establish independent sleep. There are plenty of sleep problems (night weaning, waking too early, crappy naps) that can't be readily solved with sleep training.

Unfortunately, the negative mythology of sleep training is so pervasive that it can be hard to unpack it all. Which is why I reached out to Dr. Ruid to share her clinical perspective on parent–child attachment and sleep training.

Rebecca Ruid, PhD, is a licensed clinical child psychologist in practice for 10 years at the University of Vermont Medical Center. She also offers parenting services through a community health team at a local pediatrics practice. Dr. Ruid specializes in working with parents to resolve concerns with behavior (including sleep!) as well as with children and adolescents dealing with both internalizing and externalizing concerns. She lives with her two young boys and husband in Williston, Vermont.

Attachment and Sleep Training: A Psychologist's Perspective—Dr. Rebecca Ruid

My parents gave my sisters and me a framed statement when we were very young, and this now sits in my older son's bedroom. It reads, "Parents may try to make your world better, but the only thing they can truly give you is life and love. The rest you must earn for yourself." Perhaps it was this parenting style, in addition to my training and professional development, which led me to be the type of clinician and parent that I am. Though some may interpret and equate "love" with co-sleeping and other attachment-based parenting practices, I do not view it in that way. To me there is not a specific list of behaviors that demonstrate our love for our children.

I am neither for nor against attachment parenting as a general concept. It is a valid and appropriate practice for children who have a history of trauma, for example, and one that I recommend in my work with such families. However, I believe that many people adopt attachment parenting because it limits child distress in the moment, a popular concept in our current parenting climate. In this context I struggle to see how this accurately applies the attachment theory upon which the practice is based, or how this approach will ultimately benefit our untraumatized children. I do not believe that attachment theorists would argue that we should not allow our children to experience distress or that there is a list of very specific practices necessary to lead to healthy attachment. I feel that theorists such as Bowlby[4] may argue that, barring adverse experience that interferes with attachment (on the part of the parent or the child), attachment naturally deepens and strengthens over time. To me, this will look different in different homes.

I am a great believer in encouraging children to recognize that they, and only they, have control over their thoughts and emotional functioning (the ability to regulate emotional states is closely linked to our ability to fall asleep independently). We encourage recognition of this by modeling and teaching coping skills, and then providing space for them to be used. A parent is not able to manage emotions for their child; it is an inside job. I strongly believe that part of being an emotionally healthy individual includes feeling a multitude of emotions (over time or even, sometimes, all at once!), recognizing they are normal and healthy, and being able to cope with all of them. To learn how to do this, we need to be given the space to practice—we need to feel sadness and disappointment as much as we need to feel happiness and joy, anger as much as love. We need to be able to screw up how we handle those emotions and learn from that. We need to feel pride when we handle them independently, and recognize that we have that skill. If a parent never allows their child to experience distress, that child never learns that they can experience distress and, ultimately, resolve it (whether they do something to make that happen or it happens organically). All feelings come and all feelings go—I think of them like passing clouds. Unfortunately, this is as true for the good emotions as for the bad. So it is my opinion that teaching a child to self-soothe for independent sleep is one of the first ways we can teach this, and a great gift we can bestow upon them.

There is ample evidence that sleep training or cio doesn't scar children or cause issues with attachment.[5] A multitude of factors inhibit or lead to healthy attachment: abuse, neglect, and loss of a primary attachment figure in early life, on the one hand, and support, love, and consistency, on the other. Not responding to our child every time she experiences distress is not going to ruin a bond. If done appropriately and with confidence, it can do something very different. It can send a message that you are safe and okay because I have set the stage for that and you can trust me to ensure your well-being (this message is strengthened when I do respond when necessary). It can send a message that we are separate entities, however connected we may be, and that you do not "need" me 24 hours a day every day. In this way it begins establishing important boundaries. It can send a message that I have confidence in your ability to manage this task successfully. On a concrete level, it sends a message that nighttime is a time for sleep, which is a solitary act—there are so many other hours in the day to be socially connected. It sends a message that sleep is important!

To SLIP or Not to SLIP
. . . .

For both clarity and specificity, I'm going to call this strategy the Sleep Learning Independence Plan (SLIP). Because that's what it is: a plan to learn to sleep independent of parental involvement, because parental involvement is no longer helping or is possibly hindering your child's ability to establish healthy sleep.

SLIP is a mindful parenting strategy used to foster independent sleep that generally involves some degree of tears or complaint and that is appropriate for families who have not met with success using SWAPs or for whom severe sleep deprivation is causing such significant problems that the timescale of the SWAP is not reasonable for physical or mental health.

Is SLIP for *your* family? Here's a 10-point checklist that will help you and your partner reach a conclusion. If the answer to most of these questions is "yes," SLIP might be appropriate.

1. Baby has a well-developed circadian rhythm.
The signs of this include having a consistent (within 15–30 minutes) bedtime that is followed by the longest stretch of uninterrupted sleep in the day. Bedtime is generally preceded by the longest stretch of wake time during the day.

2. Baby is chronically sleep deprived.
If your baby is getting significantly less sleep than they should or is waking excessively during the night, then they're probably sleep deprived.

3. The root issue is lack of independent sleep.
SLIP is a technique to foster independent sleep. It sometimes is applied to night weaning or excessively early waking, but it is primarily for issues related to an inability to fall asleep alone.

4. You've tried everything possible and it hasn't worked.

SLIP is generally the option of last resort. You've tried everything—made a committed effort with one or more SWAPs—yet nobody is sleeping.

5. Baby doesn't have any medical complications.

Colds, fevers, and reflux will exacerbate your child's inability to sleep independently.

6. Baby is in a safe place.

Your baby is sleeping in an empty crib.

7. The vote is unanimous.

This is not the time to have a marital squabble or to guilt-trip each other. If you and your partner are in vehement disagreement about how to approach sleep training, you aren't ready to do it.

8. You'll be able to maintain a consistent schedule.

Sleep training is not something to launch into the weekend before you hop on a plane to Morocco. Find a few weeks when you'll be able to maintain a consistent schedule and sleep location for day and night sleep.

9. You have a night vision monitor.

This is not an absolute must, but it's helpful. These expensive items answer the essential question, "Is she asleep yet?"

10. You are committed.

"Do or do not. There is no try." —Yoda

#10 is the most important item on the list. This is a good time to go to a quiet place and have an honest conversation with yourself. It may go something like this:

"Hey, self, how's it going?"

"Truth? I've been better. You?"

"Pretty haggard, if I'm being honest."

"Ayup."

"So, are we doing this? Like, for real?"

"I don't know. What do you think?"

"I guess we could try…"

"Like, put our love nugget down at bedtime and see how things go?"

"Yeah. That sounds like a good plan."

No. No it doesn't.

There is no try. There is no "let's see how things go." Do or do not.

Go for a quiet walk by yourself and *really listen* to your inner voice. If you or your partner will rush in to "rescue" your crying child after 20 minutes, you aren't ready. And that's totally okay. In fact, it's great that you *know* you aren't ready. It just means this strategy isn't for you—at least not right now.

If, instead, you understand that your child doesn't require rescuing, that they're capable of figuring out how to do this, that you have confidence in them, then you're ready to move forward… then SLIP is for you. As long as you and your partner are ready to fully commit. Like, "getting a tattoo"-level commitment.

How to SLIP at Night
. . . .

As with our SWAPs, it's best to start with SLIP at bedtime due to the powerful biological drive for sleep at that time. To be clear: you SLIP into sleep at bedtime. It's not fair to cheat the system by helping your child fall asleep at bedtime and then hoping for SLIP to salvage things later. How your child falls asleep at the start of the night is essential.

When you're ready to SLIP…

1. Make naps happen by any means necessary. You want your child well rested going into bedtime because tired kids sleep poorly. Does your baby take great naps in the car? In a stroller? Great! For the next few days do what you need to do so those naps happen. For the moment, you are not concerned with independent sleep at naptime, simply with ensuring that reasonable naps happen.

2. Corollary: Avoid catnaps. Catnaps undermine your goal of quality nappage. Don't drive to the grocery store at naptime: that 5-minute

car nap is working against Step 1. Further, don't begin SLIP when your nap schedule is likely to be wonky.

3. Do your relaxing, consistent bedtime routine but leave out the final "soothe to sleep" step. Whatever you're working to wean off—rocking, cuddling, nursing, eating—should be entirely removed from the process. If the sleep association you're working to remove involves food (bottle or boob), it should occur 20 minutes before your child is put down to sleep: thus "bath, books, boob, bed" routine will now be "boob, bath, books, bed." If you have historically rocked or bounced but not cuddled your child to sleep, remove any rocking or bouncing from the routine; quietly cuddling while reading books is fine.

4. If Baby is swaddled, continue to use the swaddle as long as you are confident that they can't or won't flip over. If your child is older and potentially capable of flipping onto their stomach, swaddling is inadvisable for sleep training.

5. If your child has been using the pacifier, now is the time to stop. While some children can fall asleep with the pacifier and happily sleep all night, eventually pacifiers tend to cause sleep association problems.

6. Ensure that baby's sleep location is absolutely safe. Are there dangling cords within reach of the crib? Unprotected outlets? Can baby climb or fall out? The crib should be clear of any possible entrapment hazards—no stuffed animals, blankets, bumpers, or pillows. The only thing allowed in there other than your baby is a small lovey—if Baby is old enough to use one safely. If your child is old enough to sleep in a big-kid bed, put on your anal-retentive hat and look at the whole room. Does the furniture present tip-over hazards? Are there toys that could break into sharp pieces? Choking hazards?

7. Make sure you are putting baby down to sleep at the appropriate bedtime. This should be the time your child has historically been falling asleep (now is when the Goddess of Consistency will reward

your devotion). The key word here is *sleep*. If you've been bouncing your child on a yoga ball for 60 minutes every night, his bedtime is not when you begin the bouncing, but when he's a limp piece of bacon sleeping in your arms.

8. Use your consistent bedtime words. Your baby's receptive language develops far earlier than their expressive language:[6] they understand what you are saying long before they can speak themselves. Use the same words every night as part of your bedtime routine. "It's time for you to sleep, buddy. Mommy and Daddy love you. We're right next door. We'll see you with big hugs and kisses in the morning. But for now we're going to leave so your body can get the sleep it needs to be strong and healthy. I love you, little dude!" Be firm, loving, and consistent.

9. Put Baby in their bed and leave the room. Some strategies suggest that camping out in the room is preferable because your loving presence can provide helpful soothing. In my experience, staying in the room has the opposite effect, making Baby more upset: "Why aren't you picking me up! HELLO?!? I can see you sitting RIGHT THERE!" It also has the potential unintended consequence of creating a new object permanence problem for you, in that Baby will expect to see you sitting there when they wake up at night. For these reasons I suggest that you put Baby down and leave.

10. Decide which parent is more likely to turn into an emotional jellyfish at the sound of crying. Lots of parents feel that they need to sit in the hallway, curled into a fetal position, crying tear for tear with their baby as some sort of penance for their failure to teach independent sleep. Crying in the hallway serves no purpose other than to make you miserable. Worse, it creates the opportunity for the dark strains of guilt to muddle your thinking—"I feel horrible! Maybe I'll just nurse him to sleep one last time?" Backsliding won't solve any problems, and it guarantees you even more crying in the future. Leave it to your partner and get out of the house.

11. Allow your child the space to figure out how to fall asleep without you. She may get angry, sad, furious, or some combination thereof.

Is she safe? Fed? Loved? If the answers are "yes," you've done your job. She's working on something new, and from her perspective, it's a frustrating challenge. It's okay for her to be frustrated.

12. Don't give up! Have faith that your child is fully capable of figuring out how to sleep without you. She may not want to, and it may not be easy, but she's absolutely capable. Going in now will sabotage the goal of improving sleep and guarantee that next time (and I promise you, there will be a next time) will be worse. You can do this. They can do it!

To Check or Not to Check?

SLIP is based on the principle that your child needs to learn to sleep without an unsustainable sleep association. Typically, you are the provider of that sleep association (rocking, nursing, feeding, cuddling, reinserting the pacifier, etc.). If you return to your child before they've fallen asleep, they're going to expect you to provide the sleep association they are used to.

And when you fail to provide this (which you will, because you are fully committed to not going back to the old way of doing things), your child is going to go *bananas*. They're going to be *furious* that you're right there but not doing what they want and expect you to— not because they're incapable of doing this without you, but because they're used to doing things the old way.

For most kids, going back in to check makes things more difficult. I'm suggesting, therefore, a method known as *full extinction:* you put your child down fully awake in a safe and comfortable place at bedtime, and you don't return until they are asleep.

Contrary to this plan, Dr. Ferber,[7] first of his name, suggested a popular and well-known method of *graduated extinction*, in which you come back for brief "checks" at progressively longer intervals (3 minutes, 5, 10, etc.). With this graduated extinction approach, your child may—and likely will—cry vociferously throughout every visit. Regardless, you remind them that it's time for sleep and leave the room.

There is ample evidence that both full and graduated extinction are extremely effective in improving sleep outcomes.[8] However, there is no evidence that one is more effective than the other. My experience has been that parents overwhelmingly prefer graduated extinction: they feel that visiting periodically is more loving, and they fear that their baby will otherwise feel abandoned. There is no evidence to suggest that kids feel forgotten if you aren't popping in every 5 minutes, but if making checks feels right in your heart, I fully support your choice.

I will, however, share that my own experience (not backed by data from a double-blind twin study or anything) with untold numbers of families is that *full extinction works better*:

- It works more quickly. Going to your crying baby can have the unintended consequence of reinforcing the crying. Psychology majors are probably familiar with the term *intermittent reinforcement from operant conditioning.*[9] The basic idea is that if you reinforce (by coming in to soothe) the negative behavior (crying) intermittently (every 5, 7, 10 minutes), that behavior will last longer than if you never went back into the room at all. My observation from working with a range of families is that full extinction leads to less crying overall and a more rapid cessation of crying.

- It results in less crying. Some, perhaps even most, babies amp up when they see you. On a 10-point scale, if a baby is crying at level 7 and Mom walks in the door, that baby is often going to jump to 11: Mom's well-meaning presence is working against the goal of minimizing tears.

If you're feeling conflicted about the two methods, know that you can begin your SLIP with graduated extinction (visits) and, depending on how your child responds, switch to full extinction (no visits). It is inadvisable, however, to switch from full to graduated. If you start with full extinction, you are committed to that path. Full stop.

The 5-minute plan

If you feel you must make brief visits to your child, I suggest the following approach. There is no "ideal" schedule for checking in on your child during SLIP, but there are some key elements for a good graduated extinction plan:

- It's simple (no user error).

- Each interval is longer than the previous interval.

- The intervals are all long enough to give your child a chance to settle to sleep.

Any schedule of visits that meets those criteria can work, so you're welcome to make up your own if so inclined. If you're too sleep deprived to derive your own, I suggest you use the 5-Minute Plan in this chart. Each check-in is a brief visit—no more than 1 or 2 minutes. You do not pick up your child, but reiterate the soothing words you used at bedtime. And (this is crucial!) you must depart while they are still awake. Continue with the schedule of increasingly long gaps between check-ins until your child has fallen asleep.

What Will Happen during SLIP?

All parents have one big question about SLIP: "How long will baby cry?" I could answer this question, but it would require that I use up my last wish with the Genie, and I'm saving that one for "ageless beauty."

Experience has taught me that my ability to predict how long it will take a baby to SLIP into sleep is incredibly poor. With that disclaimer out of the way, if you follow the plan outlined here, more often than not what will happen is this:

Night #1: 45 minutes to 1.5 hours of crying at bedtime

Night #2: 20 to 45 minutes of crying at bedtime

Night #3: zero to 25 minutes of complaint at bedtime

Although extremely rare, there *are* babies who will complain for hours. I share this not to frighten you, but to prepare you for the idea that it's not entirely outside the realm of possibility. *Most* children, however, will struggle for about an hour and then figure out how to fall asleep.

Keep track of how long it takes your child to fall asleep each night, but instead of obsessing about how long it takes on any *given* night, pay attention to the trend across days. You're looking for a trend line where things are vastly better on night #3 than they were on night

The 5-Minute Plan

	First Visit	Second Visit	Third Visit	Continue (+5)*
Night 1	5 mins. after bedtime	10 mins. after 1st visit	15 mins. after 2nd visit	20, 25, 30, ...
Night 2	10 mins. after bedtime	15 mins. after 1st visit	20 mins. after 2nd visit	25, 30, 35, ...
Night 3	15 mins. after bedtime	20 mins. after 1st visit	25 mins. after 2nd visit	30, 35, 40, ...
Night 4	20 mins. after bedtime	25 mins. after 1st visit	30 mins. after 2nd visit	35, 40, 45, ...
Night 5	25 mins. after bedtime	30 mins. after 1st visit	35 mins. after 2nd visit	40, 45, 50, ...

*These numbers look distressingly high, and you are probably looking at them, thinking, "Holy cr@p—we'll be checking in for hours!" Possibly—although it is highly unlikely that you will be checking in for hours after the first night. This chart is not intended to freak you out but simply to clarify that the pattern of adding 5 minutes to each interval continues as needed.

#1. (The possible exception to this is extinction bursts; more on this below.) The improvement is typically unambiguous and dramatic.

Dealing with Your Fear

Let's be honest—this is scary stuff! It's a package of unknown all wrapped up with guilt and judgment with a big bow of "sense of failure" on top. These are all things parents have said to me about SLIP:

> *"Well, at least I know what my kid will be talking about with his therapist in 20 years!"*

> *"I am so sleep obsessed that the worry, confusion, stress, and uncertainty are starting to bleed into every aspect of my life. Not good."*

> *"You can never ever tell any of our friends that we're sleep training our child because then we would have to move."*

> *"I'm afraid she won't trust me anymore."*

> *"This sucks."*

SLIP: Have Faith It'll Work!

Sometimes it feels as if parenting is the only occupation where other people are allowed to critique your performance regardless of their credentials (or lack thereof). And because parenting is something we care so desperately about, any comment, internet post, side-eye, or well-intended suggestion feels like a gut-punch to your very soul. We would rather have others question anything else—our career, our housekeeping abilities, our personal appearance—than throw shade on our parenting.

Because parenting is so deep, it's nestled right into our bone marrow.

And when we're in a vulnerable place (and you are never more vulnerable than when you're exhausted), we fear judgment more than we fear physical pain. Worse, we judge ourselves. The fear demons notice; they start circling, and they spread their untruths about the room like confetti.

You aren't good enough.

Your child doesn't love you.

You are failing as a parent.

This is all your fault.

Those fear demons are crafty; they find us at our lowest low. It's easy to fall prey to their quiet whisperings. But *none of what they say is true.*

You *are* the best parent for your child, and you're *more* than good enough.

SLIP isn't a symptom of failure—it's simply an acknowledgment of where things are today for your family and what you need to do to make things better. The easy path is to keep on doing what you're doing. And the vast majority of people will keep shuffling along the easy path, hoping things will just get better if they wait long enough, ignoring the dramatic, measurable negative consequences to that choice.[10] You are not a failure. You're wise enough to see that things as they stand aren't working for your family, that change is a necessary and positive thing for all of you.

As parents, we also have this huge sense of angst about abandonment. We're leaving our child in the crib! THE CRIB! Our fear is so great, you'd think "the crib" is a jagged cave lined with bat guano. No, the crib is the safest sleep space, a piece of furniture you lovingly picked out, assembled (no mean task), and situated in a comfy room you spent months crafting into the ideal love nest for your child.

Yes, your child will have to figure out how to fall asleep without your ministrations. This is one of many skills they will have to figure out, and certainly not the last that will result in tears. Do you believe your child incapable of mastering a skill that literally every person on the planet before them has mastered? Of course not!

Ask yourself, "Is my child starving, in pain, in an unsafe place, or unloved?" No? Then you've met your child's needs. These tears are about wants, not needs. Our job as parents isn't to meet every want our child will have, nor is it to prevent them from having sad or angry feelings. Withholding your assistance here isn't being a bad parent— it's being a conscientious one.

If you and I were friends, I would take you out for coffee and a pastry (preferably one with frosting), and I would tell you this:

You are not a bad parent, nor are you a failure. Some kids struggle with this, and no matter what you do or don't do, they need to sort things out for themselves. Maybe this isn't what you planned, but parenting *rarely* turns out the way we expect it to.

You are a loving parent. You've spent months holding, adoring, and being responsive to your child. Nothing that happens tonight will undo that. You know you love her; *she* knows you love her. Sleep training doesn't come from selfishness or bad parenting—it comes from love. Just as you have been responsive to her need to be held, to eat, to have your love and attention, you are now being responsive to her need for sleep.

And how wise you are to take this step to make things better! Sure, you could let this whole thing drag on for months or even years. But let's be honest—that wouldn't be doing anybody any favors. Parenting is one of life's great joys, but when you're exhausted and caring for a chronically sleep-deprived child, a lot of that joy gets tarnished. When you think about it from that perspective, why would you wait to make things better?

(And then I would give you a big hug, because I'm a hugger.)

Sleep Training for the Long Haul

Any sleep training, SLIP or SWAP, is a commitment to stop doing what you used to do, such as rocking, feeding, or nursing to sleep. The whole point of sleep training is to help your child understand that "we aren't going to fall asleep that way anymore." So you don't want to start down this path unless you are fully committed to never rock or feed or nurse your child to sleep again. Forever. This is your new normal.

Yes, there will be hiccups. You will be feeling sassy one day and decide it's a grand idea to travel across five time zones with your baby. Teeth will erupt. The plague of the tummy bug will descend upon your house. Does this mean you go back to cuddling, rocking, or nursing your child to sleep?

No.

You can temporarily *stretch* the bedtime rules a bit when you hit a travel or illness speed bump. Maybe linger while gently rubbing his back until he's drowsy, or tenderly place your hand on his tummy and sing to him while he settles into a calm state. Sometimes kids need extra care, and that's okay. But don't let these obstacles derail all your hard work by falling back into old habits.

(Although if you do, don't panic—you sorted things out once, and you can do so again.)

Picking the Right Time

Because SLIP is a scary prospect for most people, they want to find the optimal time for it. I think the mental dialogue goes something like this: "If we can triangulate the ideal time for sleep training, we can minimize the crying, get things sorted out before starting daycare, and maybe get a night or two of sleep before the in-laws show up and start critiquing how messy the house is."

But there really is no optimal time. There's *always* a growth spurt/ separation anxiety/travel/developmental milestone/daycare/teeth-ing/ear infection/head cold/shots looming in the dark to trip you up.

Here's the truth: babies are largely unknowable. You don't know when they're going to get a raging ear infection or five teeth will simultaneously erupt. So there *is* no ideal time. Much like the search for the perfect haircut or a winter coat that is both warm and slimming, the search for the ideal time is futile. Sometimes you just need to work with what you've got. There is no guarantee that waiting till next week or next month will make things any easier than they would be today. But there *is* a guarantee that waiting will prolong the anxiety and intensify the accumulated sleep deprivation.

Beware the Extinction Burst

For most babies, SLIP will be characterized by a few challenging nights followed by a dramatic and immediate improvement in sleep. Other babies, though, will continue to cry progressively longer and louder. You will feel confident that SLIP is not working for your baby, that I am just another idiot "expert," and that the only solution is to go back to whatever "up all night" routine you had going before you attempted to SLIP in the first place—horrendous as it was, it's got to be better than THIS.

Or maybe you successfully implemented SLIP and have been popping a nightly bottle of Champagne ever since, only to suddenly find that your previously happy baby is crying again. You and your partner have stopped your happy jig and are now wondering what the heck just happened?

What just happened is an *extinction burst*.

This is a great phrase to casually drop at a playgroup to establish yourself as someone capable of pronouncing multisyllabic phrases and thus very smart (*military industrial complex* and *LIBOR* are also good). But these two words also explain a common behavior that trips up many a well-intentioned parent.

SLIP is essentially a form of "extinction therapy," in which you work to make the undesirable behavior (unsustainable sleep-onset associations) become extinct by no longer rewarding (reinforcing) the behavior with visits/cuddling/nursing/etc. And for roughly 70% of you,[11] it will be spectacularly effective.

However, for the remaining 30%, your child will amp up the crying. Or frustratingly, will take a break for a few days and then resume

Extinction Burst

the crying. This resumption is an extinction burst.[12] Basically, your child is doing even *more* of the behavior you are trying to extinguish now that you have removed the reinforcer.

Awesome, right? Well, no.

So what can you do about this?

Nothing, really. Stick to the plan. Put the cork back in the Champagne bottle and wait it out. It *will* pass.

Also, file the idea of extinction bursts away for future reference because this is not the last one you're going to see. Hitting, whining, demands for treats/toys/ponies—are all behaviors prone to extinction bursts.

Say your child whines for a cookie every time you go to the grocery store. The first few times you give her a cookie because, really, it's just a cookie, right? Then you realize you have your own personal Cookie Monster, who is now demanding a cookie every time you pop out for a gallon of milk. So you calmly explain that cookies aren't everyday food and you're not going to buy them anymore.

Will your child quietly acquiesce? Give you a hug and thank you for being so mindful of their health? Or will she go from whining to screaming? And if screaming doesn't work, how about adding in some throwing? Or (please say it isn't so!) spitting and biting? You power through the tantrum, get a few quiet weeks of grocery trips, and think, *phew! That's over with...* only to have the cookie fight start anew.

That, my friend, is the joy of the extinction burst.

Common Issues

For the vast majority of families, SLIP is a relatively straightforward strategy that results in immediate and positive change. Except for babies who have a brief extinction burst, the amount of crying at bedtime and the number of subsequent wakings dramatically decreases with each subsequent night.

Generally... but not always. For those of you who've been at it for at least a week and things are still rocky, let's look at some possible culprits.

Baby continues to cry a lot at bedtime.

Some babies spout off for anywhere from 5 to 15 minutes at bedtime. You do your beloved bedtime routine and everybody is happy, then that butt hits the mattress and your beloved child instantly morphs into Mr. Screamy.

If Mr. Screamy hangs out for only 5 to 15 minutes, *you don't actually have a problem*. Some babies just need to blow off a little steam before they fall asleep. Others complain because they don't *want* to go to sleep, they don't *want* to hang out in a dark room without you, and they are unhappy about your decision to foist this unpleasantness upon them. This is not a "sleep problem," nor is it some terrible side effect of sleep training. It is simply your child nonverbally expressing their displeasure with your plan. When they're 3, they'll be verbal—instead of tears, it'll be, "MOM! I'm not *tired!* I don't want to go to BED!" If this brief session is followed by a long stretch of sleep, ignore it.

But what if Mr. Screamy sticks around for 20 minutes or more? Substantial post-SLIP crying at bedtime can be caused by a number of things:

1. You're doing check-ins/graduated extinction. Any sort of visit from you can result in persistent crying. While coming from a loving place, your visits disrupt Baby's ability to fall asleep and reward their fighting of sleep. Switch to full extinction.

2. Bedtime is at the wrong time. Your child needs to be awake long enough before bedtime to easily fall asleep. It may be time to cut out a late nap or shift bedtime later. Try a schedule change for 3 to 5 days.

3. Your bedtime routine is too short or too lively. Most bedtime routines are great as long as you and your child enjoy them. As a general rule, your bedtime routine should last 20 to 30 minutes, long enough to enable your child to successfully transition to a calm state. Sometimes it's hard to carve out enough time, and you might be tempted to shortchange the routine for a pithy "diaper change, two books, bed" sort of thing. But (and this is rare) if there's a lot of crying at bedtime, this may not be enough time for

your child to transition from play to sleep. Similarly, your pre-bed activities should be relatively dark and serene. Outside play, ticklefests, and dance parties are all awesome... unless it's prior to bedtime, in which case, no.

Baby wakes up soon, requiring assistance to fall back to sleep.

Some babies do great falling asleep on their own at bedtime (say, at 7:30) but then wake up soon after (1 to 3 hours later, say, at 9:30) and demand [nursing/ rocking/bouncing] to fall back to sleep. Then they continue to wake periodically through the night demanding more [nursing/rocking/bouncing], and despite your best efforts, nothing else will do. Things are better than they were before SLIP, but it hasn't been the transformative experience you were hoping for.

The problem is that the way you're handling the early-evening wakeup is *re-establishing* the sleep association you worked so hard to get out of at bedtime. This probably feels super unfair. However, you've likely already realized that this is only one of *many* things that are unfair about having children (such as stretch marks, inability to sleep past 6 a.m., having to share every cookie you will ever eat for the rest of your life...).

This one, however, you can fix. You'll need to change how you handle the first wakeup of the night. You probably need to entirely stop whatever activity is being demanded of you (no rocking, nursing, patting, etc.). And you *definitely* need your child to fall back to sleep at this waking without you present.

Baby still demands food all night long.

SLIP is a technique to help your child learn to fall asleep on their own. It is not a magic elixir that erases all of your night feedings (currently, the only known magic elixir is coffee). A child who was eating all night long prior to SLIP should demand less food once they're going to sleep without a boob or bottle. But a kid who was used to eating a lot at night is still going to be hungry because their body is used to getting a substantial amount of calories at night. (See more on that in Chapter 9, Eating and Not Sleeping.)

Baby wakes frequently at night and cries for 5–15 minutes.

Babies wake up every 45 to 90 minutes all night long. Most of the time, you don't realize they're doing this because they fall back to sleep without your knowledge. Sometimes, however, they grumble a bit first. A baby who periodically cries or complains for 5 to 15 minutes is simply expressing their displeasure about this whole sleep business. Parents may describe this as "crying all night" when, really, their baby is just grumping as they cycle through a light-sleep phase.

Some babies will cry with great gusto for 5 minutes before falling back to sleep for another 3 hours. You may feel the need to race to the rescue, but I strongly encourage you not to. Instead, get a timer and keep notes. If your baby has a serious need (hunger, discomfort, etc.), it won't be expressed in a brief blip of crying. In this case your well-intended rescue will likely prevent baby from falling back to sleep, exacerbating the whole situation.

Baby is making a stand against sleep, literally.

There are three types of babies: those who can't stand, those who can stand but can't sit back down, and those who have achieved mastery of both standing and sitting. (And also babies I like to squeeze, but that describes all babies.)

Your "can stand but not sit" babies will often pull themselves up and get stuck there. You go in to help them get back down off the crib rail only to have them pop back up like a Jack in the Box. Your baby will impress you with their masterful intellect as they will quickly figure out that "the standing game" is an enjoyable way to spend time with Mom and Dad, and they will happily play with you for *hours*.

To solve this, you'll need to help your baby practice their sitting skills during the day. Stand them up next to something soft (a couch, a cushioned chair) and encourage them to sit back down unassisted. Put a favorite toy or snack on the floor so they can reach it only by sitting. Practice this skill multiple times a day until you are convinced that Baby can sit down without your help.

Baby may still invite you to play "the standing game," but now you can respectfully decline, confident that Baby is fully capable of sitting down without you. The first time Baby seems to get "stuck" standing in the crib, remind her how to get down by taking her hands and letting her bend at the knees until she sits or lies down in the crib. Don't lay her down—she's already mastered that skill, and you don't want to confuse matters by doing it for her. After this brief reminder, you're out and "the standing game" is over (or at least your participation in it is).

Some stalwart kiddos will continue to stand in the crib despite their mastery of the sitting skill. Some will even fall asleep standing there. If this happens, you may want to creep into the room and gently settle them down on the mattress. You'll have the best chance of success if they're deeply asleep. If they wake up, use your words to reinforce the idea that it's time for sleep. Feel free to rub their back or pat their belly, but keep it to no more than a minute. Then leave the room. Sticking around longer than that rewards the standing, which then becomes a great way to get Mom or Dad to come play.

Unlike the throwing-food game or the taking-off-shoes game, babies will generally get tired of the standing game after a few days.

The past two chapters have covered the technical details of handling bedtime. But what happens *after* bedtime? Falling asleep independently doesn't guarantee that your child will happily sleep till dawn (in fact, I can all but promise they *won't*). We still need a plan for what to do when your child wakes later in the night. Which leads us to...

8

Handling Night Waking after SWAP or SLIP

ONGRATULATIONS! YOU'VE successfully used SWAP or SLIP to foster independent sleep at bedtime. You've taken the single most important step toward establishing healthy sleep habits for your child. You have taught your child a crucial life skill. Take a victory lap—or a victory nap!

Chances are, you will see an immediate and dramatic reduction in the number of times your child wakes at night. Take a moment to celebrate this. We often don't pause to put a check in the "win" column, but you should, 'cuz it's a biggie.

This isn't, however, the whole sleep story. SWAP and SLIP are about learning how to fall asleep independent of unsustainable sleep association. They are not, typically, a free pass to sleeping through the night. You have created the *possibility* for your child to sleep through the night. In the short run, you should expect a few night wakings.

You will need a plan to address these, and that plan will be highly dependent upon why and when your child is waking up. Typically, there are two reasons your child is waking up post-SWAP/SLIP:

1. Food (nursing or bottle)

2. Sleep association (rocking, cuddling, paci, etc.)

Let's break it down.

Waking and Eating
. . . .

If your child was routinely eating during the night, they'll need or expect to do so even after independent sleep has been established. A younger baby may not be developmentally ready to sleep till dawn without food. An older baby may be capable of a longer fast but habituated to eating a lot at night, so shifting all those calories to daylight hours is going to take time.

If your child is nursing, you may not know how much they've been eating. Some can guzzle gallons in two minutes; some take a few minutes just to get the ball rolling—you can't easily triangulate "how much they eat" from "how long they nurse." Some parents spend months functioning as a human pacifier with a baby latched to their breast all night, so "how much food is consumed at what time" is an udder mystery (*badum ching!*).

If your child takes a bottle, though, you'll know exactly how much food is consumed at night. Maybe your child drinks only a few ounces per feeding but demands multiple bottles at night, or maybe your child guzzles one or two large bottles. Consider the total volume consumed at night as a percentage of daily intake. Say your 6-month-old drinks 28 ounces of formula a day and wakes four times a night for a 2-ounce snack each time. Although her individual night feedings are small, over the course of the night she's drinking 8 ounces, or a substantial 30% of her daily intake.

Regardless of age, if your child has been eating frequently or camps on the boob all night, you can and should assume that she's been consuming a substantial amount of food. If you aren't sure, here are some indicators that your baby has been a copious eater at night:

• Middle-of-the-night diaper changes are necessary to avoid leaking.

- The morning diaper is so full, it could sink a boat (because it's huge like a cannonball, is what I'm saying).

- They aren't clamoring for food first thing in the morning.

It's entirely possible that your baby has been eating the equivalent of five cheeseburgers at night. And a baby who is used to five cheeseburgers every night will think poorly of you should you fail to provide them.

In this case, you should plan on feeding your child during the night. But this raises the question: *When* at night do you feed your baby in a post-SWAP/SLIP world?

Feeding Schedules

Predictable feeding schedules
If your kiddo has been eating on a semi-predictable schedule, your job is fairly easy: they wake at a typical feeding time, you feed them. They sleep through a feeding, you make a small offering to your Sleep Fairy (cotton candy is a popular option) and let Baby sleep.

Some parents have predictable feeding schedules that are masquerading as unpredictable ones. Take, for example, a baby who wakes frequently demanding a bottle, sucks down an ounce, then falls back to sleep but who, twice a night, takes a full 6-ounce bottle. The 1-ounce bottles were related to the bedtime bottle = sleep association. The 6-ounce bottles, though, are "real" feedings: you would go in to offer those two bottles as you did previously, while ignoring all other requests.

The same applies to a nursing mom: typically, there are many brief demands to nurse or suck, with up to three "real" nursing sessions interspersed. It's not uncommon for babies to nurse for a minute or two all night long, but twice a night to have a hearty 20-minute nursing session. Thus baby is snacking constantly but has two "real" feedings. If the long nursing session occurred at consistent times, you would offer your child the chance to nurse at *those* times.

If Baby wakes up at times other than typical feeding times, don't feed them. See the section "Night Waking Unrelated to Food" for more on this.

Unpredictable feeding schedules

For some of you, of course, your child's feeding schedule is a bigger mystery than Stonehenge. Some babies have patterns of night feeding so random that the schedule looks like a Jackson Pollock scatter painting. Other babies spend the whole night glued to Mom's boob, so there is no schedule—Baby is never not nursing. Some babies wake constantly to take itty-bitty bottles, an ounce or two, or to nurse for a minute, such that the total amount consumed over the course of the night may be significant but without any full, real feeds in the mix.

Clearly, the challenge is figuring out *when* to feed your baby or knowing when they're truly hungry. How is it possible that an app for this does not yet exist? *Sigh.*

A baby who was previously eating constantly or randomly will likely continue to wake somewhat frequently at first. Although sorting out when to feed them is challenging, your goal is to create a feeding plan that respects the fact that your child is a habitual night eater and thus is legitimately hungry but that also creates some boundaries to reduce the frequency of feedings, with the *ultimate* goal of moving some, if not all, of those feedings to daytime hours.

You should develop a feeding plan that feels right to you based on your knowledge of your child. However, consider the following guidelines:

- No food prior to midnight (ideally). Early feedings are not always problematic but they *can* re-establish the food = sleep association you used SWAP/SLIP to break out of.

- Keep stretches between feedings similar to daytime ones. The typical gap between daytime feedings is 3 to 4 hours. A baby who can go 3 hours between feeds during the day can certainly do 3 or more hours at night.

- Be flexible . . . at first. The first few nights post-SWAP/SLIP, you can be a bit flexible—this is new for everyone. But after night 2 or 3, you want to stick to your plan. For example, if after 3 nights your baby is not nursing until midnight, then there will be no more nursing until midnight. Next week, when your baby starts teething and wants to nurse at 10 p.m., you can choose to offer some gentle comfort (brief cuddle, send in the non-nursing partner, medicate), but the breastaurant is closed for business.

- Wait before feeding. If your baby wakes up, complains for 5 to 10 minutes, and falls back to sleep for 3 hours, she wasn't really hungry. Don't rush in at the first peep—see what develops.

- An early-morning snooze-button feed may be required (see the last section of Chapter 9, Eating and Not Sleeping, for more details).

Night feeding is highly individual, but here's a hypothetical example of what it might look like:

1. Baby falls asleep independently at 7:30. The last bottle was offered at 7:00.

2. Baby wakes at 9:45. Left to her own devices, she complains about the matter for 20 minutes and falls back to sleep.

3. Baby wakes at 11:40. Because it's not yet midnight, Dad holds off on giving her a bottle. She grumbles a while, falling back to sleep around midnight.

4. Baby wakes again at 1:15. This is the first post-midnight waking, so Dad offers a 6-ounce bottle. Baby drinks 4 ounces and falls back to sleep.

5. Baby wakes up at 4:30. This is more than 3 hours after the last feeding, so Dad returns with another 6-ounce bottle. Baby drinks 4 and falls back to sleep.

6. Baby wakes for the day at 6:30.

Sticking to the schedule

In either scenario—predictable or unpredictable feeding—if your child wakes up, you should either feed them relatively promptly (5 to 10 minutes max) or commit to not feeding until the next time they wake. You want to avoid the scenario where you let Baby complain for a while and then feed him. This sends mixed messages and almost always leads to more upset on subsequent nights.

Once things settle into a more regular pattern, if your child is older than about 6 months, you can choose to move on to gentle night weaning to reduce the number of night feedings (see Chapter 9, Eating and Not Sleeping).

Feeding to Sleep during the Night

Many parents who are diligently using SWAP or SLIP to establish healthy sleep associations are justifiably concerned about the possibility that night feedings can re-establish food=sleep associations. If you can't nurse to sleep at bedtime, is it really okay to do so later?

In fact, nursing or feeding to sleep later in the night does not typically disrupt your independent sleep goals. For most babies, the crucial aspect of independent sleep is removing sucking, eating, or nursing *from bedtime.* When your child eats at 1:30 in the morning, on the other hand, you can feed them until they are drowsy or asleep without issue.

Occasionally, when a child's first post-bedtime feeding happens *early* in the night (say, before midnight), those early feedings *can* re-establish the food/nurse = sleep association. This is less common, though, so start with the assumption it won't be a problem for you—you can adjust later if it becomes one. Typically, there are two clear indicators that earlyish night feedings are blowing up your well-laid plans:

1. Baby wakes early for the first feed of the night and then demands to eat frequently (every hour or two) from that point on.

2. If you try to stop feeding or nursing your child before they are 100% asleep, they become terribly upset and remain so until fed or nursed fully to sleep.

If you're seeing either of these behaviors and your child's first meal of the night comes relatively close on the heels of bedtime, you may need to wake your child fully after each night feeding or push the first feeding past midnight so that the food/nurse = sleep association is fully resolved.

Waking and Not Eating
· ·

Kids also wake up for reasons beyond "I'm hungry." Initially, they might wake because they haven't quite mastered navigating back into deep sleep without your assistance—rocking, cuddling, bouncing, paci reinsertion, etc. While you've made a valiant first step by removing these activities from bedtime, your child will likely continue to wake periodically for the first few nights expecting you to return to your previous rocking/cuddling/bouncing/paci reinsertion behaviors.

Establishing independent sleep means being steadfast and *not doing* whatever it was that you used SLIP/SWAP to wean off. When you embarked on SLIP/SWAP, you committed to no longer doing those things at or near sleep—and that includes during the night, especially for the first few weeks after independent sleep has been established.

In general, you should handle night wakings unrelated to food in the same way you handled falling asleep at bedtime. If you're working on SLIP, you should allow your child to navigate these periods of awakening independently. You know they're capable of doing so—they just *showed* you that by falling asleep independently at bedtime. It may simply take a few days before the act of effortlessly falling back to sleep becomes routine. Conversely, if you worked on a SWAP that had you rubbing their back until they were fully asleep at bedtime, you may be required to provide back-rubbing services in the middle of the night.

In addition, consider the following guidelines:

· If it's only been 2 or 3 hours since bedtime, let them resettle independently. The compulsion to sleep at this time is potent, and often your intervention will reinforce the waking. See what develops if you give your child some space. It may just be a blip for a day or two.

· When your child wakes, your decision tree has just two options: (1) go to your baby 5 to 10 minutes after they wake up or (2) wait until they fall back to sleep without your assistance. Having your baby complain for 40 minutes and then going in to feed or cuddle leads to lots of future crying.

- If you're convinced your intervention is required, repeat the process you used at bedtime. As a general rule, before midnight, you'll want to have your child fall back to sleep without you; after midnight, you may be able to offer a bit of assistance (brief cuddle, back rub, etc.). If you are using a SWAP, try to use the same approach when intervening at night.

- Be super stingy about helping your child fall asleep during the night. Yes, your child will continue to wake up: we're changing things up, and it will take time for that change to lead to uninterrupted sleep. But every time you rush to cuddle or bounce your child who has woken up, you are rewarding the behavior. What if I suggested you give your child a cookie every time they woke up? You would think I was bananapants—"They'll wake up all the time because I'm giving them a cookie!" Exactly.

- Commit to less involvement on subsequent nights. For example, if you're using a SWAP at bedtime that involves patting your child's back until they fall asleep, you should pat their back if they wake up during the night. However, just as you're working to do less and less at bedtime, you should also do less and less for night wakings. If it takes 20 minutes of back rubs on night #1, aim for no more than 15 on night #2.

To be clear, these are simply guidelines to help inform your plan for night parenting. As always, adjust to your particular circumstances. Listen to your gut—it's almost always giving you good advice.

Early-Morning Wakeups

The biological compulsion to sleep is very strong at bedtime, but it peters out closer to morning. Many babies wake up very early in the morning (4 or 5 a.m.) because their sleep drive is pretty dinky at that point.

If your child wakes at an unreasonably rude hour, you are welcome to see if the SWAP or SLIP you employed at bedtime can help them navigate back to sleep until a more sensible time. It is not guaranteed to work, however, and you will have to commit to your trial for a week or two to see results. In some cases, your child will simply grump in bed until it's time to start the day.

Many parents opt to offer Baby a quick snack (a "snooze-button feeding") to buy everybody a few more hours of sleep. Nursing or feeding to sleep in the early morning generally does not undermine your independent sleep goals. Strategies for navigating early-morning waking are addressed in further detail in Chapter 12, (Un)Common Sleep Setbacks.

As mentioned, the goal of independent sleep is not night weaning. Typically the requests to eat during the night diminish substantially once independent sleep is established, but most kids will still demand to eat 1–3 times a night. You're welcome to continue feeding your child during the night for as long as you care to. Eventually, however, you and your partner will likely decide that it's time to eliminate a feeding or two, if not fully night wean.

9

Eating and Not Sleeping

~~~

MOST PARENTS ACCEPT waking up at night to feed a hungry baby as part of Life with Baby. However, as the months slide by, the charm of getting up at night begins to tarnish and parents start to wonder, "Does my baby really need to eat quite so often?"

The answer to this question is a bit more complex than you were hoping. A simple math version might go something like this: Baby asks for food, you feed Baby, Baby is happy, thus Baby was hungry and, obviously, we feed hungry babies, so you should continue to do so. But the reality is less simple. Babies demand to eat for many reasons, not only hunger. To determine whether your baby really *needs* to eat so often at night, you need to figure out *why* baby is asking to eat.

Why Does Your Baby Eat at Night?

There are many reasons kids wake to eat at night:

1. They need more soothing to navigate a brief sleep arousal, and nursing or eating is a great source of comfort.

2. They have a strong food = sleep or suck = sleep association. If Baby eats or sucks at bedtime while or near to falling asleep, every time they cycle through a brief sleep arousal, they may need to eat or suck to fall back to sleep.

3. They are legitimately hungry. If you were tripling your weight in one year,[1] you would probably be hungry at night too.

4. It's a habit.

So there you go—problem solved!

Points 1 and 2 have been addressed in Chapters 4 and 5 (How Babies Sleep and Baby Sleep Power Tools), so let's delve into points 3 and 4: "Baby is hungry" and "It's a habit."

Baby Is Hungry

The question "Is Baby hungry?" has plagued every parent since the invention of babies. It is generally understood that feeding on demand—offering your baby breast or bottle whenever they seem to indicate an interest—is a healthy, responsive, and reasonable way to care for babies. But babies have a poorly designed communication system: crying can mean tired, gassy, wet, hungry, or *just because*. How do you know if they're actually hungry?

Most parents try to come up with an equation to determine when to feed their child at night, something like:

$$F = T \times O$$

where
F = Time to feed? {yes:no}
T = Time since last night feeding
O = Oh My God You Are Killing Me {1:0}

It *is* entirely possible that your baby wakes to eat at night because they're legitimately hungry, especially when they're newborns. It's the plague of the all-liquid diet combined with an elfin-sized stomach.

Newborns often require food every 2 to 3 hours around the clock. You might get a few 4-hour stretches between meals in there, but those longer windows may not happen at convenient times. Premature babies often need to eat even *more* frequently for the first few months. And breastfed babies will wake to eat more frequently than bottle-fed babies.[2]

As newborns grow older (between 6 and 8 weeks), they often develop a 4- to 6-hour fast early in the night. Unfortunately, babies tend to have an early bedtime, so this 4- to 6-hour stretch rarely overlaps with *your* sleep. While at 8 weeks you may have only three feedings a night, they're often clustered around the time when *you're* trying to sleep, say, midnight, 3 a.m., and 5 a.m. This staccato night-feeding pattern continues until Baby gets a bit older and is able to consume more calories during the day and eat less at night.

What every parent *really* wants to know is this: When is it reasonable to ask a baby to *stop* eating for most or all of the night? Sadly, there is no consensus on when your child is capable of fully fasting through the night (by which I mean an entire night, 10 to 12 hours). Some studies suggest that babies are fully capable of an 11- to 12-hour fast by 2 or 3 months.[3] My own experience is that while some 3-month-olds will indeed go without food for 11 hours, a much larger percentage won't readily do that until closer to 6 to 8 months. And for most of you, trying to coax your 3-month-old into an 11-hour fast would be like toilet training your cat: it seems possible, but in reality it's a huge mess. As a data point, only 50% of 6-month-olds are sleeping 8 hours without eating.[4]

The bottom line is there *is* no hard-and-fast answer to "how much does baby need to eat at night" or "when can they sleep through the night without food."

I will, however, suggest the guidelines on the facing page for your consideration.

To be clear, I'm not suggesting that it's a problem if you nurse or feed more times than is indicated here. Night feeding is only a problem if it's a problem *for you*. If you enjoy feeding your child at night and want to continue to do so for any reason (you enjoy the quiet cuddle time, it's your last child so you're not in a rush, you have cause to worry about potential supply issues, etc.), I fully support it.

How Many Night Feedings Does Your Baby Need?*

	NUMBER OF FEEDINGS		
	Low	Average	High
0–3 Months**	1–2	3–4	6
3–6 Months	0	2–3	4
6–9 Months	0	0–2	2–3
9–12 Months	0	0–1	2

* The numbers in this table reflect what I've observed across thousands of families. They don't suggest that your 6- to 9-month-old needs to eat or should be eating two or three times a night, just that many still are (frequently, this is linked to a food = sleep association issue and could be resolved by modifying what happens at bedtime). Breastfed babies more commonly fall in the average or high range, bottle-fed babies on the low or average side.

**Newborns are highly variable: some eat huge, gulping meals a few times a day, others are persistent snackers. Babies may need to eat quite frequently for the first few weeks, but things tend to taper off by about 6 weeks. So while it is not entirely uncommon for a 2-week-old to eat four or five times at night, you should expect your 3-month-old to fall closer to the low or average number of feedings per night.

On the other hand, if fully night weaning is something you *want* to do, almost all full-term babies over 6 months of age are fully capable of making it through the night without eating.

Additional notes on night feedings:

- Most babies will typically have the longest stretch of uninterrupted sleep just after bedtime, followed by more frequent requests to eat as you progress toward morning.

- Most healthy, full-term 6- to 8-month-old babies can sleep from bedtime till about 4 a.m. without eating. Many babies maintain this early-morning (4 to 5 a.m.) "snooze button" feeding.

- Typically, once your child has dropped a feed, you are done offering food at that time. However, occasionally, due to illness, regressions, and the like, a feeding will pop back up like a malignant monkey.

In general, if your baby is older than ~2 months and is eating more frequently at night than the table here suggests (or maybe just your instinct tells you something is off), it's time to consider possible reasons your baby might be extra hungry at night, such as the following.

Baby Is a Distracted Eater

As babies get older (generally around 6 to 8 months), they figure out that the world is far too fabulous to miss out on while eating. So they eat just barely enough during the day and instead tank up at night, when there's nothing good on TV. This is universally challenging, but there are a few things you can try:

- Feed Baby in a dark room with white noise and no other people in it. Babies are fascinated by older siblings in particular—your dancing toddler is far more interesting than life-giving sustenance.

- Feed Baby at home. New environments or being outside will provide an unignorable distraction.

- Drape a baby blanket over Baby while she eats so there is nothing to look at.

- Feed Baby just after waking from a nap when she's still a bit groggy and more likely to stay on task.

- Swaddle Baby at feeding times, even if she is too old or too big for sleep swaddling. It removes [playing with your hair/pulling your necklace/picking at your sweater] from the set of available distractions.

Baby Has a Preferred Source

Sometimes nursing moms find that their baby is choosing not to partake of their carefully cultivated, pumped breast-milk stores while at daycare and instead hold out till the evening, when their favorite breastaurant is open for business. Often these are babies who previously slept with minimal night feedings but who, since Mom's return to work, are night nursing like they've been trekking through the Sahara. This creates a bit of a quandary for Mom, who may feel conflicted about returning to work, is getting less baby time during the day, and may hesitate to give up the opportunity to connect at night, but who is miserably exhausted as a result.

If increasing demands to eat at night (and daytime bottle refusal) are turning you into a shambling mess, then you'll need to change your breastaurant from an all-you-can-eat buffet into a more civilized limited-service scenario, using the night-weaning techniques discussed later in this chapter.

Baby Is on Solid Food

There is nothing more fun than watching a baby squeegee applesauce through their hair, so it's no surprise that many parents are excited about the adventure of starting on solid foods. However, sometimes those new solids can inadvertently result in more demands to eat at night.

While the number of calories in breast milk can vary wildly depending on the mom and the time of day,[5] on average an ounce of breast milk or formula has about 20 calories.[6] In comparison, many popular baby foods (apples, carrots, squash) have only 10 to 15 calories per ounce.[7] Baby food also has a high fiber content, which can leave baby feeling full and thus uninterested in later offers of breast or bottle. So unless your baby is a big fan of high-calorie foods (pasta, mashed avocado, soft cheese), solid meals are generally anywhere from 25% to 50% lower in calories than liquid meals.

This is not to suggest that you should forgo the captivating joys of feeding your baby solids. But you want to be mindful that solids are almost always higher in fiber and lower in calories than bottle or breastmilk. Offer solid foods *after* a full liquid feeding. It's like dessert: always enjoyable, rarely skipped, but best after a healthy meal.

As your baby gets older and is routinely eating more calorie-rich foods, you can become more flexible about the order of solids and liquids at mealtime.

Baby Has Nursing Issues

Every mom who has ever nursed a baby has, at one time or another, been convinced that Baby isn't getting enough milk. This is entirely understandable. Those breasts, which have been hanging there forever, are suddenly, mystically, inexplicably producing food! And what's more, it's food for the most precious, tiny, beloved creature who has ever existed in all of history. Because you can't see the mystery food flowing from boob to belly, much of nursing relies on trust, growth, and wet diapers. So in general, you need to have faith that since baby is growing and producing wet diapers, all is going to plan.

However, sometimes things *don't* go according to plan. It's entirely possible to have a baby who is growing, thriving, and producing sufficient wet diapers and yet demanding to nurse constantly at night due to nursing issues, such as:

- fast letdown
- oversupply
- undersupply
- poor latch
- tongue tie

Before you freak out (seriously, I can tell you're freaking out—deep breaths, in with the good air out with the bad), keep in mind that nursing issues as an underlying cause of frequent night feeds are rare. However, if you have significant concerns, ask for a referral for a local IBCLC (International Board Certified Lactation Consultant),[8] who can help you sort things out.

Baby Has a Night Eating Habit

If you have a baby 6 months or older who eats well during the day and falls asleep independently, congratulations! Your baby's night feeding is likely just habit. Which is pretty reasonable when you think about it.

When they're itty-bitty, babies wake up a *lot*, due to their immature circadian rhythm, liquid diet, and thimble-sized tummies. They wake up and gulp down the baby equivalent of a holiday dinner periodically throughout the night. As they grow, they no longer need a holiday dinner every night, but they've been doing it their entire life, so their body has gotten *used* to that huge meal. If you try to suddenly withhold this enormous meal because "Seriously, kiddo, nobody needs to eat that much every night," it'll lead to some pretty raw feelings all around.

But that doesn't mean you can't and shouldn't work toward gentle weaning to shuffle those nighttime feasts into a more civilized daytime eating schedule.

Nightly Holiday Meal

Night-Weaning Strategies

You've likely heard many a fireside tale from parents who struggled to wean off night feeding, their faces ashen with dark circles under their eyes, their voices hushed as they describe their nighttime misadventures...

"I'll never forget the time, back when she was 9 months old. The pediatrician confidently told us it was time for our hale and hearty girl to stop eating three times a night. We started with the 2 a.m. feed, because we knew she couldn't be *that* hungry after just downing a full bottle at 12:30. We refused to give her a bottle but instead went in to comfort her with gentle words and back rubs. Our gentle daughter turned into a rampaging rock troll. It was like petting a honey badger. We tried for a full 3 weeks before relenting. I still have nightmares about it. When we finally gave her another bottle, she grabbed it with furious frenzy. We haven't had the courage to try again. She's 3 now."

These stories (and we've *all* heard them) may leave you hesitant to launch into night weaning. But let me assure you, *most* night-weaning struggles are linked to the root issue that Baby has a raging food/nurse/suck = sleep association linked to bedtime. If you've tackled that issue (and you have, right?), then you've already done the hard part.

If you are the parent of a healthy 4- to 6-month-old baby who is falling asleep independently without any food or suck association at bedtime and you want to gradually reduce the number of night feedings or to fully night wean, you've come to the right place.

Traditionally, the long-term goal of night weaning is for Baby to sleep without food for the entire night. But your baby might be younger, or you might simply be looking to remove one or two feedings but keep the rest. The strategies here will work for any of these night-weaning goals.

Pick the Right Starting Point

It's best to focus on a short-term strategy that creates longer uninterrupted stretches of sleep for you. Overall sleep duration matters, but uninterrupted sleep matters more.[9] As adults, we need 6 hours of continuous sleep to feel like functional human beings. Look at the pattern of night feeds, and focus on weaning off the feeding that will create the longest possible stretch of uninterrupted sleep for you.

As an example, suppose you have a 6-month-old baby who goes to bed at 7:30, then wakes to nurse at 10:00, 2:00, and 5:00. You might think it's best to start weaning with the 10 p.m. feeding because it's only a few hours after bedtime and, logically, a 6-month-old baby can go longer than two and a half hours without eating. However, it's the 2 a.m. feeding that is the most disruptive to your sleep. Assuming you go to bed at 10:00, removing the 10 p.m. feed makes no substantial difference in sleep, because the longest stretch left is a pithy 4 hours (10 to 2). If, however, you wean off the 2 a.m. feeding, you could go to bed at 10 and then sleep a full 7 hours. And tah-*rust* me, those 7 hours are going to make everybody feel a lot less crotchety.

So consider your night-weaning strategy from this perspective: "What would it take for *me* to get 6 hours of sleep in a row?"

A Starting Point Is a Single Point

Start with one feeding. Some people like to jump in and try to wean off all feedings at once. But tackling two or more night feedings simultaneously can get messy, in part because it's a dramatic shift in consumption. Take, for example, a baby who has three 6-ounce bottles during the night. Removing 2 ounces from each of three bottles results in a net loss of 6 ounces across the night, or the equivalent of one less bottle in one fell swoop. Some babies are malleable enough to roll with this expedited change, but others will get hungry and grumpy. If you're nursing and make the jump too quickly, you can end up engorged, with clogged ducts, or worse.

So while you're understandably looking for a quick solution, experience suggests that more gradual weaning leads to better outcomes.

Weaning Off a Bottle Feed

Night #1. Offer 2 ounces less formula than you normally would. If Baby was typically taking a 6-ounce bottle, offer a 4-ounce bottle instead. Keep all other bottles at their regular volume.

Night #2. Decrease the volume by an additional 2 ounces. The 4-ounce bottle is now a 2-ounce bottle.

Night #3 and on. Continue until you are finished. In our hypothetical example, you would offer no formula at this time as you would have fully weaned off this feeding.

Once you've gotten to zero to 2 ounces, most babies simply stop waking up. If yours continues to wake, ignore them. There may be some brief grumbles because Baby is habituated to waking at this time. But because they know how to fall asleep without bottles, and because you've diligently and gradually decreased the amount they've been eating at this time, you can be confident they aren't starving. Most babies make the adjustment without significant fanfare. Let things settle in for a few days, then move on to the next night feeding.

Closing the Breastaurant: Weaning Off a Breast Feed

Gradually reduce the amount of time you allow Baby to feed by 1 minute a night. If your baby is nursing for 10 minutes a side, start popping him off at 9 minutes, 8 minutes, 7... By the time you are nursing for 2 to 3 minutes a side, he may stop waking up on his own. Whoopee!

If you get down to ~2 minutes per side and your baby *still* demands to nurse, at this point you have a couple of options:

- Send in the Milkless Boob (a.k.a. the non-nursing parent) for a minute or two of gentle soothing. Babies are much more adaptive to the "No more food, buddy!" message when it's gently delivered by the non-nursing parent. If your child is still grumpy after a few minutes of gentle soothing...

- Let Baby complain. Your baby no longer has a nurse = sleep association and is now used to not eating at this time. There may be some brief grumbles, then they'll get bored with the whole scene and fall back to sleep.

- Move on to the next night feeding.

After Night Weaning

When you have successfully established that food is off the menu at a specific time, don't offer food at that time. The milk bar is now closed.

Depending on their age, your child may occasionally request to eat at times you have previously weaned off. How you handle these requests, of course, is up to you. If your child is younger (4 to 6 months) or has recently been sick and is possibly dehydrated, you may lean toward being more generous with night feeding, confident that you can re-wean those feedings once everybody is feeling better.

But don't *rush* to feed your child at a time when they've been reliably *not* eating. Maybe they're having a rough night (like pimples on prom night, these are simply an unfortunate part of life); maybe they just need a gentle back rub; maybe the diaper leaked and they aren't too keen about it; maybe they just need to grump for a few minutes before falling back to sleep. Feeding should no longer be your default response to a mysterious night waking.

As you get closer to the 9- to 12-month zone, I would encourage you to be stingy about going back to feeding your child at times that you've already weaned off. People often get stuck in a cycle of endless night weaning because they periodically convince themselves that their older baby, who has been comfortably not eating at night, is now likely starving and MUST. BE. FED. Night weaning turns into night-nursing whack-a-mole.* You know your child can and will get all their food in during the day—deviating from the "milk bar is closed" plan at night risks flagrant disregard of the Goddess of Consistency.

When Baby Doesn't Have a Regular Feeding Schedule

What if your baby has no discernable pattern to night feeds? If every night is a bad game of Baby Sleep Bingo? How do you wean off the 2 a.m. feed if it never actually happens at 2 a.m.?

This is a trickier scenario, but many families have had good success using the following night-feeding plan:

- Shorten the first feeding of the night, whenever it happens.

- Maintain a reasonable gap between feeds—say, 3 hours.

- When Baby requests to eat at night, respond promptly (within 5 minutes), or send in the non-nursing parent for some food-free soothing, or fully ignore the situation until Baby falls back to sleep again.

- Once the first feeding has been fully eliminated, no longer offer food before or at that time. There is no going back.

- Repeat the process with the next feeding.

A variable schedule case study

Let's say you're the parent of a healthy 7-month-old who wakes up three times a night with zero predictability. Sometimes there are only

---

* Whack-a-mole is one of those "you might be a child of the '80s" carnival games that you've likely never heard of because you're too young. Aaaaand now I feel super old.

two feedings, sometimes four, and the times they happen may vary by as much as 2 hours in either direction. Mom is night nursing in a sleep-deprived haze but has the general sense that the sessions last about 15 minutes—7 or 8 minutes per side.

Your initial goal is to shorten the first feed of the night, regardless of *when* that happens. Your secondary goal is to work toward spacing the feeds out. In practice, it might look like this:

Night #1. Baby wakes at 11:45 p.m. Mom promptly responds but uses a timer and pops Baby off the breast at 6 minutes per side. Baby wakes again at 2 a.m., only two and a quarter hours since the previous feeding, so the breastaurant is closed. The non-nursing parent goes in to gently rub Baby's back for 5 minutes. Baby grumbles a bit but eventually goes back to sleep, until 3:10 a.m. Because it's been 3 hours since the last feed, Mom offers a full feeding. Baby sleeps till morning.

Night #2. Baby wakes for food at 11:30. Mom feeds but pops baby off the breast at 5 minutes per side (1 minute less than the night before). Baby wakes again at 1 a.m. Because it's only been an hour and a half since the last feeding, the non-nursing parent is once again on the case. Baby is fairly cross about this, and it takes her 25 minutes to fall back to sleep. Baby wakes again at 3:10. As it has been over 3 hours, Mom goes to offer a full feeding. Baby sleeps till morning.

Night #3. Baby wakes for food at 12:15. Mom feeds Baby but pops off the breast at 4 minutes. Baby wakes again at 1:45. Non-nursing parent is once again called upon to go calm cranky baby. It takes 30 minutes, but eventually Baby goes back to sleep until 3:45. Mom feeds Baby, who then sleeps till morning.

It may not seem like things are going swimmingly, but in fact, a positive pattern is emerging:

- The early-evening feeding is getting shorter.
- The second request for food is being gently refused.

- Baby is able to sleep for a long stretch after the second night waking. This makes it clear that this request is more about want than need (Baby isn't really hungry).

· While the time fluctuates, we're establishing a pattern of two feeds per night. The first is gradually getting shorter, and the second is falling somewhat predictably in the 3 to 4 a.m. zone.

A few nights later...

Night #6. Having diligently shortened the duration of the first feeding to a minute per side, tonight is the first night no food will be offered. Baby wakes at 10:45. Both parents agree to wait and see what happens. Baby complains for 15 minutes before falling back to sleep. Parents do a silent victory dance, whisper-singing, "We are the champions!" Baby sleeps through till 2 a.m. Now what? She hasn't been eating before 3:00. What do we do? Panic ensues! Go back to the night-feeding rules. Is it past the time we drew the line in the sand (about 11 p.m.)? Ayup. Has it been 3 hours since she last ate? Ayup. So it's feeding time. Sure, 3 a.m. was a good goal, but we just weaned off the first feeding of the night. A child who was previously only spacing out night feeds between 3 and 4 hours has just successfully slept *7 hours*. This is crazy great! Two a.m., roughly, is the new first feeding. Repeat the process at this time.

Feel free to adjust the night-feeding rules to align with your own parenting philosophy and your specific child. It's far less important to have the "right" rules than it is to fully commit to them. Your success with this and most parenting endeavors will be almost entirely dictated by commitment and consistency.

How and When to Use Dream Feeds

A dream feed is when you feed your mostly asleep baby at a time that suits your own nefarious purposes rather than when Baby wakes up and requests it. This means setting your alarm to wake up and feed your baby when they're fully asleep. It's a technique that is unnecessary for 87% of babies, but it can be useful for a few specific scenarios:

For shuffling feedings

Often the night-feeding schedule of a newborn or younger baby (less than 6 months) makes it impossible for you to get anything approaching a human level of uninterrupted sleep. Dream feeds are a great tool to shuffle those feedings to a schedule more conducive to your sleep.

The most common scenario is a baby who wakes to eat 1 to 2 hours after the parents go to bed—the parents barely get a quick nap in, which is a foggy form of sleep torture, before being awoken to feed Baby.

In this instance, the parents could offer Baby a dream feed when *they* go to bed, removing the need for Baby to eat an hour later, and creating the potential for everybody to get a longer stretch of uninterrupted sleep. The feeding isn't removed—it's simply *moved*.

For weaning a boob baby

What is a boob baby, you ask?

No, I didn't just call your baby a boob. Some babies are simply exceptionally *into* the boob. (Some babies are huge bottle babies, so this issue is not exclusive to breastfed babies!)

Let's say your boobs were chocolate caramel cupcakes. Who doesn't enjoy a nice chocolate caramel cupcake? Your weaning plan involves trying to convince your boob baby to eat less cupcake. So they get pretty cross with you: "Gimme my full-sized cupcake, woman!" It's not that they're starving; it's not that they don't know how to sleep without a mouth full of cupcake—it's just that cupcakes are fantastic and they *adore* those cupcakes.

Boob babies may be more responsive to weaning in the context of a dream feed. They still get their cupcake, but since they're half asleep while they're eating it, it's less of a struggle to cut back.

For discouraging waking

Additionally, dream feeds meet your child's need for food without encouraging them to wake up. Babies who like cupcakes are apt to wake themselves fully as they cycle through a light-sleep phase in the hopes that another cupcake will appear. Every time you run in to feed them, you reinforce the drive to fight sleep by handing them another cupcake. This is a fairly compelling reward system so, unsurprisingly, the demands for cupcakes continue. The dream feed may help to break this cycle.

Parents often blanch at this idea of dream feeds—after all, they require that you wake your child, something we've been conditioned to avoid. And your baby is probably still going to wake up at other times seeking that cupcake (seriously, what do you put in these things?). So the dream-feed strategy is not the ultimate magical cure for all night-feeding woes. It may do some helpful things, though:

- It ensures that your baby isn't hungry. When Baby wakes up an hour after a dream feed looking for a cupcake, you can be confident that she's not really starving. She may be grouchy about the cupcake, but you know this is about want, not need.

- It removes the reward system. For some babies, eating at night is a powerful incentive.

- It enables you to continue with your night-weaning plan. You can gently wean off dream feeds using the same methods you would for regular feeds. Typically, dream-fed babies are more amenable to being popped off early because they're mostly asleep while it's happening.

As with everything, dream feeds don't always work. Your child may resolutely continue to wake to eat at other times, or they may be too tired to actually eat during the dream feed. But it's a worthy tool for your night-feeding toolbox.

Common Issues in Night Weaning

For most of you, night weaning an older baby who falls asleep without eating or sucking is an effort that will pay dividends with nothing more than a bit of patience and persistence. If gradually weaning off night feeds isn't going smoothly for you, here are some additional thoughts to consider.

Moving Food to Daytime
As you're working on night weaning, make sure you're offering additional opportunities for Baby to eat during the day. Your baby could

be getting as much as 25% to 50% of their calories at night. You won't be able to successfully wean off those feeds without reinserting them elsewhere.

Snooze-Button Feedings

Sometimes babies have a feeding that's close to the time they start the day, about 4:30 to 5:30 a.m. Some babies can successfully wean off this early-morning feed and contentedly sleep through till their normal wake time. Others will respond to your weaning plan by staunchly insisting on starting the day unreasonably early. Given the unpleasant choice between a 5 a.m. feeding and a 5 a.m. wakeup, most parents choose to keep the snooze-button feeding to buy everybody an extra hour of sleep.

Using SLIP to Stop Night Feedings

Many parents (and a surprising number of pediatricians) suggest using sleep training or extinction to stop night feedings. Truthfully, this method works. If you simply close the night milk bar—no gradual weaning, full stop—after a couple of days, everybody will be sleeping soundly. The problem is what happens over those couple of days (hint: many tears). Hungry kids tend to cry a lot. As a general rule, it's best to take a more gradual path out of night feedings. Caveat: if you've diligently tried all the gradual night-weaning techniques and are getting nowhere, it may be that the more direct route is better for your child. There are times when cold turkey is the best plan for all involved.

Inconsistency

Your goal for your naturally inconsistent baby is to keep the Goddess of Consistency appeased as frequently as possible (baskets of dates, salted nuts, and fine silks are recommended offerings). Unfortunately, inconsistency is often an unavoidable part of the weaning process.

Night weaning a baby with a variable feeding schedule may lead to Baby waking up at one time and *not* getting fed until they fall back to sleep, but being fed at *other* wakeup times. This may be necessary as you temporarily move through weaning off a specific night feeding. The key word here is *temporarily*.

The Goddess of Consistency may overlook a short-term affront, but if inconsistency continues for weeks, it's time to re-evaluate the strategy.

Baby Is Too Young

There is absolutely zero consensus on when babies are capable of going without food all night, and some experts will even suggest that if you're still night feeding your 3-month-old you're a big doofus. My own experience is that most babies are reliably capable of going all night sans food somewhere between 6 and 8 months (snooze-button feedings don't count). If your baby is under 6 months and your efforts to night wean are going miserably, maybe he's just not ready. Wait a bit and then try again. (Or maybe I'm the doofus. Who knows?)

Night Weaning Is Endless

Many parents describe night weaning as an endless cycle of cutting back on feedings only to have them come back like a petulant zombie. This chapter provides strategies to address the most common causes of frequent night feeding in older babies. Most are well within the realm of parental control. Most... but not all.

There are many things that can hinder your diligent night-weaning efforts. Teething, travel, and illness are the top three. Kids get sick, and sick kids don't eat well during the day and don't sleep well at night. Travel almost always leads to disrupted night sleep and increased demands for food at night. Teething is a thing that happens, and it's almost always unpleasant. All of these things may undermine your efforts. Don't worry if there's some occasional backsliding on night weaning. Have faith: eventually you'll get where you're trying to go.

Parental Guilt

Many parents return to work earlier than they might like. While having time away from a young baby can be a bit of a blessing (yay, adult interaction!), it can also represent an enormous loss (he took his first steps at daycare?!). The necessities of life can reduce your weekday time with your child to a few paltry hours that can be best described as "not nearly enough." It's not surprising that despite the extreme exhaustion that results from frequent night feedings, some parents of older babies are reluctant to end them—while fatiguing, those night feedings represent precious cuddle time, which is, in its own way, sweet and beautiful.

Sometimes parenting feels like a competitive sport with clearly defined winners and losers, with the winners proudly proclaiming that their child is "sleeping through the night." And we can feel obliged to work toward night weaning due to well-intentioned questions from family and neighbors—"How's he sleeping?"

But the reality is that there is no *requirement* that you wean off night feedings if you enjoy them and are able to get enough sleep. There is nothing inherently wrong with feeding a baby at night. College applications do not ask "At what age did you sleep through the night?" The only reason to wean off night feedings is because your child no longer biologically needs them *and they aren't working for you.*

If they *are* working for you, then tally ho!

10

Becoming the Zen
Nap Ninja Master

T HE KOBAYASHI MARU is a famous training test in Starfleet
(yes, that Starfleet). Star Trek's Starfleet cadets are faced with a
command decision: A civilian ship has become disabled and is
stranded in the Klingon Neutral Zone. If you choose to save the ship,
all the civilians are rescued but local Klingon warships blow you to
smithereens; if you choose to not save the ship, local Klingon warships
will blow the civilian ship into smithereens while you cowardly watch
from a safe distance. The Kobayashi Maru is a classic no-win scenario.

For some of you, naps will feel like the Kobayashi Maru, which may
be enormously depressing. But Captain Kirk found a way to beat the
Kobayashi Maru (spoiler alert . . . he cheats), and you will too.

If your child is an Olympic-grade napper, the world is your oyster—
you get predictably chunky naps during the day, giving you precious
kid-free time. Your well-rested baby will be less fussy and more pleasant to spend time with. And as there is much truth in the old adage
"sleep begets sleep," your brilliantly napping baby is far more likely

to sleep well at night. Mastering naps is essentially the Valhalla of baby sleep.

However, for many parents, naps are truly challenging to sort out. Babies can *and will* successfully fight naps. Sleep drive is relatively dinky during the day. Trying to get your child to nap too early or late can result in epic nap battles. A short or missed nap can set you up for a rough slog for the rest of the day. An unintended 5-minute catnap in the car can result in no later nap at all—a serious crap nap day.

And the result of a crap nap day is often an increasingly overtired and fussy baby who then heads into bedtime primed for a rough night.

Thus, you might feel enormous pressure to become a world-renowned Zen nap master: the benefits of success are substantial, and the penalty of failure is … well … nap pandemonium.

Why Good Naps Are So Challenging

Sorting out naps is hard for a lot of reasons.

1. The baby-sleep universe is filled with conflicting advice. Your child should be sleeping every 90 minutes. Your child should be napping on the 2–3–4-hour schedule. Your baby should be napping on a rigid schedule. Naps should float about like a drunken monarch. Car naps are evil. Car naps are awesome. There is a 5-second window where your baby will easily fall asleep and stay asleep and if you miss it you are a FAILURE AS A PARENT AND A HUMAN BEING. Honestly. It's exhausting.

2. Day sleep is primarily regulated by Baby's sleep drive, which accumulates the longer they are awake. Unfortunately, day sleep drive is pretty dinky, thus it's easy to forgo sleeping at naptime (relative to bedtime).

3. Your baby's nap schedule is constantly changing. So while bedtime (once it gets locked in) is a relative constant for years, naps are fluid. You are aiming at a moving target.

4. Babies can and will fight sleep. Life is exciting, naps are not. At no point in the history of life on our planet has any child anywhere

Car Naps Happen

ever said, "Playing with stacking cups is enchanting, but I think I would like to go to a dark, quiet room for some 'me' time in the crib now."

5. Naps are susceptible to even small sleep disruptions. Travel, appointments, teething, illness, car naps or even a nap skipped in order to make a particularly fun playdate can all throw a monkey wrench into your well-laid nap plans.

So getting and keeping great naps is hard (you probably already know that). But it *can* be done (you likely don't believe that). It will just take a little time, faith, and commitment.

Setting Realistic Nap Expectations

How many naps should your child be taking and how long should they be? Your neighbor's baby is taking two 3-hour naps a day—should yours be too?

Everybody has that friend with the unicorn baby who is charming every second of the day, is a nap and night-sleep champion, and poops jellybeans. Don't get drawn into your comparisons with this unicorn baby. Your non-jellybean-pooping baby is perfect too!

Naps are also hugely age-dependent, so let's break it down:

Newborn Naps: Zero–3 Months

For the first few weeks, naps are a bit of a crapshoot. Your newborn might nap for 10 minutes and then be resolutely awake for 4 hours. She might then nap for 4 hours, wake up for 45 minutes, and go back down for another 2 hour nap. It's hard to nail down a normal newborn nap schedule because there is no "normal." Newborn naps may be 10 minutes or 4 hours long, and that's okay.

Note: Newborns can and will sleep just about anywhere. While your 6-month-old can only sleep at home under a very specific set of circumstances (white noise, pre-nap routine, sacrificing a live chicken to the nap gods), your newborn is pretty portable. This is a great time to take advantage of this fact and get out of the house.

Newborn nap homework

Your focus is on using the Power Tools and not letting your baby stay awake too long between naps. If you're feeling sassy and want to start experimenting with putting your newborn down for naps awake, go for it. If the thought makes you blanch with terror, don't sweat it (for now).

3- to 6-Month Naps

By 3 months, your baby should be substantially less fussy and more predictable. They're also a lot less floppy and a lot more chubby. Some people love the newborn phase because they're tiny and portable, but me? I love a happy chunky monkey. The Ben & Jerry's ice cream, I mean. Obviously.

Some 3-month-olds will naturally establish a fairly predictable "by the clock" schedule of naps and bedtime. Others will be more erratic, mixing long and short naps, resulting in a somewhat unpredictable bedtime. Naps can still be highly variable at this age. Consolidated nap sleep is a developmental milestone[1] involving brain chemistry and the establishment of a more mature sleep cycle. You can't make babies take long, chunky naps until they're ready.[2]

3- to 6-Month nap homework

Three months is a fantastic time to make solid nap habits a priority. I would even go so far as to use the word *ideal*.

Why 3 months is the ideal time to establish nap mastery:

- You've had a few months to heal from birth and have conquered essential feeding and baby-care skills. You may not yet realize this, but you are officially a baby pro. Congratulations!

- Your newborn is no longer a newborn—she's a baby. She's less fussy, has a somewhat more regular sleep/wake cycle, and is settling into a predictable feeding pattern.

- You've still got lots of soothing tools in your baby sleep arsenal.

- Your child doesn't yet have substantial issues with object permanence and separation anxiety.

- You probably don't have teething in the mix yet.

Continue to use as much age-appropriate soothing as possible and ensure that Baby isn't awake too long. But note that your baby (who is no longer a newborn and now is just a regular old baby) is not as portable as he once was. Naps will now be more successful if they occur in the same dark, safe place every day. By now, you also should have committed to a brief but consistent 10- to 15-minute pre-nap routine.

This is a great time to focus on independent sleep. No more (or dramatically less frequent) naps on your lap, on your boob, in a baby carrier, etc. Sure, you can occasionally enjoy a good cuddle-nap. But this is the time to buckle down to avoid major nap tribulations in the future.

6- to 9-Month Naps

Nap duration is often variable for the first 6 months. Some babies will lock into long naps early, but many are still taking short (40- to 50-minute) naps. However, somewhere between 6 and 9 months, those

45-minute naps should extend into lengthier hour-and-a-half naps. The third nap, if it's still happening, is often a tiny 15–20-minute affair.

Most 6- to 9-month-old babies are taking three naps a day, although some particularly gifted nappers might already be down to two. Others will still take short crap naps and thus will resolutely need three. Still others will *need* the third nap but won't easily *take* the third nap, resulting in an overly long wake time prior to bedtime. Thus there's often a lot of active "nap yoga" happening at this age—capping naps, forcing the third nap via babywearing or stroller walks, bedtime adjustments on particularly bad nap days, etc.

If naps have been a bit shaky to date, they might start to fall apart at this age. This is a particularly challenging nap zone for many parents for several reasons:

- Older babies are BUSY. Far too busy working on [crawling/standing/ catching the cat's tail] to bother with napping.

- Separation anxiety peaks. Your baby will start freaking out when you leave the room long enough to blow your nose. The last thing your baby wants to do is separate from you to nap. Nap battles ensue.

- Object permanence blows up on you. If your 6- to 9-month-old baby isn't falling asleep independently at naptime, you're headed into the danger zone of crap naps.

6- to 9-Month nap homework

By this age, you should have a well-established pre-nap routine and naps should (generally) occur in the same place every day. Your flexible, portable newborn has become a full-fledged baby, and babies thrive on routine and predictability (see also: why babies make terrible traveling companions). This means it's a bit harder to get out of the house, and playdates often mean blowing a nap. You'll have to determine which is more critical to household harmony: a solid nap for your baby or the desperate bliss of adult interaction for you. As a general rule, try not to blow too many naps, unless you're feeling like Jack Nicholson in *The Shining*, in which case get thee to the nearest coffee shop, pronto.

Your 6- to 9-month-old baby really needs to be falling to sleep at naptime without your assistance. I know, I keep harping on this! You're looking for some easier option so you can avoid this step. You can't.

9- to 12-Month Naps

Most 9- to 12-month-old babies have happily settled into two fairly predictable hour-or-longer naps a day. Which is not to suggest that your older baby won't ever fight naps, or that your almost-a-toddler won't be too busy working on standing, crawling, or even walking to bother with something as dull as napping. But hopefully your naps have settled into a nice chunky pattern. (If they haven't, hang on— we'll troubleshoot naps soon.)

9- to 12-Month nap homework

With luck your naps are by now a fairly well-oiled machine. They should happen on a relatively predictable and consistent schedule, and mostly at home. The Goddess of Consistency will reward your devotion with longer naps, or will at least refrain from further smiting. Thus your homework is just to keep doing what you're doing!

12- to 18-Month Naps

Celebrating your child's first birthday is a bigger deal than just the joy of watching a baby double-fisting birthday cake. (Truthfully, giving babies cake is one of the best things in the world, and any older baby I'm asked to babysit is totally getting cake. Or some grapefruit. Good times.)

Your 1-year-old toddler is full of boundless energy and will, between 12 and 18 months, drop to one nap. She will sometimes fight you on naps because *life is happening.* Now is when your consistency and routine schedule pay off. Toddlers don't transition well. The child who was happily playing with blocks morphs into the Dread Pirate Roberts when it's time to leave the playdate. Luckily, you've established fantastic groundwork by being so rigid about sleep for the first 12 months that now it's smooth sailing.

(Why are you laughing? Stop laughing. I didn't say anything funny.)

12- to 18-Month nap homework

Keep an eye out for signs that your kiddo is ready to drop a nap (more on this later). Use a 20-minute or longer pre-nap routine to help your child transition from playtime to sleep. Bright outside light is not your friend in this, so consider keeping the pre-nap activities inside. If white noise is helpful, there is no need to stop using it, although many parents of toddlers do.

18-Month to 3-Year Naps

The vast majority of babies are napping at their third birthday,[3] so don't be too quick to buy into it when your not-yet-3-year-old tries to convince you that they're ready to stop napping. Many kids at this age will temporarily fight naps then fall back into a happy nap pattern. They're tricky like that. (Although . . . some kiddos do stop napping by the time they're 3—more on this later.)

As a rule, however, 3-year-olds don't want to do *lots* of things (wear shoes, share toys, eat anything that's not a cracker). Don't let them easily sway you on napping.

18-Month to 3-Year nap homework

Stay the course. Consistency, commitment, all that good stuff. Do that.

3- to 5-Year Naps

Some lucky parents will have kids who nap until the end of kindergarten, but most kids will be done with napping far before then. While having a child who doesn't nap frees up your schedule, it also means you no longer get a midday breather. Most people (read: me) look back on the halcyon days of napping as a time filled with the golden glow of a Norman Rockwell painting.

3- to 5-Year nap homework

Make a toast to your departing naptime and wish it a fond farewell!

The Three Conventions of Nap Nirvana
· ·

When it comes to children, there are things you can and can't control. Unsurprisingly, most of the things you care about fall in the "outside your control" bucket (such as how many hours their fingers spend in their nose, and what they do with the stuff they find in there). As a parent, you have to accept that you can't entirely control napping. Kids can and will fight naps. Some days will be terrible nap days, even if you do all the right things.

And what *are* "all the right things"? When it comes to napping, you have three very potent and specific jobs that I'm calling the Conventions of Nap Nirvana:

1. *Give your child as much age-appropriate soothing (a.k.a. Power Tools) as you can.* Plunking your 4-week-old down awake in a crib with nothing more than happy thoughts and pixie dust is unlikely to work well. Neither is having your 14-month-old nap exclusively on your chest while you bounce on an exercise ball. The key term here is "age-appropriate."

2. *Use the same pre-nap routine for each nap of the day.* It doesn't need to be an elaborate 60-minute affair involving massage, a Turkish bath, interpretive dance, and a musical puppet show. But you need more of a transition from playtime than "Well, time for your nap—into the bed you go, my friend!"

3. *Timing is everything.* Try too *early* and your child won't be tired, but will be justifiably annoyed with you. Wait too *long* and your cranky, overtired baby will be unable to easily fall asleep, but there is nothing left for it but to press on like Shackleton.

Simple, right? Theoretically, it is.
Theoretically.
Let's break them down into some specifics that will help get you from where you are (desperately short, hard-won, inconsistent naps) to where you want to be (nap nirvana).

Age-Appropriate Soothing

The biological compulsion to sleep is not nearly as strong at naptime as it is at bedtime. Plus, your baby wants to hang with you, because you are a delightful person to hang out with. So you need to gently convince your child to forgo your charming company for a while—but without the advantage of powerful biology.

The Baby Sleep Power Tools discussed in Chapter 5 are your allies in encouraging healthy naps. Many people are eager to quickly wean off the Power Tools as though you get a free Starbucks gift card by being the first on the block to have a child who can sleep without any soothing tools. As far as Starbucks and I are aware, this is not the case.

Your baby will, however, likely require *more* soothing at naptime than at bedtime. Don't worry about being consistent between how your baby naps and how they sleep at night—it's okay if naptime and bedtime aren't the same. The Goddess of Consistency will not punish you for this!

Consistency

Nap consistency is like dog poop on the carpet: ignore it and your house will be an unpleasant place to hang out in. The Goddess of Consistency might overlook a few small insults during the night, but she will clobber you should you flout her at naptime.

What does "nap consistency" even mean?

- Your child naps in the same location, with the same pre-nap routine, most of the time.

- You take advantage of a single set of nap cues (white noise, swaddle, lovey, etc.) for all naps.

- For older babies, you nap at the same(ish) time every day.

- You don't skip naps.

Being consistent is a drag. It requires that you organize your entire life around your child's nap schedule, which can be inconvenient if not sometimes impossible.

You'll be inclined to do what works instead. Or to nurse your child to sleep without any routine or additional soothing association. Or to have your baby nap in the stroller, while babywearing, or in the car, depending on where you and your older kiddos are off to for the day. Which is fine ... on occasion. But beware the Goddess of Consistency: she holds a grudge and doesn't take insult lightly.

Some days you will find yourself repeatedly writing "all work and no play" on the walls with a Sharpie. When that happens, it's time to toss consistency and get out of the house. But if naps are the ever-loving bane of your existence, those days will be the exception to the rule.

Starting at about 2 months, you'll want to have a consistent pre-nap routine. Generally, 10 to 15 minutes of quiet wind-down activity is plenty, but it will be a sequence of activities that you will do before *all* naps, *all* the time.

Most babies (and certainly most older kids) struggle with transitions. Being yanked from a game of "hide Cheerios in the couch" and getting plunked into a dark crib asks a lot of a 1-year-old. The pre-nap routine helps to create space for your child to successfully transition from play to sleep.

A regular dull, dark, safe place is another important foundation for nap success. Location becomes a powerful sleep cue as your child comes to understand the activities, sights, and sounds of their sleep place. As anybody who has ever attempted to travel with a baby will attest, most children struggle to nap in new places. Once they're no longer newborns, napping at home will be crucial.

Fortunately, the Goddess of Consistency will abide the occasional small indignity. A good goal is to have your child nap in the same place, with the same routine, and sleep associations 80% of the time.

Timing Is Everything

Timing is crucial to nap success. This is one of the most frustrating elements to baby sleep, as it often feels like throwing darts at tiny balloons in a windstorm.

There is a persistent idea that there is a "magic sleep window" for naps: if you can hit it *just right*, your baby will easily drop off to sleep with nary a whisper, but miss the "magic sleep window" by a few minutes and *you are screwed*. And there is some truth to this, for two key reasons:

1. A baby who hasn't been awake long enough won't have accrued sufficient sleep drive to fall asleep.[4]

2. Babies who have been awake too long accrue a sleep debt, which has many negative impacts[5] and, paradoxically, will make it challenging to fall asleep.

Many parents are frustrated by their inability to triangulate this magic window. But the issue is not that the parents are incompetent, it's that babies are mysterious and the magic window is often an unknowable thing. And further, for some babies, even if the nap is timed perfectly, there is no "baby easily nods off to sleep" payoff.

So to be clear: timing *is* everything. It creates the foundation for a good nap, and ignoring it all but dooms you to nap failure. However, while nailing the ideal time for naps may result in stupendous naps for some babies, for other, more challenging tykes, it is simply the first step of *many* needed to get to nap utopia.

In an ideal scenario, you aim for this magic window by following Baby's lead. When your baby starts to yawn, get fussy, and rub their eyes, when their eyes look unfocused, when they cease to make eye contact, etc., it's time for nap. Following Baby's lead, however, is rarely straightforward. Some babies don't give good sleepy signs. Or they give sleepy signs when they're already *over*tired, so that if you begin your 15-minute pre-nap ritual when your baby has started to become fussy and rub their eyes, it's already too late.

If you're finding this to be the case for *your* baby, instead of watching for cues, focus instead on how long they've been awake. In fact, I generally find wake time to be more straightforward and less error-prone than following cues.

The Wake-Time Method

The Wake-Time Method involves calculating the time your child should be taking a nap based on how long they've been awake to ensure:

- that your child isn't awake too long between naps;

- that your child is awake long enough between naps to accrue sufficient sleep debt; and

- that your nap schedule is flexible enough to comfortably accommo-
date a high degree of variability in nap duration.

The ideal wake-time duration will vary by baby, but the chart here
provides some general guidelines.

Wake-Time Duration

	Wake Time*	Nap Duration	Naps per Day
Birth–6 weeks	30 mins.–1 hr.	15 mins.–4 hrs.	4–8
6 Weeks–3 Months	45 mins.–1 hr., 45 mins.	30 mins.–2 hrs.	3–5
4 Months	1–2 hrs.	30 mins.–2 hrs.	3–4
5 Months	1 hr., 15 mins.–2.5 hrs.	30 mins.–2 hrs.	3
6 Months	1.5–3 hrs.	45 mins. –2 hrs.	3
7 Months	1 hr., 45 mins.– 3.5 hrs.	45 mins. –2 hrs.	2–3
8 Months	2–3.5 hrs.	1–2 hrs.	2–3
9–12 Months	2–4 hrs.	1–2 hrs.	2
12–18 Months	5–6 hrs. (if 1 nap) 3–4 hrs. (if 2 naps)	1–3 hrs.	1–2
18 Months–Done Napping	5 hrs.	1–3 hrs.	0–1

*Most babies need to stay awake progressively longer as the day goes on. Thus, the amount of time
between when your baby wakes for the day and nap #1 will generally be shorter than that between
the end of nap #1 and the start of nap #2. And the amount of time between the last nap of the day
and bedtime should be the longest time your baby is awake. Hence, the lowest number would most
likely apply to the first wake time and the highest number to the last wake time.

Use the chart as a touchstone, but adjust the times based on your
observations with your child. Most parents are pretty canny when
it comes to figuring out how long their child needs to be awake between naps.

As noted in the chart, the optimal time is a moving target (babies
can remain awake longer as they get older), so be prepared to regularly
re-evaluate your nap timing.

"Time Awake" vs. "By the Clock"

When your baby is younger (generally under 6 months), naps will flutter about like a drunken mosquito. As your baby gets older, though, things will become more regular: Baby will tend to wake at the same time every day, nap duration will become more consistent, and bedtime will happen at the same time every day.

As sleep becomes more predictable (usually sometime between 4 and 9 months), you can segue from the Wake-Time Method to the By-the-Clock Method. "By the clock" is just what it sounds like: napping at a specific time every day. Having a consistent by-the-clock nap schedule simplifies your ability to plan around naps and creates a predictable rhythm to your child's sleep/wake pattern. It's clearly an appealing alternative for parents, who are often fatigued by the pandemonium of random nap schedules.

The transition from Wake Time to By the Clock is often a gradual process that happens without your involvement. Predictability in sleep schedules begins with a consistent bedtime, which will commonly lead to a consistent morning wake up, which in turn creates the opportunity to make nap #1 happen by the clock. For example, if your child is routinely waking at 6 a.m. and can comfortably remain awake for 2 hours until nap #1, you can peg nap #1 at 8 a.m.

Nap #1 is often the first to fall into a predictable duration. When this happens, you can now have a "by the clock" time for nap #2. Continuing with our example, if your child is consistently waking from nap #1 at 10 a.m. and needs to be awake for 3 hours before nap #2, you can lock in the second nap at 1 p.m.

Parents often ask, "When should we shift to napping by the clock?"
Answer: "When you reasonably can."

Most parents are pretty keen to have *some* idea of what to expect during the day, so mindfully working toward By the Clock (when appropriate) is a great goal that appeases both the Goddess of Consistency as well as your own sanity.

Sleep Schedules

When you're desperately sleep deprived, your brain stops working efficiently; higher functions like math and critical thinking become as challenging as *spellin* and *calkulus*. Unsurprisingly, chronically sleep-deprived parents like concrete baby sleep schedules, ones that don't require math or decision making. But I want to caution you that sleep schedules are not as concrete and easy as you might hope…

Newborn sleep is a capricious hummingbird. One nap might be 30 minutes, the next, 3 hours. Trying to shoehorn a younger baby into a fixed schedule leads to bedlam for the following reasons:

1. Variability in nap duration will sabotage your attempt at locking in on a schedule.

2. Younger babies are particularly vulnerable to "awake too long/too short" issues. If you've picked the wrong sleep schedule, it's easy to unintentionally end up with a baby who takes crap naps because they've been awake too long or not long enough.

3. The amount of time your baby can be awake is constantly expanding, which means that the schedule that works today may not work next week. A baby who mysteriously fights naps is often simply on a schedule that no longer fits that child.

Take, for example, the popular 2–3–4 schedule (babies are awake 2 hours before nap #1, 3 hours before nap #2, and 4 hours before bedtime). This is a great schedule… provided you are the parent of an 8-month-old. Trying to implement the 2–3–4 plan with a 4-month-old would be a mess, pushing your baby to stay awake far longer than they can handle.

Similarly, some approaches tout having babies nap every 90 minutes throughout the day. This will work like gangbusters for your 4-month-old, who is developmentally ready to be awake about 90 minutes between naps. But it'll keep your newborn awake far too long and will frustrate your older baby, who won't be ready to sleep so soon.

I'm not saying schedules are bad per se, but they're challenging for babies with unpredictable nap durations. Make sure you're applying the *right* schedule at the *right* age. And be mindful that your rapidly changing baby may outgrow the current schedule in the twinkling of a mischievous monkey's eye.

Rather than taking a preset schedule and trying to fit your child into it, if you follow your child's lead as they establish their own predictable nap durations, they'll *tell* you what their schedule is.

The Newborn Exception to the Rule

The Three Conventions of Nap Nirvana apply to all babies all the time. If, however, you gave birth yesterday and have only been home from the hospital for 5 minutes, feel free to relax. You get a 2-week "I Just Had a Baby" pass that allows you to be inconsistent and go with the flow.

The Fourth Convention of Nap Nirvana
. . . .

What? You thought there were only three? Perchance I said "three." I just didn't want to overwhelm you. "Three" sounds cute and achievable. Like three itty-bitty widdle things. Four sounds like AAARGH, FOUR THINGS? I CAN'T EVEN GET FOUR PIECES OF CLOTHING ON MY BODY!

The Fourth Convention of Nap Nirvana is that by about 3 to 6 months, your baby *must* fall asleep independently.* Failure to heed the almighty Fourth Convention of Nap Nirvana leads to short naps and persistent nap battles.

Teaching your child to fall asleep independently at naptime is the second biggest challenge you will face in the first year of parenting. (The *first* biggest challenge is, of course, growing a baby and then getting Baby out of your body. The third biggest challenge is funding your new coffee habit. Because there is nothing more critical than a hot cup of coffee in the morning. Can't pay the heating bill? I can wear a sweater. But keep the hot coffee coming or I will punch you in the mouth.) It is critical that you work toward putting your child down for naptime awake and that they fall asleep on their own.

All of the things discussed in Chapter 4, How Babies Sleep, apply

---

*If you've read the whole book, this shouldn't come as a big surprise, but some people prefer to skip ahead, in which case this is news.

to naps. Soothing, consistency, and timing are fantastic, but as your child grows older than 3 to 6 months, independent sleep is crucial.

Frustratingly, a child who has learned how to sleep at bedtime cannot transfer that knowledge to naptime. You are probably thinking, "What. The. Ever-Loving Blazes. *Is* This Madness?!" I cannot give you a compelling scientific explanation for it, but babies need to learn independent sleep *twice*.

The happy corollary to this, however, is that rocking/feeding/cuddling to sleep at *naptime* will not confuse the issue at *bedtime*. Sleeping one way for naps and another for bedtime will not incite the ire of the Goddess of Consistency.

How to Put Your Child Down Awake at Naptime

I will tell you exactly how to put your child down awake at naptime. However, the price for this information is $1,000.

Or, you could flip back to the chapters on teaching your child how to fall asleep without you (Chapters 6 and 7 on SLIP/SWAP). Either works great for me.

Nap success with SLIP/SWAP will be entirely predicated on *your* commitment to the first three nap conventions. Trying to teach independent sleep at naptime without adherence to those would be, in the immortal words of Vizzini,* "Inconceivable!"

Additionally, you'll likely want to address naps *after* you've successfully established independent sleep at bedtime. Why?

· Establishing independent sleep is far easier at bedtime than at naptime. You can make mistakes, be inconsistent, etc., and still end up with a successful outcome. Naps are a greater challenge. Tackle the easy stuff first to bolster your confidence and firmly establish that, yes, this is a possible thing.

· Independent sleep at bedtime leads to better nighttime sleep for everyone. You and your child will have better success with independent sleep at naptime when you're all well rested.

---

*From *The Princess Bride*.

- Short term, working to establish independent sleep at naptime often results in crap naps. Crap naps combined with short or splintered night sleep can create a huge sleep debt for your child, which is counter to your goals of establishing healthy sleep. Having healthy sleep established at bedtime helps to reduce the crap-nap sleep debt.

If you've nailed the first three conventions and your child is confidently sleeping independently at bedtime, it's time to kick off your Nap Master Plan!

Your Nap Master Plan

Step 1: Select the SWAP/SLIP you want to commit to.
- If you had success with one of the SWAPs at bedtime, start with the same method at naptime.

- If you found your attempts with bedtime SWAP to be a frustrating mess, feel free to skip them all and move on to SLIP.

- If you started directly with SLIP at bedtime, you could continue with SLIP at naptime or consider one of the SWAPs as a starting point for naps.

I generally prefer initially approaching naps with one of the SWAPs. Fostering independent sleep is more challenging at naptime than at bedtime because the drive to sleep at naptime is relatively dinky; your child will likely struggle far longer to master it. With both SWAP and SLIP, you should expect that it will take many days or weeks to fully establish independent nap sleep. While things often go surprisingly smoothly, it's possible that your nap SLIP plan may involve weeks of tears.

So if you've got SWAP alternatives that might work, *try those first*. Your mother-in-law is coming to visit for a month? Babies often go down more easily for people who are not their parents—put Grandma on the case and see what happens. Get creative.

But what if you've tried everything and are getting nowhere? Or you're going back to work and your 9-month-old only sleeps latched on your boob and the lovely daycare ladies refuse to offer this service?

Or you're finding that the methods that *used* to work aren't working *at all* anymore? Then start with SLIP.

As discussed previously, you can start with any of the SWAPs and switch to SLIP later. If, however, you begin your nap plan with SLIP, you are firmly committed and should stay the course.

Step 2: Fully commit to your new plan for at least 5 days.

It will take more than a few days to see whether your new plan is working. Your child has been falling asleep one way for most or all of their life. Adjusting to a new way will take time. Accept that, at first, naps may be hard or nonexistent.

Start with the first nap of the day. Do your wonderful wind-down routine, use your words, and use the SLIP/SWAP you've committed to for 1 hour.

If your baby falls asleep *before* the 60-minute mark, then *huzzah!* Let your child sleep until approximately the time they would have normally awoken from this nap. Generally, this means letting them sleep as long as they want. But don't let baby sleep *so* long that they won't reasonably be ready to go down for their next nap. If your 9-month-old baby is still asleep at 11 a.m. and they typically take a second nap at 2, you'll need to wake them to stay on schedule.

If, on the other hand, baby falls asleep briefly (more than 20 minutes) before waking, naptime is *over.* Sometimes parents feel that the nap was too short and they attempt to extend the nap. This rarely works out, although you're welcome to try. A micronap is better than no nap: this mini-nap is a win. Your child has just fallen asleep a new way. This is huge!

If your baby is still not asleep after 60 minutes, naptime is over. Go about your day until the next scheduled naptime. Yes, your child will be tired and fussy. And keeping them awake until the next naptime is no picnic: it means no stroller rides, no car trips... Even a 5-minute nursing (or feeding) nap can throw things off—if they start falling asleep, you may need to tickle their feet, take off their jammies, etc. Do what you can to ensure that they aren't sleeping before the next nap.

If your child is taking two naps a day, repeat the process for nap #2.

If your child is still taking three naps, you *may* want to deviate slightly for nap #3. If the results of naps #1 and #2 are encouraging, experiment by continuing the process for the third nap. If, however, the first two naps were a bit of a slog, it's often better to have the third nap happen on the go—in a stroller, in the car, or while babywearing. It's okay in *this instance* to break the cardinal rule of consistency. Often babies still *need* a third nap but won't easily take one, so even parents of champion nappers find themselves taking Baby out for a 20-minute stroll around the block. Nevertheless, while it's fine to be a bit loose in how the third nap happens, *don't* go back to whatever it is you're trying to wean off. If you have a baby who only naps on your chest on the sofa, don't let Baby sleep on your chest for nap #3 (and in this case, babywearing would be off limits too). If you have a baby who only naps if being nursed to sleep, don't nurse to sleep for nap #3.

Some babies will get through day 1 with many tears and little to no sleep. You may both be feeling fatigued and stressed out. As a general rule, you want bedtime to happen at the same time every day, but in this case it is often wise to shift bedtime 30 to 60 minutes earlier.

For some babies, rough naps will continue. *Most* kids will start falling asleep within a few days, but *some* particularly strong-willed babies will successfully fight naps for *weeks*. I say this not to scare you but to let you know that it's possible.

Puny sleep drive + ingrained sleep habits + change = time.

Each time you give your child the opportunity to practice napping in the *new way*, you're strengthening her ability to do it the *new way* and you're weakening the propensity to do it the *old way*. Try to resist the temptation to go back to the *old way* just this once.

Step 3: Evaluate your progress.

Take detailed notes about what happened at each nap for your 5- to 7-day trial run. Here are some signs that you're on the right track:

- It takes less patting/visits/tears for your child to fall asleep than it did when you first started. We're not looking for perfection—just a trend from more to less.

- Naps are longer than when you first started. Don't compare to what they were before you started your plan—compare to day 1 of the new way of doing things.

- Your child is falling asleep independently. Depending on the starting point for your nap plan, any independent nap sleep should be viewed as a positive sign!

Don't get too freaked out about short naps right now. It's like riding a bike without training wheels: things will be a bit wobbly the first time, but they'll even out with practice. Any independent sleep is a huge accomplishment—your child did something they couldn't do before!

Here are some signs that your plan *isn't* working:

- It's been a full week of absolutely no naps.

- Your instincts tell you that the SWAP you've been working with isn't right for you and/or your child.

In an ideal world, I would provide you with a clear, user-friendly flow chart to determine the best path forward. But the reality is that naps are a challenge. If you've been diligent with the first three nap conventions, you should see some nap sleep occurring no matter which SWAP/SLIP you selected for your plan. However, it is possible that you could do things perfectly and still have a child who refuses to nap for a full 7 days.

This may be a sign that the SWAP you're using isn't the right one for your child or that you haven't given it enough time. It's time for a gut-check: What do *you* think?

If you elected to SLIP, it may be that your child needs more time. Kids can and do fight naps. You put them in a dull, safe place with as much soothing as you can, at a time when they should reasonably be ready to sleep, but the rest is up to your child. Most kids will figure things out within 7 days. Others will need longer.

Once you start down the path of SLIP, you are committed. Before you start, you and your partner need to be clear that [nursing or feeding to sleep/co-sleeping/rocking to sleep/pacifier use] is no longer on the table for naptime. Full stop. Even it if takes longer than you might hope.

Stuck with Craptastic Naps?
. . . .

What if your baby is 6 months old or more, you've nailed independent sleep, you've got a big gold star on the Nap Ninja sticker chart, and your child still can't nap longer than 35 minutes?

It may be that your child has become habituated to short naps. But habits are not forever things: you can change them. Except for the coffee habit—you're stuck with that for life.

There are two methods to break the short nap habit.

Method 1: Disrupt the sleep cycle

Nap duration is usually military-precision predictable: you know exactly when your child is going to wake up. This is helpful, because you're now going to wake them 5 to 10 minutes before they regularly wake up. Slightly jostle your child while they're still in the crib—not enough so that they're standing there waiting for you to pick them up, but enough so that you see a bit of eye fluttering. Often this will disrupt your baby's sleep/wake pattern just enough so that they fall back into deep sleep. Continue this pattern for 5 to 7 days, after which your child should have re-habituated to the new, longer nap sleep pattern and voilà! no more short naps for you.

People are resistant to this strategy because they fear that waking their child up just a little bit will result in even shorter naps. But it's often extremely effective, and, worst case, if you *do* inadvertently wake them up fully, you've only shaved a few minutes off an already short nap.

Method 2: Bore to sleep

It's not easy to fall back to sleep after a short nap—even a micronap can deflate all your accrued sleep pressure. It's even harder when the alternative is "play with Mom or Dad." You are catnip to your child. This is a good thing: it's evidence that you have a closely attuned relationship, that you are properly stimulating and responsive to your child's interests, and that you're a veritable chocolate fountain of fun. The downside, however, is that your child will happily forgo sleep to enjoy your enchanting company.

When you're initially teaching your child to nap independently, you go get them when they wake from a nap, even if it was inordinately short and was clearly *not enough sleep*. You've asked them to figure out how to nap independently, and they've done so! Celebrate the win and go on with your day.

That being said, this is one area where I am often proven wrong (this is the *one and only one instance*—on everything else I am 100% right), so you may want to experiment with giving your child a chance to fall back to sleep after a micronap (anything under 30 minutes). Leave them alone in their quiet, dark, safe sleep space, which should be inherently boring. Ideally, it's so boring they fall back to sleep.

How long you wait is up to you, but I would encourage waiting at least 15 to 30 minutes. If your child complains for 20 minutes then falls back to sleep for an additional 30, consider that a success. If your child complains for the full 30 minutes after every nap for weeks, you may graciously concede defeat.

This applies for only the first two naps of the day. The third nap (if your child is still taking one) is generally short no matter what. Get them promptly when they wake from the third nap.

Lastly, have faith: your child *will* figure out how to take longer naps eventually. Or they'll go to kindergarten. But definitely one of those things will happen, and probably both.

When Your Child Drops a Nap

After months of working on your nap ninja skills, you will have developed a certain degree of confidence in your nap ninjaness. It is precisely at this moment that your child will start fighting naps, making you feel like you need to turn in your nap ninja blackbelt because, clearly, you are a ninja fraud.

Don't do this. You have earned your ninja blackbelt and should wear it with pride! (Also, it helps hide postpartum muffin top.)

Chances are, your child is getting ready to drop a nap. Dropping a nap is rarely a binary process where one day Baby needs and will happily take a nap and the next day, not. Sometimes the transition is rocky. It's also difficult to deduce if your child is ready to drop a nap or you're simply facing one of the thousands of other niggling issues that can plague naptime (regression, illness, phase of the moon...).

Luckily, dropping naps falls roughly on a predictable(ish) schedule.

Schedule of Nap Dropping

3–6 Months

Newborn babies often take as many as six to eight naps a day, but by about 3 months of age, your baby should have settled into a three- or four-nap-a-day pattern. By 4 to 6 months, they're down to just three. Usually, this is a nontraumatic event. In fact, it's generally a happy one, as bedtime shifts earlier.

6–12 Months

Somewhere in this 6-month period, your child will drop the third nap.

If your baby is taking long, chunky naps at 6 months (an hour and a half or more each), they may be getting sufficient daytime sleep with only two naps. However, many babies take shorter naps and thus need the third nap until closer to 9 or even 12 months. Chances are that as your child gets older, that third nap will not happen in the crib but will be more of an on-the-go event: napping while being carried, in the car, in the stroller... or even a pithy 10-minute drowse while eating. Which raises the question, "Am I supposed to be driving my child around every afternoon forever?"

No. You will get a brief reprieve until they start school, at which point you'll be driving to baseball, swim lessons, dance class, etc. as a matter of course until they go to college. But I digress...

There often comes a time when Baby *needs* but won't easily *take* a third nap. You can force the issue by taking a leisurely walk in the stroller or you can choose to skip it. Feel free to skip it if nap #2 is late or is long enough that Baby can comfortably make it to bedtime. However, for some babies, skipping nap #3 leads to "awake too long" or "bedtime too early" problems, making a brisk walkabout generally the better choice.

12–18 Months

Babies drop from two naps to one somewhere between their first birthday and 18 months. Do some babies drop to one nap earlier than this? Yes, but it's rare. Don't assume your less-than-1-year-old is ready to drop to one nap just because they throw a couple of rough nap days at you.

Let's be honest here: the two-to-one nap transition is often a bit sloppy and can drag on for weeks. Many parents get stuck with a toddler who takes nap #1 from 9:00 to 10:30 but is steadfast in their refusal to take a second nap... which is challenging, as now they're awake from 10:30 in the morning till 7:30 in the evening, an eternity for a toddler. Conversely, if you try to keep them awake until it's time for their afternoon nap, they're melting down like Jell-O in the sun.

There is no sleep alchemy to navigating this transition. Mostly you just push through and have faith that on the other side is a verdant Narnia where your toddler happily subsists on only one nap.

18 Months–3 Years

Most kids are still napping on their third birthday. Sure, lots of 2-year-olds prefer not to take a nap. But if your child is under 3, it's more likely that while they may not want to nap, they still need a nap. Remember the cardinal rule of kids: you can't make them eat, sleep, or poop. But you can make them go to a dark, comfortable, safe, dull place every day at the same time. What they do in there is their business. It's your business not to confuse their desire to not nap with not needing to nap.

There is a small percentage of toddlers who are done napping as early as two. If it seems like yours might be one of them, you have my sincere condolences.

3–5 Years

Most kids stop napping entirely somewhere between the ages of 3 and 5. Some lucky parents are weaning their kids off napping just before kindergarten. But for most of us, the Age of Napping will end between 3 and 4 years. Trust me when I tell you that no matter how frustrated you may feel right now with your progress on the nap front, when naps finally do fade off into the distance, it'll be like saying goodbye to your best friend.

Here are some signs that your child may be ready to drop a nap:

- Afternoon and/or evening naps are making it hard for Baby to easily fall asleep at bedtime.

- Naptime becomes a battle.

- Long naps become short naps.

- The morning nap is fine, but Baby can't fall or stay asleep for the afternoon nap.

- The morning nap gets short or ceases to exist.

- Kiddo refuses to nap no matter what.

- Bedtime is becoming a battle.

- Your child is falling asleep fine but waking up and staying awake for a long window during the night.

- Morning wakeup time is creeping up on you (6:30 a.m. becomes 6:00 a.m., then 5:30 a.m., then 5:00 a.m.).

Surviving the Transition Phase

There may be a few weeks or even a month when your child needs a nap but adamantly refuses to take one, or when a previously long nap is resolutely stuck at 20 minutes. During this phase it's a tossup as to who will feel more cantankerous about the nap situation: Baby or you.

There is no magic elixir to make the nap-dropping phase go more smoothly (if there were, I would sell it and be rich as Croesus), but here are some things that may help:

- Sometimes even a catnap is enough to take the edge off and make evening and bedtime more pleasant for all involved.

- Sometimes, however, catnaps complicate matters, and even a short car nap will throw off the rest of the day. (Confusing, I know!)

- When Baby drops a nap, the whole sleep schedule (naps + bedtime) might need to be temporarily shifted earlier.

- Temporarily shortening the nap that is on the way out can mean that your child still gets some sleep at that time but not so much as to prevent later naps from happening easily or on schedule.

- Try heading outside at the time when your child was previously napping. This will distract your fussy toddler, and exposure to bright light will help produce "it's awake time" hormones in their body.

- Some older kids transition best going from napping every day to napping every other day.

- Kids who are moving out of the nap phase altogether may need to have a slightly earlier bedtime.

When your child is fully done napping, consider a transition to "quiet time." Quiet time is essentially naptime with a tiny bit more light and a few board books. Your child is still alone in a dull, dim place. They can have a few safe toys to play with, but nothing that makes noise or lights up. Quiet time is generally 1 hour. It's often helpful to provide your preschooler with a tangible cue (like a kitchen timer or an old radio alarm clock) so they know when quiet time is over (and when it's not).

Bad Nap Days
. . . .

Bad nap days are like bad hair days: they always happen when you run into an ex at the mall. (Wait, what?) Some days, for reasons entirely beyond your control, naps will become an unmitigated mess. If you're diligent about the Four Conventions of Nap Nirvana, your bad nap days will be infrequent. But even strict adherence to the Conventions doesn't fully inoculate you from the occasional bad nap day.

Bad naps have a lot of possible causes:

- Not following the conventions. The most common root cause is Convention #4: older babies and toddlers aren't falling asleep independently.

- Inconsistency. You get a few months where your baby can sleep wherever and however. After this grace period, however, you need to embrace your inner nap police. Yes, it can be isolating to miss out on

Bad Nap Days

fun stuff because your precious tulip can sleep only in her bedroom. And no, it's not fun to leave the nice park and all the cool moms who hang there because it's naptime. But naps are like Crock-Pots: you only get out what you put in.

• Teething. There is a substantial body of research that proves that teething doesn't impact sleep. Millions of parents ardently disagree.

• Separation anxiety. This is when your 8-month-old wants to be with you constantly. And truthfully, there isn't much you can do about it. Day drinking will get you shunned by other parents, plus you can't put your kiddo down long enough to mix a good cocktail.

• Sleep deprivation. Anything that substantially reduces the amount of sleep your child gets (illness, travel, etc.) can result in a sleep debt, which leads to a vicious cycle where they're tired but can't fall asleep.

• Catnaps. This morning when your child fell asleep for 3 minutes on the way home? Yep, that did it.

• Hunger. This is rarely an issue, but sometimes babies are eating on a schedule (such as E.A.S.Y.)[6] on which their last feeding is quite a bit before naptime. If you have a large gap between the last meal and nap or if your child wakes up from naps ravenous, hunger may be the root cause of short naps.

• Environmental issues. This is rare, because most parents are almost obsessively compulsive about making sure their child's sleep environment is more luxurious than a Turkish spa, but anything that makes your child uncomfortable—itchy jammies, too cold or hot, ambient light, household noise—could hinder naps.

• No pre-nap routine. Newborns don't need help to transition from play to sleep time; older babies do.

• Shiftless Sleep Fairies. Seriously, fairies—why can't you take a page from the shoemaker's elves?

So there are lots of reasons bad naps can happen. But the truth is that if you can embrace the nap conventions, you've really done all you can do.

11

Why, When, and How to Wean Off Your Sleep Power Tools

PERMS WERE A big thing when I was in high school (yes, I'm that old). You had to keep your hair fully permed at all times to maintain maximum bang height (stop judging me). Perms were expensive and stinky and they damaged your hair, but you got them every 3 months regardless. I maintained my perm all the way through my sophomore year of college, when abject poverty forced me to stop. As modern parents, you probably can't imagine this, but it was cool at the time, and then it wasn't, and now I'm done with perms for good.

The Sleep Power Tools are a lot like perms is what I'm saying—cool until they aren't, and eventually you'll be done with them for good.

The Sleep Power Tools have hopefully stood you in good stead, lo these many months. But eventually you're going to stop using them, because eventually your child will outgrow their *need* for them.

Fears of getting "stuck" with pacifiers, swaddles, etc. have led people to aggressively try to wean off these powerful soothing tools sooner than they should. Which is understandable. When you see

Weaning Off the Power Tools

other parents decrying the fact that their 5-year-old is heading off to kindergarten with a travel bag of pacis, it's easy to think, "Best to get rid of these things now!"

And eventually you *do* need to gently wean off your use of soothing sleep tools. Continued swaddling will make it challenging for your 8-year-old to have sleepovers, and ongoing pacifier use will hinder your 16-year-old's ability to get a date. So let's talk about when, why, and how to gently wean off your Sleep Power Tools.

Weaning Off the Pacifier

Why

Many babies can happily use a pacifier for months or even years. Some babies use it just to fall asleep and don't need it reinserted later. Others become proficient at reinserting their own pacifier (or switching to sucking on their own appendages) at an early age.

Other babies, however, will require a pacifier to fall asleep and *then* will require your pacifier reinsertion services hourly throughout the night (typically, this becomes an issue between 4 and 8 months). Which means their parents will need to get up 4,380 times to reinsert the paci before their child figures out how to do it themselves. If your life has devolved into nightly paci-fueled pandemonium, it's time for that thing to go.

Pacifier use has also been linked to chronic ear infections.[1] If your child is a die-hard pacifier kid and suffers from *chronic* ear infections, it's time for the paci to go.

Even if your child is sleeping well with a pacifier, consider getting rid of it before your child's second birthday. Recommendations about dental care and pacifier use vary, but there is some evidence that consistent pacifier use past 2 years can lead to tooth misalignment and palate malformation.[2] Pacis have also been linked to tooth decay.[3]

When

The easiest time to stop using the pacifier is just before 4 or 5 months. Babies (mostly) don't remember things exist at this point, so the beloved paci is quickly forgotten. If you've been giving your baby lots of soothing sleep cues (swaddle, white noise, sleep routine), the loss of pacifier at 4 months may go virtually unnoticed.

However, if you stop using the pacifier *before* 4 months, you:

- miss out on the potential SIDS protection provided by pacifier use at the time when the risk of SIDS peaks (the risk significantly decreases after 6 months)[4];

- remove a powerful tool from your arsenal for successfully navigating the dreaded 4-month sleep regression; and

- may see more night waking and shorter naps.

Still, for most babies, gradually weaning off the pacifier before 5 to 6 months is probably the easiest and least error-prone option. I would encourage you to weigh the potential advantages and disadvantages with your pediatrician. Babies at greater risk of SIDS (preemies, babies exposed to smoking, etc.) might be encouraged to continue to use the pacifier past this point.

Alternatively, you could wait until the pacifier causes significant sleep disruptions. This often begins at about 6 to 8 months, but it may not happen at all. Or you could wait till Baby turns 2 and your dentist starts giving you the stink-eye.

How

There are two basic strategies to wean a baby or younger toddler off the pacifier (I've included a third strategy for older kids as well). But before you actually wean off the pacifier, it's helpful to lay some groundwork:

1. Give your baby many sleep associations. If you've been popping in a paci then plunking baby in bed, you've been teaching your baby that pacifier = sleep. When you then remove the paci, you've left . . . nothing! So before you wean off the paci, make sure you're using as many age-appropriate alternate sleep cues (routine, white noise, etc.) as possible.

2. Cut back on paci use during the day. For many babies, the pacifier is like a mustache: if it's missing, you almost don't recognize them. But if you're ready to drop the pacifier for sleep, it'll go easier if you start using it less during the day. Begin with small windows of time and use lots of distraction (songs, play, going outside) to distract Baby from the loss of the beloved pacifier. Gradually increase those windows until there is minimal paci use during the day. (It's okay to keep using the paci for particularly rough spots if you need to.)

Once you've established a strong foundation, it's time to politely show the pacifier the door.

Option 1: Cold turkey

As anybody who has ever jumped into a cold lake can attest, sometimes it's far better just to take the plunge—tuck up into a cannonball and leap in. The baby equivalent is this: no pacifiers at bedtime, no pacifiers in the crib, no pacifiers at night. Yes, there will be some tears, but if you've embraced all the sleep fundamentals discussed in this book, the process will be generally less dramatic than you expect. Often, falling asleep without the pacifier for just a day or two is enough to get your child used to sleeping without it. Sometimes temporarily pushing bedtime later (15 to 20 minutes) helps so that Baby is extra sleepy (but not an overtired mess) at bedtime.

Depending on your baby's age and temperament, and on just how exhausted everybody is, this is definitely an option to consider. But first you might want to have a go with . . .

Option 2: The pull-out method

Of course, if you were successful with this strategy, you wouldn't have a baby to begin with *badum-CHING!* You'll find this method fully detailed in Chapter 6, Teaching Baby to Sleep, Part 1: SWAP.

If you feel the method is not getting you anywhere or your baby is just getting frustrated or angry with you and you're ready to give up and just pop the pacifier back in, don't feel bad. You aren't the first parent who couldn't make the pull-out work. Many factors feed into your ability to make this method successful, and most of them (temperament, level of attachment to the pacifier, sleep deprivation) are beyond your control. If you're hitting the wall of your commitment and patience, that's okay. Your fallback plan is Cold Turkey.

Option 3: Pacifier weaning for older kids

If your child is 18 months or older, you have some fun options to wean off the paci. Admittedly, I'm using the term *fun* in a very general sense: it isn't mojitos-with-John-Oliver fun, but it's more fun than diaper rash.

Begin by talking to your child about *why* we're going to stop using the pacifier *before you actually stop using it*. There are good surprises and bad surprises. Coming home from work to find your partner has picked up takeout from your favorite Indian restaurant = good surprise. Startling your toddler with the announcement that the pacifier is going bye-bye at bedtime = bad surprise. So set a deadline, perhaps 5 days hence, and start casually discussing the pending transition to paci-free sleep. Don't make a big production about it—just drop it into conversation over lunch.

It's okay if she disagrees with your sentiments. You can be empathetic. "I know, I love ba-ba too. But it's important that your teeth grow in healthy and strong! You need strong teeth to eat all the foods you like."*

---

*Obviously this is a joke. I know your toddler subsists on Goldfish crackers and positive thinking.

Then, depending on the age and personality of your child, you can add in a little theater. Some ideas to consider:

· Mail the pacifiers to Santa so he can give them to the new babies. Wrap the pacis up in paper, put them in a box, and take them to the post office (most post office staff will happily play along with you). Celebrate your outing with some ice cream! (Pro tip: Never pass on an excuse to enjoy a nice frozen treat.)

· Trade the pacifiers for something awesome—a toy your child is enthralled by, a trip to the petting zoo... It's helpful if your child can see the pacifiers leaving the house, so you may want to enlist the help of a friend to bring the special toy over and take the pacifiers in exchange.

· Put the pacifiers in a basket out on the front step for the Paci Fairy, who comes when you're asleep and leaves behind something awesome.

Feel free to get creative. I would caution you, though, against using the "you're a big girl [or boy] now" argument to support your cause. Kids often have ambivalent or even negative feelings about being a big girl or boy. What are the advantages? When you're a little kid, everybody thinks you're adorable, food-tossing is an acceptable thing, and pants are optional. Who wants to give that up?

When you get rid of the pacifier, make sure you don't have any pacis hiding behind the couch cushions: if your child finds one later, it'll undermine the special "bon voyage" ceremony you so meticulously crafted.

Weaning Off the Swaddle
. . . .

Swaddling is wonderful, and if your baby responds to swaddling, I encourage you to embrace it. But eventually, it will need to go.

Why

There are three essential reasons to wean off the swaddle:

1. You don't believe Baby needs it anymore. Ideally, you would test this theory out to confirm if it holds up. But yes, eventually all babies outgrow the need to be swaddled!

2. Despite your Herculean efforts, you are unable to keep Baby from popping out. Generally, a better solution is to change your swaddling technique or try a different swaddling blanket. But if you've exhausted every possible strategy and your future power-lifter baby is busting out, you may be done.

3. Your baby is flipping from back to front while swaddled. Sleeping facedown while swaddled is unsafe and has been linked with a dramatically higher incidence of SIDS. If your baby has figured out how to flip onto their stomach while swaddled or is showing signs that they're close (such as getting up on their side, which is a precarious position) you should:

- Stop swaddling immediately. You never want a swaddled baby sleeping facedown. Not even if you are watching. Not ever. Or...

- Consider moving baby to a sleep space where they can be strapped on their backs and thus are incapable of flipping. If the swaddle is a critical component of your child's sleep and weaning results in a miserable mess for all involved, you can continue to swaddle only if you have a safe place for baby to sleep where flipping over is impossible.

For most families, Baby flipping from back to front or flipping onto their side means the immediate and permanent end of swaddling.

When

The answer to "when" comes down to this: whenever you think they're ready or they start flipping over. If you have the option, consider maintaining the swaddle until after independent sleep is established.

How

Option 1: Swaddle with one arm out at bedtime.

It's okay if there are a few grumbles as Baby sorts out this new situation. But you're looking to see whether they can successfully fall asleep and stay asleep with roughly the same success as when fully swaddled. If it normally takes 10 minutes to fall asleep and it now takes 20, fabulous! They're just figuring out how to fall asleep with this arm thingy flapping about. If, however, it's an arduous process or they wake excessively, they may not be ready. Go back to your normal swaddle routine. Try again next week.

Option 2: Use a transition swaddle.

In recent years, a new category of "swaddle transition" alternatives have come to market, and based on feedback from parents, they're extremely helpful. Essentially, these allow a baby's arm to move but restrict movement just enough to keep those pesky arms from batting Baby in the face and waking her up. These are, however, yet another baby item that is useful for only a very short time, so you may choose to skip buying one.

Option 3: Just stop swaddling.

If your baby has a great consistent bedtime routine and is falling asleep independently, simply removing the swaddle may be the easiest and most direct route. *Boom*, done.

Swaddling and SWAP/SLIP

Often, people have the mistaken impression that swaddling and SWAP/SLIP cannot coexist. But as long as your child isn't flipping over, swaddling can be an enormously helpful tool while fostering independent sleep. You want to give your child as much soothing as possible as they navigate the unfamiliar waters of learning to sleep without you.

Safety Note. Swaddling is often an effective tool to lessen the amount of crying involved with SLIP. However, angry babies can kick and inadvertently flip themselves from back to stomach, which is an enormously risky position from a SIDS perspective. Swaddling during SLIP is *only* for babies who are still sleeping in a place where they can be safely strapped in or for parents who have a working night-vision monitor to ensure Baby is safely on her back.

Weaning Off White Noise

Most babies benefit from the use of white noise until their first birthday. There is no compelling reason to stop using white noise after Baby turns 1, either, although you're welcome to do so. Simply gradually turn down the volume of your white noise over a few days until it's off. This is quick and painless, and kids adapt well to the normal ambient noise in the house. If the occasional unusual noise (garbage trucks, barking dogs, etc.) starts to cause sleep disruptions for your toddler, go back to using white noise.

Weaning Off Managing the Schedule

"We can never get out of the house because we *are captive to this child's sleep schedule!*"

Ayup.

When

In a word, never.

Truthfully, as your child nears adolescence, your ability to maintain a consistent and age-appropriate bedtime will fade away as bedtime will be determined by extracurricular activities, homework load, etc. At this point, you won't wean off managing the schedule—it'll simply be wrested away from you.

The good news is that as kids get older, they can tolerate the occasional missed nap or delayed bedtime. So while your 6-month-old is a puddle of misery if you blow bedtime by an hour, your 4-year-old will barely blink about the periodic late bedtime.

However, don't let this fact leave the impression that these events are no big deal. Some kids are amazingly adept at navigating a blown nap or bedtime without any subsequent degradation in behavior, creating the perception that you no longer need to be as strict about the sleep schedule. This can lead to late bedtimes becoming a semi-regular phenomenon or a common "as long as it's not a school night" thing.

Which is a problem, because inconsistent bedtimes with older kids have been linked with:

- behavioral problems,[5]
- poor academic performance, and[6]
- ADHD.[7]

So you'll want to establish and maintain an early and consistent bedtime[8] for your child as long as you feasibly can. Even when it's unpleasant. Even when your friends don't understand why you're being such a stickler about things.

Not everybody understands that this is really important. But that's okay—you and I do. And that's what matters.

12

(Un)Common
Sleep Setbacks

~~~~~~~~~~~~~~~~~~~~

FOR MOST THINGS in life, you set a goal (finish college, learn to knit, climb Kilimanjaro...), work diligently toward that goal, and, if you're lucky and determined, you'll achieve it.

Baby sleep does not work like this. You can do all the "right" things, starting from the second you give birth, and *still* have everything go terribly wrong. You can have a 3-week-old who sleeps 10 hours a night turn into a 4 ½-month-old who wakes up so often it's like they're giving free ponies to the kid who wakes up the most, and she's determined to win.

I don't say this to push you into a pit of depression. I say this because bad sleep is sometimes unavoidable. And also, hopefully, to give you some tools to navigate setbacks that might arise.

Note: Most of the things in this chapter assume your child is already falling asleep independently. If your child is struggling with sleep and has not begun to fall asleep independently, go back to Chapters 6 and 7, Teaching Baby to Sleep, Parts 1 and 2.

The Dreaded Sleep Regression

Every once in a while your baby's sleep will mysteriously become a disastrous mess. At the same time, your baby will become really fussy, which is either the cause or a result of the sleep deprivation. The slender thread of normalcy you've been clinging to will disappear and you will stumble into the void of parenting despair, wondering, "Why did we think this baby thing was such a great idea anyway?!"

If you've ruled out all the obvious causes of sleep stoppage, then what is probably going on is a *sleep regression*.[1]

Sleep regressions are also known as *growth spurts, developmental bursts,* or *wonder weeks*.[2] I'm not a fan of the term *regression* because (a) it sounds pretty negative and (b) it doesn't really describe what is going on. "Needy volcano" would probably be a better term.

Regression is actually the opposite of what is happening. While your child's behavior might "regress," your child is actually *expanding* their skills and understanding, even if that expansion is internal and thus not immediately observable.

There is some consensus that regressions occur in a roughly predictable pattern across the first 20 months of life, with at least half of all babies studied showing indications such as fussiness, decreased sleep, increased awakenings, wants to nurse/eat constantly, cannot be put down, etc. However, there is no firm consensus on *how many* regression periods there are or *when* they occur. Various studies have come up with as many as ten or as few as three to five.[3] During these periods, 40% to 60% of babies were considered to be having a regression (meaning that 40% to 60% *weren't*).

The bottom line is that your child will likely have a handful of regression periods. While we don't have strong evidence for exactly when they'll occur, the most common regressions seem to come around 4 months, 6 months, and 8 to 10 months. Sometimes you'll get dustups at 1 year, 18 months, and 2 years.

This seems like a lot, and the idea of weathering a string of sleep regressions is probably giving you the vapors. But before you faint like a delicate petunia, let me assure you: it's likely not nearly as bad as you imagine. Remember that "common" means that roughly half of babies will have a regression period at any one of these times ... this also means half *won't*.

So while it's easy to see every rough week as a regression, most of us will experience only a few *true* regressions. Typically, you'll know you're in the midst of one when you see a consistent pattern like this:

1. Sleep stops. Naps get short, helping Baby fall asleep takes forever, Baby wakes up constantly, Baby wakes up miserable, Baby simply won't sleep, etc.

2. Fussiness starts. Perhaps it's due to sleep deprivation or maybe it's the massive jumps their brain is making, but your sweet, happy baby will morph into a cranky, clinging starfish.

3. Nursing or feeding is endless. Sometimes regressions are called "growth spurts"; the idea (especially for nursing moms) is that your baby is demanding more from you to amp up your supply because they're getting bigger and need more food. If you're nursing, you may find that your baby is glued to your boobs endlessly. At least it feels endless because even a few days with a baby attached to your boob seems like an eternity. Bottle-fed babies also demand to eat more. And while this process can leave you feeling like the saddest mommy cow in the barnyard, the solution is to let them have at it.

4. Must. Be. Held. Babies often become clingy during regressions. No longer content with some playtime on a mat or in the bouncy seat, your baby only wants to be held.

On average, regressions last 1 or 2 weeks. I won't lie to you—sometimes they can be really rough. Especially if things were feeling a bit shaky to begin with. But ...

1. Don't panic! This is temporary. It's a bad week or two. It's shorter than having the flu, right? You can do this!

2. Do what works (for now). It's OK to use a stroller nap to smooth out a rocky day. If a night feeding sneaks back in on you, you have the knowledge to gradually wean off it later.

3. Get back on the sleep path. Sleep regressions are temporary... unless you let them derail you permanently. Some regressions are fairly mild and manageable, while others are a tsunami of fussy sleeplessness. However, you don't want to relinquish independent sleep if at all possible. If you do go back to "the old way," pivot back to independent sleep as soon as you reasonably can. If a month has gone by and you're still rocking/cuddling/feeding to sleep, then you've fallen into the classic sleep regression trap: you let a temporary survival tactic become the new norm.

Sadly, babies do not come with alarms that signal the end of a sleep regression. Sometimes you'll know it's over because miraculously your baby will sleep a ton (for a day or two) and everybody will breathe a heady sigh of relief. Sometimes things will just gradually (and thus more subtly) improve. Be mindful about getting the sleep bus back on course.

Baby Learns Cool New Stuff
. . . .

Your cool little dude is learning amazing new skills all the time. Huzzah! Except those new skills often need practice. And what better time to practice than naptime and bedtime?

You think you've successfully figured out this sleep stuff and then, mysteriously, your perfectly healthy baby will start fighting bedtime, waking up frequently at night, or resolutely staying awake for hours at a time in the middle of the night.[4] Often this will continue for a few days until, as if by magic, your child will delightedly show off their new skill (standing up, flipping over, crawling, walking) and will (thankfully) go back to sleeping through the night.

Separation Anxiety
. . . .

The term *separation anxiety* comes from a large body of research starting in the 1960s[5] that observed that babies cry or cling when parents start to leave the room. You'll know your child has separation anxiety when you find yourself pooping with an 8-month-old on your lap.

Baby Acquires New Skills!

Your once social baby now is happy only when they're *with you*. While it's an enormous compliment to be so adored by a beloved child, it frequently means that you can't put them down or leave them alone (in a safe space or with other familiar caregivers) without major upset.

There is no concrete evidence of when separation anxiety develops, but anecdotally, parents report it beginning around 6 months and peaking around 8 to 9 months. This makes sense, as separation anxiety would naturally develop along with your baby's emerging skills with object permanence.

Many parents report that the emergence of separation anxiety leads to a bump in sleep disturbances. But does it? There has been insufficient research on sleep and separation anxiety,[6] and most of it has focused on older children with anxiety disorders[7] rather than on garden-variety infant separation anxiety.

Further complicating matters, separation anxiety develops or peaks during the same timeframe as object permanence and sleep onset association issues. So a child who hasn't mastered independent sleep will scream bloody murder when their parents try to put them down awake. "Oh no, our peanut has serious separation anxiety!" the parents might say. Well, possibly. But your peanut *definitely* doesn't know how to fall asleep. And "I'm pissed at you and don't know how to do this sleep thing" is almost identical to "I have separation anxiety." For many families, the bedtime behavior that was previously attributed to separation anxiety evaporates like the fog at dawn once their child has learned how to fall asleep independently.

If your child is a Master of Independent Sleep and is struggling to separate from you at bedtime, take it as the compliment that it is: you are *extraordinary*, and your child wants to be with you! But here are some things you can do to help minimize separation anxiety:

- Ensure that your pre-nap or bedtime routine is long enough to help your child transition from play to sleep. Use your words to reinforce the idea that you're nearby even when they can't see you, and to reassure them that you'll be there with big hugs and kisses in the morning.

- Hold or wear Baby as much as possible during non-sleep hours. Fill your child's bucket of "you time" as much as you can.

- Practice separating for brief periods (2 or 3 minutes) throughout the day, to help your child become accustomed to the idea that she's okay when you're not directly nearby and that when you say you will be back, you will. Leave your child alone in a safe space, and use your words to make it clear that you're leaving and will be back shortly: "Sweetie, I need to put the laundry in the dryer, I'll be back in 2 minutes." Sometimes it's helpful to sing while you're out of sight so that your child can hear that you're nearby.

- Don't feed the anxiety. Remain loving but consistent about separating at naptimes and bedtime. Your child is picking up cues from you, so you want to respond to their feelings of anxiety with loving confidence: "I love you, bubs, and I'm always nearby. Now it's time to sleep." Often separation anxiety behaviors (clinging, whining, crying) tweaks our own emotional baggage,* and if we're feeling nervous about things, so will they.

- Try not to let your response to separation anxiety draw you into bedtime battles. Your child doesn't want you to go, so you're going to see an increase in protests at bedtime. But deviating from your rock-solid bedtime routine is a slippery slope. One more cuddle quickly becomes five more cuddles.

- Read to them about separation. For toddlers and preschool-aged children, consider adding books that feature themes of separation into your sleep routine. *Llama Llama Red Pajama*, *Goodnight Moon*, and *The Kissing Hand* are all good options.

Travel
. . . .

Here's a pro tip for travel with babies:
    Never travel with babies.

Most babies don't sleep well in an unfamiliar environment. I don't care how much gear you schlep from home, most babies are going to sleep poorly in a new place. Further, travel almost always disrupts their sleep schedule. This is exacerbated if you cross time zones. Thus travel is the perfect storm for interrupted sleep.

And a sleepless vacation leads to PTSD: Post-Travel Sleep Disruption. Even a moderate reduction in daily sleep can, over the duration of a holiday, accumulate into a significant sleep debt. This accrued sleep debt becomes the unwanted souvenir you bring home with you, resulting in crap sleep even after the trip is over.

Worse, when babies sleep poorly, parents are often forced to go to great lengths to keep the peace: reintroducing night feeds, soothing

---

*I don't mean to suggest that *you* have emotional baggage. I'm saying we *all* have emotional baggage. Separating isn't hard just for our kids—it's often hard for *us* too.

previously independent sleepers fully to sleep at bedtime, co-sleeping, etc. This can lead to the frustrating realization that it takes only a single trip to undo all the hard work you've invested in fostering healthy sleep associations. Yes, this is entirely unfair. Here—let us be jointly indignant about it for a moment. It doesn't change anything, but sometimes having a buddy who shares your frustration helps.

Is the solution to never leave the house? No. Travel is a great way to recharge *your* batteries, and nobody's batteries need to be recharged more than parents of babies.

However, I would be cautious about travel that isn't restorative for *you*. When evaluating an opportunity, consider if you will have enough fun to outweigh the (potential) sleep deprivation. Put off any trips that aren't going to fill you with delight.

Avoiding Post-Travel Sleep Disorder

While there is nothing to guarantee you perfect sleep while you travel, these strategies will substantially increase the odds of things going well:

Stick to your normal sleep schedule.
Do so as militantly as possible.

Adjust your schedule to account for time zones.
Travel to different time zones messes up your circadian rhythm. It typically takes 1 day for your body to adjust 1 hour, so if you travel across five time zones, it'll take 5 days to fully adjust to the new local time.[8] Luckily, our bodies respond dramatically to light exposure therapy,[9] which is a fancy way of saying "go play outside at the right time." Bright outdoor light can help your child's body adjust even more quickly if you time it appropriately. That, however, is trickier to figure out than you might think, as there are specific times during the day and night when our bodies are most responsive to light.[10] Here are some tips:

- If you are crossing only one time zone (a 1-hour time difference) for a brief time (less than a week), consider keeping Baby on your home time zone. This also helps you avoid having to readjust when you return home.

- If you are traveling two or more time zones west (bedtime needs to shift later), try to expose Baby to bright outside light during your home time zone's late afternoon or early evening. For example, if you fly from New York to San Francisco, try to play outside in a park at 6 p.m. EST (New York time), which is 3 p.m. PST (San Francisco time).[11]

- If you are traveling two or more time zones to the east (bedtime shifts earlier), try to expose Baby to bright light during your home time zone's early morning. So, flying from New York to London, you would strive to play outside at 6 a.m. EST (New York time), which is 11 a.m. BST (London time).

- Employ the same technique in the opposite direction when you return home.

- Get outside at the right times on a sunny day for the most help. If that's impossible, bright indoor light will work,[12] although SAD (seasonal affective disorder) lamps are better.[13]

Don't let Baby sleep overly long during the day.

Keep day sleep normal(ish) so that excess napping doesn't stick you in the "up all night" penalty box.

Bring as many familiar items as is feasible.
It's worth the extra checked-bag fee to have them with you, if you can swing it.

If your child falls asleep independently, try to ensure that they keep doing so.
This is the #1 thing that trips up traveling parents. It's harder for children to fall asleep in unfamiliar environments, so they may struggle a bit at bedtime. You can be more generous or more involved as your child falls asleep than you are at home. However, don't get *overly* involved. Many a well-meaning parent has turned their independent sleeper into a dependent sleeper because travel threw them off their game.

Practice first.

If you'll be bringing a travel bed (Pack 'n Play, etc.) with you, experiment with having your child nap in it a few times at home so it's familiar.

Avoid skipping naps.

If naps aren't going well, consider making them happen in the car or stroller or via babywearing. A solid stroller nap is preferable to a skipped nap.

Expect to have a few setbacks. Even if you do all the right things, your child likely won't sleep as well as they do at home. Naps will be shorter. Morning will start earlier. Developing a bit of a sleep debt is common. This will carry over into sleep at home, so things may be a bit off for a few days or weeks after your return. Stay focused on your core sleep goals (soothing, consistency, independent sleep)—you'll get things sorted out.

Daylight Saving Time
. . . .

"Daylight Saving Time is something I thoroughly look forward to," said no parent ever.

Daylight Saving Time (DST) brings the sleep disruption of jet lag without the perk of travel. *Any* change in clock time results in sleep problems because the clock time is no longer aligned with our circadian rhythm. And it makes you feel like a boob when you can't figure out how to change the dashboard clock in the car. Or maybe that's just me. Anyhoo...

Spring Forward

In spring, we (except those fortunate enough to live where DST isn't a thing) set the clocks later by 1 hour, which means asking your child to go to sleep 1 hour earlier than they are used to.

Falling asleep 1 hour early is hugely challenging because our bodies are wired for wakefulness during the time leading up to sleep (this is referred to as the *forbidden zone for sleep*).[14] Asking your child to fall asleep during this time is like asking them to cut your hair: it's guaranteed to end badly.

To avoid this problem:

- Spread the time change across 4 days, shifting your child's sleep earlier by 15 minutes a day. If your current schedule is to sleep from 7 p.m. to 6 a.m., shift the first day to 6:45 p.m. and 5:45 a.m. This may mean waking your child up in the morning (I know!), as you need them waking up at the new target time, not their old normal time. Continue shifting all sleep—naps and bedtime—15 minutes a day for another 3 days, at which point your child's post-time-change sleep schedule should be the same as their pre-time-change sleep schedule (in the earlier example, 7 p.m. to 6 a.m. clock time).

- Keep the lights dim in the hour before bedtime. This means no outside playtime, exposure to bright screens (TVs, iPads, etc.), or bright indoor light. Dim lights will help your child's hormonal regulatory system adjust to a sleepier state.

- Try to get bright outside light exposure early in the morning. This can help shift your child's clock up, so they're readily able to fall asleep as you increasingly shift bedtime earlier.

If your baby is routinely waking at an uncivilized hour—say, 4 or 5 in the morning—you may want to use the spring time change to shift their sleep to a slightly less horrible time of 5 or 5:30 a.m. To do this, change the clocks forward but keep your child's sleep schedule where it was.

The same thing can help for babies who go to bed quite early—say, 6 p.m.—preventing working parents from spending time with them in the evening. Keeping Baby on their current schedule while changing the clocks (bedtime moves from 6 p.m. pre-time-change to 7 p.m. post-time-change) can carve out an additional hour of baby time at night.

Fall Back

In the fall, clocks go earlier 1 hour. Somewhat confusingly, this results in keeping your child awake 1 hour longer than they're used to at bedtime while hoping that a combination of happy thoughts and pixie dust will result in them sleeping in an additional hour in the morning so that their night sleep lines up with the new clock time.

In some ways, the fall time change is the good one: it's easier to stay awake an hour longer than it is to fall asleep an hour earlier. The kicker is that it almost always leads to earlier wakeup times because *most* kids will wake up at their "normal" time, which, due to the clock change, is now even earlier than when they woke previously.

To help your child adjust to the new clock time, you might reasonably consider ignoring them until your target wakeup time, an hour later. But ignoring them is unlikely to do anything beyond making you all feel sad and grumpy. Starting the day early also results in all naps shifting up an hour, leading to a very long stretch of wake time between last nap and bedtime, so your child continues to be an overtired blob at bedtime and the cycle continues. While most kids will stretch their night sleep out eventually, it can take weeks, leaving everybody a bit crusty in the interim. This happens because your child's circadian rhythm is entrenched in their pre-time-change wakeup time. Breaking out of this requires that you retrain your child's circadian rhythm so that their wakeup time lines up with the new clock time.

To do this, expose your child to bright light for about an hour in the evening. Ideally, play outside in the sun, but for those of us in northern climates, this may be impossible, and bright indoor lights or an SAD lamp is a reasonable fallback plan. Continue to do this until your child is comfortably sleeping until your target wakeup time.

Concurrently, in the morning, keep the lights dark and activity low, and hold off feeding your child until after your target wakeup time. For example, if your child is waking at 5:00 a.m. and you are trying to shift her wakeup time to 6:00, avoid screens and bright lights, and don't offer food until *after* 6:00.

Typically, the fall time change doesn't help *anybody*—no parents are excited to wake up earlier than they already do. However, in some (relatively rare) cases, babies have a *very late* bedtime, and parents use the fall time change to shift it earlier. You simply keep your child's bedtime the same while moving the clocks, so that a 9 p.m. bedtime now falls at 8 p.m. clock time.

Navigating DST and Naps

If your child is still napping based on wake time, continue as such. Your child's wake time will move based on the time change, and naps will organically shift forward or back.

If your child is napping by the clock and you've elected to go the 15-minute-a-day route for bedtime and wakeup time changes, you would apply the same 15-minute shift to your child's nap schedule. If instead you've chosen to just move the clock ahead or back an hour all at once, you may need to be a bit more flexible with your nap schedule—shifting temporarily to combination of By the Clock and Wake Time approaches—to avoid too long or too short periods of wakefulness during the day.

And lastly, petition your elected officials to get rid of Daylight Saving Time. DST is like bustle skirts: it seemed like a good idea at the time, but now we know better.

Chronic Sleep Deprivation
. . . .

No matter how diligent a parent you are, at some point your child is going to become sleep deprived. Illness, travel, teething, regressions, skipping naps at daycare... Life will conspire to plague your house with chronic sleep deprivation.

The cycle begins when something (say, travel or a tummy bug) throws off Baby's sleep. She has a few rough days that leave her sleep deprived. The loss of sleep leads to increased levels of cortisol,[15] a naturally occurring stimulant[16] that, paradoxically, makes it harder for babies to sleep well. So now she's struggling with naps and is waking up more frequently during the night. This exacerbates the sleep debt she accrued during the tummy bug, and you're all stranded in the Land of Not Sleeping.

The key to breaking out of that place is to make sleep happen *by any means necessary*. Ish. I meant "by any-*ish* means necessary."

You need to help your child get more sleep, both during the day and at night. Ideally, you'll help your child catch up on sleep using longer naps in a way that doesn't retrain Baby to sleep only on or with you. Often, holding or nursing a baby throughout naptime ensures a longer nap, but it also ensures that your baby will insist upon your continued naptime presence even after you've broken out of the cycle of sleep deprivation—solving the current problem creates new, longer-term issues.

A better way to encourage longer naps would be to take advantage of babywearing or stroller rides. Most babies will take a long, hearty nap if pushed in a stroller the entire time. Stroller naps are often effective and won't necessarily affect your child's ability to fall asleep in the crib once you've caught up on sleep.

Generally speaking, once your baby has settled into a consistent bedtime, that time is sacrosanct . . . except in the case of accrued sleep debt. Very overtired babies may need an early bedtime for a few days to a week while they catch up on lost sleep. While you can't always force longer naps, you *can* generally get your child to sleep slightly earlier than normal. Experiment with a bedtime that's 30 minutes earlier for a few days. With luck, you'll get your baby back to normal within a few days.

Your Child Doesn't Nap

Baby Edition: The 20-Minute Rule

If your baby is struggling with naps in general, see Chapter 10, Becoming the Zen Nap Ninja Master. If, however, you have received your Zen Nap Ninja certificate in the mail, but now your normally great-napping baby mysteriously won't (or can't) fall asleep at naptime, give that nap a solid 20-minute effort and then let it go. Similarly, if your baby wakes up after a scant 15 minutes and can't fall back to sleep even though you can tell they're still tired, let them try to fall back to sleep for 20 minutes and then let it go.

Let's call this the 20-Minute Rule. On rough days, give it 20 minutes on the front or back end. If things still aren't going your way, throw in the towel. Yes, you now have a tired, fussy baby on your hands. Some days are like that. The good news is that in a couple of hours, you'll have a chance to try again.

Try not to obsess about the occasional crap nap—you'll only make yourself and your child miserable. Occasional crap naps are The Way of Baby.

Toddler Edition: The 1-Hour Rule

Almost all children under 3 need to take a nap. Whether they want it or not, this is something their little body needs. Two-year-olds are challenging boundaries all day long, naps included. Don't confuse this with a signal that they no longer need a nap.

Toddlers often start fighting naps around their second birthday. They're *going* to fight you on it, because that's what toddlers do. They will also fight you about shoes, diaper changes, and international monetary policy. The key is to be calm and consistent. Don't get drawn into power struggles or debates. Use the same tone of voice you might when discussing the weather: "I love you, Bubs, and I'll see you when naptime is over."

Your job is to provide them a time to nap that is:

- consistently in the same place and at the same time every day
- preceded by a lovely, calming routine
- dull and dark
- safe

What they do in there is their own business. If they want to just hang out counting their toes for an hour, that's their choice. Usually after a couple of days, the toe counting will lose its appeal and they'll go back to falling asleep.

Too Long in Bed

Too much sleep is an uncommon issue, so your default assumption should be that these aren't the droids you're looking for. But sometimes your child struggles at bedtime or starts the day at an uncivilized hour because you are asking them to sleep more than their body needs and thus they're undertired.

Once your child has learned to fall asleep independently at night, they shouldn't typically have huge difficulties *falling* asleep and *staying* asleep. If you're still constantly struggling with *falling or staying* asleep, you may have a "too long in bed" issue. Here are some clues that this may be the problem:

- Baby naps significantly longer than the guidelines outlined here (see Chapter 10, Becoming the Zen Nap Ninja Master). If Baby is a mammoth napper and sleeps great at night, you don't have a problem (and we're all jealous!). But if your mammoth napper can't easily fall asleep or stay asleep at night, she might be getting so much daytime sleep that she doesn't have enough awake time to accrue sufficient sleep debt to sleep solidly at night.

- Baby isn't awake long enough before bedtime. Regardless of how long your child can be awake between naps during the day, the gap between the last nap of the day and bedtime should be the longest stretch of the day. Late naps (even catnaps) within this window can make nighttime sleep challenging.

- Baby is outgrowing the need for that much sleep. Younger babies will sleep 12 or even 13 hours at night. As they get older (around 6 to 12 months), they outgrow the need for so much sleep; most settle into the vicinity of 11 hours a night, give or take an hour. This can create the perception that there is a "problem," but really it's just your child growing up.

Night Gaps
. . . .

A nightcap is an enjoyable beverage. A night gap is something else entirely.

A night gap is a less common symptom of "too long in bed." Children with a night gap fall asleep independently just fine at bedtime but then are awake for a long period of time in the middle of the night and simply *can't* fall back to sleep. No matter what you do (ignore, feed, bounce, bribe) they're resolutely awake for 1–2 hours in the middle of the night.

If you have ruled out *all* other potential causes for this waking (sleep associations at bedtime, rewarding the behavior in the night, etc.) *and* it's persistent, the answer might be that your child has a gap in their night sleep because they're sleeping more than they need. Typically "too much sleep" manifests as an inability to fall asleep at bedtime or waking up rudely early in the morning. But sometimes the result is a gap in night sleep.

Shorten the duration of their night sleep or cap naps to reduce the amount of sleep they're getting in a day. If your child takes huge naps but sleeps 11 hours at night, focus on reducing nap sleep. If your child sleeps 13 hours at night and takes average naps, consider shortening night sleep. Experiment with decreasing sleep duration an amount equal to the size of the night gap (e.g., if the night gap is 1 hour long, cut daily sleep back by 1 hour).

Starting the Day at an Uncivilized Hour

All babies start the day at an uncivilized hour. The only question is whether that hour is unconscionably uncivilized or just "normal baby" uncivilized.

Babies wake up really early. Generally speaking, 6:00 to 6:30 a.m. is a reasonable target, although some unusually early risers can't make it much past 5:00 or 5:30.

This is what babies do. I know it can be a shock when you realize that you will be waking up at 6 a.m. every single day for the next decade. These are the sorts of painful details that are rarely covered in your "preparing for baby" class.

Does this mean that you have to *accept* waking up at 5:30 as the best you can do?

Possibly.

Your focus should be on maximizing the total amount of uninterrupted sleep your child gets at night. For most babies, this seems to be roughly 11 hours (give or take an hour).

But some babies are neither getting 11 or even 10 hours of sleep nor making it until 6 a.m. When my dude was little, he resolutely woke for the day at 4 a.m. I still have flashbacks to the miserable hours cloaked in darkness waiting for the sun to rise, knowing the whole day would be "off" because he would be ready for his first nap of the day when most babies were just waking up.

There is no amount of coffee that makes getting up at 4 a.m. feel like an okay thing to do.

So, what if baby is legitimately getting up *too early*?

Change Bedtime to Change Wakeup Time

Option 1: Make bedtime earlier

A possible cause of a baby's waking up unreasonably early is that their bedtime is too late. They go to bed overtired, leading to an early wake time.

If your child is awake far longer than the wake times suggested in this book, move bedtime earlier by 15 minutes a day until (a) you hit the zone or (b) bedtime turns into a monumental battle.

Often, an earlier bedtime results in sleeping later in the morning. Even if the morning wakeup remains at its previous hideously early time, you've still improved matters by increasing the duration of night sleep.

Commit to the earlier bedtime for at least 3 to 5 days before deciding that it worked (or didn't).

Option 2: Make bedtime later

Most babies who have dropped the late-afternoon/early-evening nap are going to bed between 7 and 8 p.m. However, some babies are happiest going to bed as early as 6:30. And for some people, a 6:00 to 6:30 bedtime is appropriate for their child.

However, a *too* early bedtime can lock you into early mornings, because a child who goes to bed at 6:00 and can only sleep 10 or 11 hours will start the day at 4 or 5 a.m. They'll have simply gotten enough sleep by that point.

Conversely, some parents seek to push bedtime later in order to try to achieve a more palatable morning wakeup. That can work: some children will sleep 11 hours regardless of what time they go to bed. If they're up till 9:00, they sleep till 8:00. If they go to bed at 7:00, they're up at 6:00.

Unfortunately, most babies are hard-wired to wake up early, so pushing bedtime late may have no effect on the time they wake.

That being said, sometimes gradually pushing bedtime back (assuming that it doesn't *overly* stretch the time awake before bedtime) can help shift the morning wakeup later. Experiment with a slightly later bedtime for 3 to 5 days. Try to expose your child to bright (ideally outdoor) light in the late afternoon or early evening to help shift their circadian rhythm, resulting in a later bedtime and later wakeup time.[17] Pushing bedtime back is unlikely to have the desired result without *also* using light therapy to shift the internal clock.

If your child can happily stay awake for the extended evening time, can easily fall and stay asleep, *and* continues to sleep for the same number of hours at night (thus resulting in a later morning wakeup), then open a bottle of celebration juice. If not, the delayed bedtime experiment didn't work; shift back to the previous earlier bedtime.

Rule Out All Possible Contributors to Early Waking

Is there a reason your child wakes up so early? Do some experiments to rule out the following:

- Environmental factors. Sunlight peeking in through shades, the sound of the neighbor's garage door opening, barking dogs, or a soggy diaper can all prompt your peanut to start the day. Sneak into your child's room about 30 minutes before morning wakeup (or better yet, assign this early-morning task to your partner!). What do you (I mean they—definitely they) notice? Sound or light issues can be easily dealt with. White noise is almost always helpful. If you've got diaper issues, try overnight disposables.

- Hunger. Sure, your child is biologically capable of fasting for 11 or 12 hours, but many babies are too busy to eat during the day so they get a bit peckish in the wee hours. A 5 a.m. snooze-button feeding might buy you all an extra hour or two of sleep. Snooze-button feedings are less fun than a box of puppies, but they're often the "least bad" alternative available to you.

- Need for soothing. Babies are cycling through deep and light sleep all night long. Earlier in the night, it's easy to cycle from light to deep sleep because the compulsion to sleep is strong. Toward morning, though, baby is less tired, so navigating those light sleep cycles becomes challenging to the point where they just can't. But sometimes babies can navigate back to sleep... with a little nudge from you. Essentially, they can either start the day at 5 a.m. or, with a bit of extra soothing, they can sleep an extra hour to hour and a half (this is especially true of younger babies). This soothing might include offering a pacifier, having a brief cuddle, etc. Nobody is thrilled to wake up and gently coax a baby back to sleep at 5 a.m., but it beats getting up for the day.

Disrupt the Sleep Pattern

This sounds like something you would not want to do—waking a sleeping child is only slightly less distasteful than licking a toilet. And truthfully, this is a bit of an Advanced Sleep Ninja technique that isn't necessary for most people. But if you've tried everything else without success, you might want to experiment with this.

Wake your child *just slightly*, before they normally wake up in the morning. For example, if your baby wakes up at 4:30, you go in at 3:45 (and by "you" I mean your partner, obviously). Wake Baby a tiny bit by rubbing their belly, unswaddling and re-swaddling them, picking them up briefly, etc. You aren't trying to get them awake and upset, but they should be awake *enough* to need to fall back asleep after you leave.

The goal of this exercise is to see whether, by disrupting the sleep/wake cycle your child has established, we can get them to break out of the pattern of waking up too early and to actually sleep later. Often it takes only a few times for a new sleep pattern to develop.

Toddler Alarm Clocks

For kids 2 years and up, toddler alarm clocks can be helpful in establishing a later wake time. Ideally, this alarm clock doesn't actually have an "alarm" but instead provides a visual cue (a red light that turns green, a picture of a sleeping or awake bunny) that lets your child know it's time to start the day. These can be purchased at most baby stores, or you can make your own by putting a nightlight on a timer.

These are sometimes known as "reverse alarm clocks" because the purpose is not to wake the child but rather to provide a gentle reminder that it's *not* time to get up yet.

Here's how to use your toddler alarm clock:

· Make the clock something of an exciting gift. It's not punitive, it's a present! When it shows up in the mail, wrap it. Let kiddo pick out where it will go in their room. Show them how cool it is.

· Talk about how it works. "Sleeping bunny means it's bedtime and you stay in bed. Awake bunny means it's time to get up and start the day." Be firm but matter-of-fact about it. "It'll tell us when it's time to have morning hugs and oatmeal!"

· Set the wakeup time 15 minutes later than your toddler currently wakes up naturally. Many people skip this step, hoping to jump immediately to a reasonable wakeup time. Don't do this—your toddler isn't going to sit there for 2 hours waiting for the clock to tell them it's time to get up. Start small. Establish the Law of the Clock and get everybody comfortable with the rules about staying in bed till it turns on. Once that's well understood by all, try adding another 15 minutes.

· When the light turns on, go into their room with your Happy Parent face on. "Honey, you stayed in bed until the light turned on! What a great way for us to start our day!"

· Let the clock be in charge of when you all get up in the morning. Morning is when the clock says, so don't go in until the clock says so. If your child calls for you, play dead. If they're mobile and they come out, quickly walk them back to bed and reiterate the rules. Establish clear parameters. If you get your child up for the day the minute they call for you, you've wasted $40 because you just taught your child that the wakeup clock is simply a fancy nightlight and morning time is still whenever they say it is.

· For older kids (3 and up), sweeten the deal with a reward chart. This isn't strictly necessary. If you decide to use a chart, though, the child gets a sticker every morning that they stay in bed until the light turns on; if they get seven stickers, they get an ice cream cone (or some other big treat)!

- Continue adding about 15 minutes to the clock every 3 to 4 days, until you get to the point where your child can no longer sleep. If you pushed your clock out to 6:30 and your child is waking each day at 6:00 regardless, you've gone too far. You don't want your child lingering in bed awake for ages—15 to 20 minutes of counting toes is fine, but pushing it too long can lead to noncompliance.

How much additional sleep will the toddler clock buy you? Anywhere from 30 to 60 minutes of additional sleep is a plausible target. When you've been waking up every day at 4:30, sleeping till 5:30 feels like a spa vacation.

13

Older Kids, Siblings, and Twins

T HE FIRST YEAR with a baby, your brain is so full of everything baby (nursing, sleeping, pooping, crying, laughing, eating, crawling) that it can be impossible to imagine a future where they aren't a baby. But while you're not looking, they're quietly turning into a toddler. And then (blink five times!) a preschooler.

As this happens, many parents start thinking about baby #2. This is result of a magical convergence of having enough time pass that you've forgotten how challenging newborns can be while you're enjoying the sparky fun of a cool little 2-year-old kid, leading to the conclusion, "We should totally have another one!"

Your growing kids, however, can have unique sleep issues as they become mobile, age out of naps, and adjust to the arrival of a new baby.

"I want to go to bed!" said no kid ever. Life is happening, and there are no [bubbles/dogs/tickles/sandboxes] to be found in bed. So, understandably, kids are pretty unenthused about sleep. And older kids are developing a growing awareness of what they do *and do not* want to do, as well as growing skills (both physical and verbal) to ensure that they *do not have to do them.*

Most of the baby sleep literature is focused on babies, presumably with the assumption that by their first birthday, you've got everything sorted out and there won't be any sort of issues in the future. Which is a shame, because a significant number of families with older kids struggle with sleep. (Parent surveys suggest that 32% of toddlers and preschoolers aren't getting enough sleep.)[1]

Luckily, with bigger kids, you've got a lot of parenting arrows in your quiver. And there are only a few primary causes of bedtime battles and older kids.

Independent Sleepers

Hopefully, you haven't skipped over the large sections of this book that highlight the importance of falling asleep independently, because it's just as key for older kids as it is for babies. If you stay and cuddle or sit in a chair in their room until older kids are asleep, they'll need you there to fall back to sleep during the night. This can manifest in various ways:

- Your child wakes up and stays awake for a long stretch in the middle of the night.

- They wake up multiple times at night and need you to come cuddle before they can fall back to sleep.

- They fall asleep in their bed but can only fall back to sleep in yours.

- Bedtime is a huge battle.

All of which traces back to what happens at bedtime. Your kid needs to learn how to fall asleep without you [cuddling/lingering/rocking/sitting in a chair nearby]. We've all seen the quiet old lady whispering "Hush" in *Goodnight Moon*, so it can seem both reasonable and loving to stay in that rocking chair while our children nod off to sleep. However, what that book *doesn't* show is the quiet old lady getting super pissed off because the bunny wakes up five times a night and can't go back to sleep without her trotting back in to hush some more.

This point has been made elsewhere, but it's something that frequently trips people up, so I'm going to make it again: *independent sleep starts at bedtime.* Many parents try to cheat the system by maintaining the status quo at bedtime while desperately trying to convince their child to stop demanding more cuddles all night long. You're not going to be able to convince your 3-year-old to go back to sleep without you at 2 a.m. until you stop providing cuddle-time services while they fall asleep at bedtime. The problem, and the solution, starts at bedtime.

The SWAP and SLIP methods presented in Chapters 6 and 7 will help you establish independent sleep for your child who is under about 18 months. If your child is 18–24 months or older, the need for sustainable sleep associations at bedtime remains, but you have a lot more tools to work with. Your baby is now a child with whom you can have a dialogue. This vastly expands your strategies for fostering and maintaining healthy sleep associations.

Strategy #1: Boundaries and Bait

Older kids are great—they don't need to be carried everywhere, they're super fun, and they can be bribed. Before you blanch at the suggestion that you bribe your children, consider the fact that parents use subtle bribes all the time. Have you ever said, "If we can finish up with our grocery shopping quickly today, we'll have time to stop by the park on the way home"? Bribe.

Here, we combine a bit of bribery with some conversations with your child to come up with the Boundaries and Bait method, which stacks up as follows:

1. Determine what your bedtime rules are and ensure
all caregivers and parents are clear about these rules.
The two key boundaries that need to be a part of your plan are (1) kiddo falls asleep without an adult in the room, and (2) kiddo stays in bed. You may have additional rules depending on your situation (no milk

after we brush teeth, lights out at X o'clock, stuffed animals that get thrown out of crib stay out all night, etc.). Everybody must be fully on board with the new plan. If your partner is going to go back to rocking your toddler to sleep the second you go out of town, you're doomed.

2. Talk to your child about what will be happening at bedtime when it's not bedtime.

This should be done over lunch or some other happy, distraction-free part of the day when you can be fully emotionally present. The time leading up to sleep should always include relaxing and enjoyable activities, so avoid anything that has the faintest whiff of nagging at that time. Explain the what, why, and when (and possibly the how) of your plan. That may look something like this: "Hey, Bubs, I love cuddling with you! But our bedtime cuddles are causing you to wake up all night and that's not okay [what]. Your body needs that sleep so it can grow strong and healthy [why]. In 3 days, we're going to make a change at bedtime [when]." Then you proceed to outline the plan you and your partner have put together for how you'll be handling bedtime. This includes the bait (yay!) and the boundaries (boo!).

What is happening at bedtime must change (this is a firm boundary). But *how* it changes is open to discussion. "We're going to change what happens with our bedtime routine. What would you like our new bedtime routine to look like? What should be the last thing we do together before we say goodnight and go to sleep?" Make a chart that pictures the steps of your new and improved bedtime routine (this doesn't need to be Pinterest-worthy, pictures printed off the internet taped on cardboard are great).

3. Connect emotionally with your child.

This may be a scary change for your child. She may feel she can sleep only with you there. Sure, you know she's entirely capable of falling asleep without you, but she doesn't. Let whatever has happened before go—this is not time to grouse about previous bedtime shenanigans. Comments like "You are screwing around for 2 hours at bedtime and we are so totally over it!" are not helpful. Instead, normalize your child's feelings about this. "I don't like it" is a common response from kids. Keep your tone gentle and matter-of-fact: "I know this will feel different at first, but I also know that you can do this and that it's an important change for our whole family. You do amazing things all the time." (Share examples—take care of fish, blow bubbles, skip rope . . .) "You can do this too."

4. Make sure bedtime is a distraction-free affair.
There are often pressures that make the evening frenetic: racing home from work, making dinner, taking older siblings to swim team, etc. But don't short change your child's bedtime routine. This is a time for them to enjoy some calm activity while getting your full attention. It's a 20- to 30-minute commitment to fill your child's emotional bucket before separating for the night.

5. Figure out what bait you want to use for motivation.
Choose some from the list below and share them with your child. This is exciting and fun stuff—emphasize the positive! Get creative! Some good incentives to consider include:

- Make your child's bed great. Ask them what would make their bed even better! Maybe the blanket is too hot, or the noise from the kitchen makes it hard to fall asleep. Maybe it's too dark, and a night-light they can turn on and off all by themselves (without getting out of bed) would help them feel in control. Take them shopping and let them pick out special sheets, a bedtime teddy, etc. Kids rarely get to make purchasing decisions, so this can be hugely empowering. Let them name their new special teddy, and talk about how Teddy will be there to cuddle with at bedtime and anytime they want during the night. Practice giving Teddy a hug if Teddy feels lonely.

- Let your child drive the bedtime routine. Give lots of choices. Do you want to brush teeth first, or take a bath? Do you want to read three books or four? What song do you want to sing? How many kisses before we say goodnight? The last step in the routine should be "Mom or Dad says goodnight and leaves." Commit firmly to the new plan. If you've agreed on four books, then four it is. Otherwise, bedtime devolves into a long bout of limit testing (more on this later).

- Use a reward chart (most productive for kids 3 and older). Get something amazeballs and put it where they can see it but can't touch it. Even better, let them pick out something they are really excited about. If you're not keen on more "stuff," it doesn't have to be a thing— it could be a special activity. After every night that your child sticks to the rules, they get to put a sticker on the chart. When they earn a sticker, make a big fuss: Great job! Family dance party! If they don't earn a sticker, don't make a big deal about it—no lectures or grumpy faces. A simple "Hey, Buddy, you can try again tonight!" will suffice. When they get seven stickers, they've earned their prize.

- For younger children, reward charts can be ineffective. Reward charts require kids to forgo something they want for days, which is an eternity when you're 2. You may have better luck with a more immediate reward system, such as offering a treat (box of goodies to pick from, pancakes, visit to the park) the next morning.

- Have one or two "bedtime tickets." Make a ticket (a square of cardboard with aluminum foil taped to it). The rule is that your kid stays in bed after bedtime. If, however, they need something (an extra hug, a drink of water, a trip to the bathroom), they can exchange one ticket for it. When the tickets are used up, no more getting out of bed (and no more parents rushing in for hugs or to pick up the stuffed animal that "fell" out of bed, etc.). Tickets can be helpful because they empower your kid—he can make you come back if he wants— but it also respects the family boundaries (you only get so many and when they're gone, you're done).

- Create a visual cue to indicate it's time to sleep, such as a nightlight on a timer. Sleep cues can be helpful in supporting your bedtime boundaries: "If the light is on, it's time to stay in bed." This may not feel like a bribe, but you can make it one with one simple addition: wrapping paper.

Often simply talking about not getting out of bed along with a few of these choice pieces of bait is enough to resolve the issue. But not always. So what happens when your peanut uses all of her "bedtime tickets" and persists in getting out of bed? Or screams when you leave the room? You'll want to think about some natural consequences* that support the bedtime rules you've agreed upon. Here are some options:

- If your child yells for you after bedtime (or after all bedtime tickets have been exhausted), gently reiterate the boundary: "I hear you, and I know you want more playtime with Daddy. But it's time for you to sleep. I can hear you but I'm not coming back in. I'll see you in the morning with big hugs and kisses!" Mean what you say; if you say "I'm not coming back in," you aren't.

- If your child is still in a crib, follow the same strategy as SLIP (see Chapter 7).

- If your child is in a big-kid bed and continues to get out, create a physical barrier—either close the bedroom door or put up a baby gate. With this strategy, the bedroom must be entirely baby-proofed. Your child may come to the door or baby gate and yell at you. She may fall asleep on the floor by the gate. Typically, within a few days, the novelty of camping on the floor will wear off and she'll stay in bed. Each subsequent night the door starts open and remains open as long as your child continues to respect the "stay in bed/room" boundary. The gate is a logical consequence to repeatedly coming out of bed/room issues.

- In a slight modification of the door/baby-gate strategy, close the door until your child gets back into bed, at which time you come in, give a quick hug and kiss, and say goodnight, with the door now open as long as kiddo stays in bed. This is a great modification as long as it doesn't turn into the door game. You'll know you've been drawn into the "door game" if the "door closed, hugs, door open" cycle continues endlessly.

---

*Parents are dealing with a myriad of scenarios at bedtime. This is at best a partial list of ideas, so feel free to use your own creativity to develop strategies that are the best fit for *you*. Ensure that your plan centers on *natural or logical consequences* rather than on punishment. A *natural* consequence flows from the digression without any action from the parent—for example, a natural consequence to tossing your stuffed bunny out of bed is that Bunny sleeps on the floor for the rest of the night. A *logical* consequence is one where the parent takes an action directly related to the digression—for example, putting up a baby gate if a young child refuses to stay in their room after bedtime. A *punishment* is unrelated to what is happening. "If you throw Bunny out of the bed again, I'm throwing Bunny away" would be a punishment.

- If there are subsequent wakings or demands or getting out of bed later in the night, handle them the way you did at bedtime. If your child still has a bedtime ticket and calls for a drink of water at 2 a.m., bring them a drink of water.** If they're out of tickets, no more visits.

- Commit fully to your plan. It's not like pink lipstick—something you try for a day or two and then give up. This plan represents the new normal for your family. You don't go back to cuddling to sleep when you travel to Grandma's house or somebody gets a tummy ache. If you really have a hankering to go back to cuddling somebody to sleep, make a new baby. Or get a puppy.

Strategy #2: The Fade

Sometimes you find yourself no longer wanting to date someone, and rather than confronting them with the inelegant "It's not you, it's me" conversation, you gradually become less and less responsive until they get the idea and stop texting you. This is called the "fade." However, that's not the fade we're talking about here.

The bedtime fade is useful to help kids who are used to sleeping with you in the room gradually become accustomed to falling asleep without you. Simply put, you progressively move yourself farther away over a series of nights.

1. As always, talk to your child about what will be happening when it's not bedtime. Highlight the why, what, and when. "I love snuggling with you at bedtime, but this is making it hard for you and I to get the sleep we need at night. You need to sleep so you can stay strong and healthy, and I need sleep to be a great mom for you! So starting Saturday, I'm going to stay with you but won't be in bed with you. I'll be nearby. And you know that I'm always here for you even if you can't see me." Reiterate the message over a few days before making the change, so everybody is clear on the plan.

**Avoid water requests by allowing kiddo to have a leak-proof sippy cup of water by their bed. The only reason *not* to do this is if they're drinking so much water, it's leading to diaper leakage. But most kids just want a sip or two here and there. It's a great way of empowering your child to take care of their own needs.

2. If appropriate, encourage your child to cuddle with a transition object (special blanket, lovey, teddy) at bedtime.

3. On the first night, take one step back from your current level of contact or presence. If you've been crawling into bed with your child, start by sitting next to the bed with your hand on their back. If you've been sitting in a chair near their bed, move that chair a few feet away.

4. If your child protests this change, warmly but firmly reiterate your bedtime boundary: "I love you and I'm here for you, but it's time for you to sleep. I'm going to stop talking now so your body can relax." You are present but only minimally engaged. Don't get drawn into a dialogue about it (this is why we had the conversation over lunch for the past 3 days). You are a loving but silent presence.

5. When your child falls asleep with you present, they will expect you to be there later in the night (see Chapter 4, How Babies Sleep). Sneaking out after they fall asleep doesn't work: it encourages kids to fight sleep at bedtime (they know you're going to sneak out the second their eyes are closed), and they'll hunt or yell for you later. Plan on remaining in your child's room for the duration of the night. THIS SUCKS, I KNOW. It's temporary.

6. On each subsequent night, be less engaged and physically farther away. If you were right next to the bed on night 1, be 2 feet away on night 2, 4 feet away on night 3, etc. Each night, move closer to the door. Don't let this stretch on indefinitely: the whole transition should take no more than 3 to 5 nights.

7. When you're no longer visibly present at bedtime, you're done.

If for some reason you feel that neither Boundaries and Bait nor The Fade will work for your particular circumstance, feel free to modify them so they do. In most cases, the specific strategy employed is less important than your commitment and consistency in execution.

Teach Self-Calming during the Day

This is not a third strategy but something that is a good idea to practice with all kids. There will be moments when your child is awake at bedtime or during the night. There will be nights when they're too wound up or worried to fall asleep. This is not a "kid thing," it's a "people thing."

Your bedtime job is to provide a consistent, enjoyable routine that happens at the same time every night, to put your child in a safe, dark, quiet, comfortable place that is conducive to sleep, and to teach your child to fall asleep independently.

What happens after that is *their* job. This is why we call it *bed*time instead of *sleep*time.

Does that mean it's okay for your 2-year-old to sit in their bed awake and talking to themselves for 20 minutes? *It sure does!*

Wait—isn't this some sort of medieval child torture? No, it isn't! Learning to entertain themselves, care for their bodies, or (*gasp!*) spend a moment of the day without constant stimulation is healthy! As adults, what do you do when you can't fall asleep? You lie there and think quiet thoughts until you *do* fall asleep. Your child is learning to do this also.

It's helpful nonetheless to teach your child coping strategies so they can meet their own needs when they're struggling with sleep. Practice these with them during the day, and offer a brief reminder that they can do them on their own at night. Here are some self-calming options:

- Belly breathing (discussed later in this chapter).

- Mindful relaxation. Have them visualize relaxing every part of their body, part by part. Start with the toes; let all the muscles in the toes relax. Now the whole foot. Now the calf. Move, part by part, all the way up to the head. Do this with them a few times (practice during the day, practice again before you leave at bedtime), then simply remind them that it's an available tool.

- Telling yourself a story. Give them some prompts for a story they can tell themselves if they can't sleep. What if there is a bear in the forest, and a dragon moves in next door? What if your garden was full of fairies? Who are the characters in your story? What happens next?

· Thinking back over your day. What were the three brightest spots in your day? What made those times so great? What are you looking forward to doing tomorrow?

If your child is struggling to fall asleep, go to them briefly to acknowledge and normalize what is happening, then encourage them to figure out a good way to calm themselves: "Sometimes it's hard to fall asleep. The other night my brain was too busy for sleep. I used belly breathing to help calm my body. What strategy are you going to use?"

Bedtime, Boundaries, and Limit Testing

In the 1970s, some dastardly professors at Stanford University concocted an evil scheme to torture preschoolers called The Marshmallow Test. They put 4-year-olds in a room with a lone marshmallow and told them, "If you don't eat the marshmallow for 15 minutes, you can have that marshmallow plus a second marshmallow. But if you eat it? No second marshmallow for you!"[2] Then they laughed evilly while backing out of the room to go bully puppies.

Most *adults* can't wait a full 15 minutes, which is why we snarf cookie dough when there's a batch baking in the oven. For 4-year-old kids, 15 minutes is quite simply an eternity. Unsurprisingly, two-thirds of the kids ate the marshmallow. Frankly, I'm amazed they didn't *all* eat the marshmallow.

When it comes to sleep, [you/snacks/Duplos/the dog] are the marshmallow. Going to bed requires forgoing this awesome marshmallow in exchange for some ambiguous concept like "health and well-being." Your increasingly opinioned 2-year-old will, at some point, likely come to the conclusion, "I am not interested in this healthy sleep stuff you keep talking about."

What will follow is referred to as *limit testing*.

From your child's perspective, you are one giant science experiment and they are continually developing, testing, and modifying hypotheses about how you "work" (What happens if I do X? How does it change if I do Y?).

This genius-level capability often manifests in limit testing at bedtime. Your child doesn't want to miss out on the marshmallow by going to bed, so they ask for *one* more book. Board books are quick, so you give in, just this once. That worked well—next time they ask for *two* more books. Or maybe you set the limit on board books to "no more than five" and your clever child changes directions and calls you back because they need another hug. Who can refuse their child's open arms? Not *this* lady, I'll tell you. So that works. But even the biggest softy is going to cut it off ten hugs later. Next, they're thirsty. That's easy enough—give your child a sippy cup of water. Then it's "I have to poop!" That's a good one, because you definitely can't say no to *that*. But eventually you figure out that their trips to the potty are, shall we say... unproductive. We move on to tummy aches, nightmares, etc. Some kids (even verbal ones) will start screaming like they're in pain when you leave their room.

Parents will swear, "Something must have happened! I've never heard him scream like that!" However, this child was perfectly happy stacking blocks on the carpet 30 minutes ago. Either he's suddenly developed an acute case of appendicitis (doubtful) or he's identified the necessary volume required to get a response from you.

Limit testing is a nefarious parenting challenge because there is always a little voice in the back of your head quietly whispering like the flutter of a maleficent moth, "But what if something really *is* wrong? What if he's sick? What if he's scared?" And kids *do* get sick. And they *do* get scared.

Here are two good clues that you're dealing with limit testing:

1. It happens every (or almost every) night. Yes, children have nightmares and night terrors. But not young children.[3] And not every night.

2. There is no evidence of a problem except at bedtime. If your kiddo is playing, eating, and thriving normally all day long but then develops a "major illness" every night at 7:30, you've got a genius who has figured out how to delay bedtime.

Limit testing tends to ebb and flow. You may feel you've put it behind you only to have it pop up again in a few weeks or months. Your genius is restarting the experiment to see if something has changed. Aren't you lucky to have such a smart kid!

Kids test limits because it works. If whatever they're doing didn't work, they would stop doing it. So the key is to make it stop working. Here are steps that will help convince your child of your resolve:

1. Mean what you say.

Sometimes we blurt out things without thinking. This is a time to be really mindful of what you say, because as soon as you say it, it's THE TRUTH. If you say "It's time for bed and I'm not coming back until it's morning," you mean it. If you come back 15 minutes later, you've just taught your child that "I'm not coming back" means "I'm not coming back unless . . ." and the "unless" part will spark the ire of the Goddess of Consistency, who FORGIVES NOTHING.

Sometimes, in a heated, unguarded moment, we blurt out something we *don't* mean: "If you throw Bunny out of the bed one more time, I'll put him in the garbage!" If words are erupting from your mouth before you've thought them through, remove yourself from the scene and take a few moments to collect yourself. What did you *mean* to say? "I'm not picking Bunny up again tonight, so if you toss him out of bed, he's going to spend the night on the floor. You can play with him again in the morning."

2. Fill their bucket.

Limit testing happens because kids are kids. But sometimes it happens because their emotional bucket is running on empty. Kids need time with you when you're emotionally present. It's easy to spend time with your children when you're physically but not emotionally present because you're [running errands/cleaning/on the phone]. Limit testing is an effective way to get your undivided attention, because negative attention is still attention.

Filling their bucket involves doing something *they're* interested in— read books, play in the sandbox, chase and tickle, etc.—and giving them your full attention while you do it. It doesn't have to last hours:

**The Goddess of Consistency Rewards
Those Who Mean What They Say**

carve out small moments throughout the day. This investment in your relationship will make it easier for your child to separate from you when it's time to sleep.

3. Don't reward limit testing.

Let's consider, for a moment, that limit testing is not just about avoiding sleep—it's also about getting your time and attention. Even negative attention trumps no attention, so your well-intended lecture on why it's critical to stop singing after bedtime is going to encourage more singing. This is why the logical consequence to most bedtime limit-testing behavior is to ignore it. While you may not be keen to have your child take off their jammies and sleep naked, returning to put the jammies back on just encourages further nakedness. You should, if you can within the bounds of safety and sanity, ignore the behavior.

4. Commitment is the foundation.
I hate the word *try*. When parents tell me they'll "try" something, it's a clue that they aren't really committed to change. You can "try" yoga or a new cake recipe, but when it comes to limit testing, it's a firm "do." We can talk about reward charts, nightlights, and bedtime routines until the stars fall from the sky, but the reality is that the details of your plan don't matter half as much as your level of commitment to making change.

5. Give your child as much control as you can.
We're constantly saying "no" to our kids. No, you can't put that in your mouth. No, I won't buy that for you. No, you can't ride the dog like a pony. Let them be the boss whenever humanly possible. Ask them what they want their bedtime routine to be. Sure, the last step is "Mom or Dad says goodnight and leaves," but everything up to that point is entirely up to them. Let them pick their jammies, books, songs to sing, etc. Say no as little as is necessary.

6. Set kids up for success.
The Marshmallow Test tells us something we already know: little kids have no self-control. Giving young children a ton of freedom at bedtime and requesting that they not take advantage of it is setting them up for failure. One of the many beautiful aspects of the crib is that it creates a physical barrier. Some people call cribs "baby jails," but that suggests your child has done something wrong and is being penalized. Putting up physical barriers (cribs, baby gates, closing doors, etc.) is just acknowledging the reality of your child's age and maturity. Speaking of which . . .

Moving to a Big-Kid Bed
· ·

Moving your toddler out of the crib and into a big-kid bed is a lot like giving them the car keys: you are presenting your child with a huge amount of freedom and power that is almost guaranteed to be used in nefarious ways.

People often think their child has "outgrown" the crib and might sleep better if they had more space. However, the best-case scenario is that your child sleeps in a bed *as well as* they do in a crib. The freedom and mobility of a big-kid bed doesn't fix sleep issues—it generally exacerbates them. It's important, therefore, to be clear with yourself about why you're moving your child out of the crib, so you can be sure it's the right move.

Good reasons to move to a big-kid bed
- Your child is continually climbing out of the crib and potentially hurting themselves in the process. You're awakened at 2 a.m. by a crash and find your 2-year-old crying on the carpet. Both of you are stunned by what has just happened. But don't panic (yet): often kids try this once or twice, realize that crashing to the floor isn't as much fun as they expected, and stop doing it. Some parents cover the floor with pillows, like a Turkish spa. If that helps bring you some peace, feel free. Also, please send pictures! If, however, your child is a committed crib climber, it's time for a big-kid bed.

- Your child is legitimately old enough to not need to sleep in the crib anymore. Typically, this is after their third birthday. As your child gets older, their ability to moderate their own behavior increases, so they're physically able to understand and execute family rules such as "Stay in bed when it's bedtime." Check your crib manufacturer's specifications for height and weight limits for your crib.

Less good reasons to move to a big-kid bed
- To solve sleep issues. As mentioned, swapping beds is unlikely to fix things and likely to make things worse.

- You need the crib for a new baby. Prepping your first baby's room was a full-time job complete with color coordination, accessories, and personal touches gleaned from your design inspiration board. Subsequent babies don't get this sort of white-glove treatment. Despite the minimal design approach for subsequent children, it's natural to think that you need to free up that crib for the new baby. However, if your child is younger than 2 ½ and it's financially feasible, I would encourage you to simply invest in a second crib. If your child will be 3 or more when the new baby arrives, or if getting a new crib is simply not realistic (due to money, logistics, etc.), you may need to transition your child to a big-kid bed. Ideally, you should make this change 3 to 6 months before the new baby's arrival so that your child has no sense of being pushed aside to make room.

Making the Move

When it's time to move to a big-kid bed, develop a solid plan so that the transition is both effortless and fun for all involved. While in theory, you could go back to the crib if things don't go smoothly, the reality is that reassembling a disassembled crib requires a PhD in mechanical engineering. So once you're done with the crib, you're done.

Make it safe.

Some kids will continue to stay in their big-kid bed until you come and get them. But others will get up to wander about on silent cat feet without your knowledge. If you haven't already done so, make sure there are no safety hazards in their bedroom (furniture that can tip over, exposed power cords, accessible electricity outlets, choking hazards, etc.), because your child will now have access to these things without you present.

If your child has access to the entire house, consider the very real possibility that they'll leave their room without waking you up. Are there safety hazards that you should be concerned about? How are you going to handle those? Is there a way to confine your child to a subset of the house by installing a baby gate at the end of a hallway? Go into each room your child could potentially access and ask yourself, "What sort of shenanigans could my 3-year-old get into here?" The answer is almost always, "A whole lot!"

Make a plan

You could just show up one afternoon with a toddler bed and say, "Look, Bubs, you're sleeping here from now on. Cool beans, right?" But I don't recommend it. Instead . . .

1. Talk to your child about moving to a big-kid bed before moving to a big-kid bed. This is a great lunchtime conversation. Never make it about the new baby. "We're giving all your cool stuff to the new baby" doesn't feel good. Imagine if your husband asked for your engagement ring back because he needed it for his new younger wife! Right?! So make it all about them. "We're getting you a new bed because you're getting bigger and you need space to grow!"

2. Get your child involved. If you're buying a new mattress or head-board, allow your child to help pick it out. Let them pick out new sheets and choose a new stuffed animal as their special "big-bed sleeping buddy." This is fun stuff, and kids love being empowered to make decisions!

3. Talk about the big-kid bed rules. (Hint: They're pretty much the same as the crib rules.) What can they do if they can't fall asleep? What can't they do? Are they allowed to get out of bed without you? Are they allowed to leave their room? Often it's helpful to make a visual chart with pictures (get out the glitter glue!).

4. Give gentle reminders. "I love you, peanut, and I'll come to get you out of bed with big hugs and kisses when it's time to wake up in the morning!"

5. Consider a visual cue to remind your now-mobile child that it's not time to get up. If you don't have one already, this is another time the nightlight on a timer comes in handy.

Frequently, the transition to the big bed is an uneventful affair and your child will be thrilled with their "fancy new bed!"

Sleep and New Siblings
· ·

No matter how long it takes you to get sleep stuff on track with your baby, there are good odds that eventually you will consider that it might be a good idea to have another one.

Even outside of the realm of sleep, bringing a new baby into your family is a huge transition for your existing children. They'll have to share you. And while preschool kids are amazingly good at a whole host of things (giggling, nose picking, exploring) they're notoriously bad at sharing. But there are many things you can work on before and after your new baby arrives to help your older kid(s) adjust more easily.

Before baby arrives
- If you've got any lingering sleep struggles with your existing child, you'll want to come up with a plan to sort those out well in advance of Baby's arrival.

- Practice patience and waiting for desired activities or results. Parenting a newborn means you won't be able to be as responsive to your existing kids, so practice delayed gratification now.

- Carry your older child less and practice safe behavior when crossing the street, in a grocery cart, etc.

- Don't do anything for your child that they are capable of doing for themselves. Step stools are helpful. Consider making an accessible snack drawer that your child can reach without your help.

- Make big changes (bed, potty) well before Baby arrives so there is pride in growing up instead of feelings of being pushed aside.

- You are in charge, the child is not. This is a great time to establish clear boundaries.

- Playgroups, preschool, and playdates are a great way to help a child get used to being around other kids.

- Have an established individual "quiet time" so your child gets used to being by themselves. Practice going out of the room (and coming back): "I'll be back to play with you in 10 minutes." This helps develop independent play and gets them used to the idea that there are other demands on your time.

• Refer to the new baby as "our baby."

• Remember that children are adaptable. They won't be scarred by this experience. This is a new kind of family life!

When you give birth

• Try to prepare your child beforehand for the idea that you will be gone for a few days. Create some transitional objects: record bedtime stories or songs, make a photo album of the two of you together, or ask them to take care of something (feed the fish) while you're away. Bake a cake together and put it in the freezer so you can have a little party when you get home from the hospital.

• Hide a surprise around the house, call from the hospital, and tell your child how to find it.

• Keep your child's routine as regular as possible.

• Give them an "important job" to do, like calling friends and family to tell them about the new baby.

• Bring a photo of them to the hospital and make sure it's somewhere they can see it when they arrive.

• Do not allow other guests to visit when your older child comes to see you in the hospital, and try not to have the baby in your arms when your child arrives. They're really most interested in seeing you!

• If you choose to get a celebration gift for your older child, pick something that reflects that they are bigger and older, which is a good thing.

Back at home

• When you come home, have somebody who is not Mom carry the baby into the house.

- Try to carve out 24 hours without visitors so you all can snuggle together and begin to establish the "new kind of family."

- No matter how well you've prepared everybody for the change, there will be some conflicting emotions. Don't tell your child how they feel about the baby—"Of course you don't really hate the baby!" Try to normalize their feelings: "Sometimes it's hard when things are different from what you're used to."

- All feelings are okay and should be validated as such: "Sometimes you miss being the only one." But also set limits: "You don't have to like the baby, but you cannot hit the baby." And don't freak out—hating the new baby is not a predictor of their future relationship!

- The older child shouldn't be made to feel guilty for feeling angry or jealous: "Sometimes it's hard to be the older child."

- Never apologize for the baby's existence or for the change in your family dynamic.

- Communicate in many ways that your child is irreplaceable: "You are my favorite 3-year-old in the whole world!" "Lindsey is so lucky to have you as an older brother!" "Look how she smiles when you talk to her!"

- Talk to the baby about the older child where the older sibling can overhear you: "Did you see your big sister at the park yesterday? She loves to climb that big tree! Someday she'll teach you how to climb it too."

- When an activity with an older sibling is interrupted, clarify that it's only temporary: "I must feed Max right now, but I'll be back to finish building this tower with you."

- Occasionally "ask" the baby to wait for you to finish something with your older child.

- Try not to deprive your older child(ren) of attention, but don't go overboard either. Don't pile on the gifts or treats associated with birth. This sends a guilt-laden message that can communicate that your child should feel uncomfortable about this change.

- Give your child more grown-up privileges.

- Schedule one-on-one time with your older child, not because of the baby but because you enjoy them and want to spend time with them. Ideally, this time is predictable and happens at the same time every day.

- Nursing or feeding tends to be the most jealous time. Keep a basket of toys, snacks, books, audiobooks, music, drawing supplies, etc. at your nursing station. These are special things that are only used when nursing or feeding.

- Invite your older child to sit next to you. Cuddle. Have them help you. Make up stories together. Have them "read" to you and the baby while you nurse.

- Use Baby's natural reflexes to show your older child how to get "finger hugs" from the baby (your newborn will clench her hand around his finger). This is a great way for them to gently interact instead of getting big, overzealous toddler bear hugs.

- Pets and lovies can be helpful.

- Imaginary playmates often emerge at this time. This is normal and totally okay!

- It is best to allow the child to take the lead. Let the sibling relationship develop at its own pace. Do not try to force or control the relationship.

- Take lots of pictures of the kids together. Have fun with it!

Beware the New Baby Bed Bounce

Most kids seem pretty unfazed by a new baby for the first 3 to 6 months. My working theory is that for a while, they view the baby's arrival in the same vein as a long visit from Aunt Matilda: vaguely unpleasant but mercifully brief. But sometimes, once your older kids come to understand that the new baby is indeed a permanent fixture, sleep problems can erupt.

This is the New Baby Bed Bounce. A few months after the new baby comes home, your older child starts fighting bedtime, skipping naps, or waking up periodically during the night. This tends to be a rough time for parents who are just getting over the challenging newborn phase (again), so it's easy to get panicky when your older child starts having sleep problems—"Et tu, Brute?"

Consider for a moment that the arrival of a new baby is a HUGE deal for your older child. At first it's exciting—people are visiting, cupcakes are involved. But eventually that ends, the baby is still there, and the baby gets All. The. Attention.

So from their perspective, it's entirely reasonable to start fighting sleep in order to garner some of your precious time and attention. When your 3-year-old starts calling for you at 2 a.m., you're going to come rushing in (nobody wants to wake the baby), so your child gets your immediate and undivided attention while expending very little energy. And it's hard for you to set firm limits at this time. It's a huge transition, and many of us feel guilty and miss having one-on-one time with our much-loved older kids.

This isn't to suggest you should let your guilty heart let things continue as they are, or that you *should* feel guilty. This is a time of transition. Your threesome just became a foursome (or your foursome a fivesome, etc.). That takes some adjustment from all parties. But it doesn't mean that kiddo gets a free pass to go romping about in the middle of the night.

The New Baby Bed Bounce is a plea for your attention. Instead of providing that attention at bedtime (or 2 a.m.), try to carve out time during the day. Ideally, this is time that your child can *predictably* count on each day that is focused entirely on them. Maybe it's 30 minutes where you play in the sandbox while a 13-year-old you've hired pushes the baby in a stroller. Maybe, instead of washing dishes, this is what you do when the baby naps. It's easy to get swept up in a new baby's needs. But it's still crucial to carve out some dedicated time to connect emotionally with your older children. Making this happen can be enormously challenging (even more so for single parents) and requires some creativity. Don't be shy about asking for help, calling in favors, or spending a little money.

All of the strategies for limit testing *also* apply to the New Baby Bed Bounce. New babies are amazing but also enormously draining, so it can be hard to find the fortitude to make glittery bedtime charts and stick to boundaries with your older children. But this investment of your limited time and energy will pay off in *not* having to coax your toddler back to bed at 3 a.m. for the next 4 months. You don't have to let waking up all night leave you and your toddler sleep deprived and cranky. Healthy sleep is no less crucial to your older child now than it was when *they* were the baby.

Sleep and Multiples

About 3% of births in the U.S. are multiples (twins, triplets, etc.).[4] If you are one of these rare families, you're probably doubly or triply interested in how to establish healthy sleep for your kids. You also have the well-earned respect of the rest of us, who struggled mightily with our singles. So may I say, we, collectively, tip our hats to you!

Happily, everything in this book applies to your multiple kids too. There are, however, some important addendums that parents of multiples should consider:

- Multiples are far more likely to be born prematurely (over 50% of twins and 90% of triplets are premature). If your baby was born prematurely, you'll need to be extra mindful about ensuring a safe sleep environment, as preemies are at higher risk of SIDS.[5] You'll also want to use their adjusted (not actual) age when following guidelines for how long they can be awake, etc. Preemies take time to catch up to their full-term peers in terms of sleep, so don't consider yourself a failure when your 3-month-old twins are still taking 20-minute naps. Swim in your own lane. Have faith. They'll get there when they're ready.

- Minimize the number of night wakings. This is a critical survival strategy for your family. If one baby wakes up hungry, both get fed. Synchronization is essential.

- Use the Sleep Power Tools—as many as are appropriate when they are younger.

- Make establishing independent sleep a priority early on. Ideally, this is an achievable goal by 2 to 4 months, before it becomes a major problem.

- The whole idea of "following Baby's lead" applies far less to you than it does to parents of singletons. Figuring out a way to tandem feed and have babies nap or sleep at the same time is vital. Don't be shy about asking for help and reaching out to experts.

- Based on anecdotal feedback, multiples do quite well sharing a room and will typically not wake each other by crying or fussing. If, however, you see overwhelming evidence that yours are routinely disrupting each other's sleep, they may need to be temporarily separated for sleep (even if this means some creative reconfiguring of your living space).

- Give each baby their own crib. Many parents of newborn twins choose to have them share a single crib (known as co-bedding). There is no compelling evidence that this is safe, nor that it is hazardous. Due to the lack of evidence, the American Academy of Pediatrics recommends against this practice.[6]

Room-Sharing

Choosing to have your kids share a room (or not) is entirely up to you. There's a lot of chatter about what's best, what ages, what genders. But the truth is that up until 100 years ago, almost everybody slept in a single room, so we are all descendants of many generations of families and siblings who successfully room-shared. According to a recent survey, about 45% of American kids aged 6 to 11 share a room (and 11% of those share a bed).[7]

So figure out what makes the most sense for your family based on the kids' temperaments and your physical options, and know that whatever choice you make will be fantastic.

That being said, there is one important consideration that should factor into your decision: *safety*. Often, newborns room-share with their parents for both practical and safety reasons. But most parents have plans for that baby to eventually move out of *their* room and, in some cases, into a room with an older sibling. Which is great, *unless* the older sibling is younger than 3.

Pairing a 2- or 3-year-old, especially one who is no longer in a crib, with a baby creates the possibility of safety issues. Two young crib-sleepers can safely share a room, but if one is not in a crib or can easily climb out, room-sharing might need to wait until the older sibling is mature enough to be trusted alone with Baby.

Younger children don't always understand safe choices for babies. They may seek to give the baby in the crib a "gift" of a small toy, unaware that it's actually a choking hazard. They might think Baby looks cold and give Baby one of their blankets, a potential SIDS hazard. Your mobile child needs to be mature enough to have a solid understanding of what is and isn't safe for the baby, in order to be trusted alone at night. Most children older than 3 have the maturity to understand safe sleep if given clear guidance.

SLIP and Siblings
. . . .

Parents are sometimes concerned that SLIP will lead to crying, which in turn will wake up siblings, etc., and then no one is sleeping. This is a fair concern but far less of a problem than you would guess.

Your baby's crying bothers you far more than it bothers anybody else. The minute you hear your child, your whole body goes on high alert, your heart racing, palms sweaty. Trust me when I tell you that your older child doesn't really care that much—which isn't to say that it's impossible for some night crying to wake an older sibling, just that it's unlikely.

Here are some tips for when you have an older child and are implementing a SLIP strategy:

• Talk to the older child about it in an age-appropriate way. "We're going to help Nugget learn to sleep better. This is really important so he can grow strong and healthy! But it may be hard at first. And because babies don't have words, you may hear him crying. But we want you to know that Mommy and Daddy are taking care of him and he is okay." Ask them if they have any questions or concerns about things. Most often you'll find they couldn't give a flying fig, and when is snack time?

• Use white noise with your older child. Explain that this will help keep the baby from waking him up.

- If some night crying does wake him, gently help him back to bed and reinforce the message that you are in charge, and you are taking care of Baby. Baby is just fine.

Nightmares and Night Terrors

Waking and Upset

Sometimes young children wake up at night visibly upset, disoriented, or even inconsolable. They might be upset for any number of reasons, many of which are discussed in this book. However, what if your child is falling asleep independently, has no problematic sleep associations, and is still routinely waking upset?

The most likely culprit is *partial arousal parasomnia*.[8] This is fancy science-speak for "Your kiddo just woke or partially woke from a non-REM sleep phase."[9] Young children wake up thrashing, confused, upset, flailing, saying things that make no sense, or behaving as though they are terrified. They may yell alarming things or fail to recognize or respond to you. These episodes usually happen early in the night. Needless to say, parents get pretty rattled when their 2-year-old doesn't seem to know who they are or screams "GET OUT!" at them. Parents often mistake these events for sleep terrors, which typically occur with older children (4 to 12 years old).[10] Also, saying "Help, my baby has sleep terrors!" is a whole lot more punchy than "Help, my baby has partial arousal parasomnia!"

Sometimes these just happen, but they can be exacerbated by travel, illness, sleep deprivation, daycare transitions, inconsistent naps, or a blown bedtime. Avoiding parasomnias is yet another reason staying consistent about Baby's sleep is an investment that pays off. (The Goddess of Consistency is always watching—*always*.)

Night Fears and Nightmares

Figuring out why your young child is waking up at night is a challenge because they don't yet have the right words to just tell you about it. They're crying, demanding to nurse, to have a snack, to come into bed with you, etc. because they lack the facility to express ideas like "I just had a scary dream!" And who wants to go to bed when they just dreamed that there are snakes in there? Also, sometimes older kids start to develop fears around the dark, night, and being alone, which is a perfectly normal developmental thing to do . . . until fear of pirates hiding in the closet results in your 3-year-old refusing to go to bed for hours.

Luckily, we've got a wonderful expert here to help you navigate these challenges.

Dr. Ruid, PhD, on Nightmares and Fears

Kids and dreaming

There are varying beliefs regarding at what age children are capable of dreaming and experiencing nightmares. Your child may be saying they had a nightmare because they actually did or because they've learned that claiming to have a nightmare is an effective way to get parental attention. When it's 2:00 a.m. and your child is crying in your doorway about having a nightmare, it's all but impossible to know which it is. Whether or not your child is actually experiencing nightmares is less important than recognizing and responding to your child's real, perceived, or desired need in a consistent and empathic manner. Luckily, the way to respond to a night waking in the moment is mostly the same, whether that waking is behavioral or fear based.

The rationale for this is that we don't want to reinforce the actions (waking, seeking a parent), whether driven by desire for attention, by avoidance, or by anxiety or fear. We want our children, and ourselves, to enjoy a great full night's sleep!

If your child is waking at night and seeking you, it is possible that your child's goal is to control where you are, gain access to something (often parent attention), and/or delay or avoid sleep, and that they have learned that falsely claiming to have had a nightmare can elicit the response they want. Thus the key to altering night waking behavior(s) you want to prevent is to not allow your child to dictate *where* you are in the home, gain access to the reinforcer (again, often parent attention), and/or delay or avoid sleep!

If the behavior is driven by fear or anxiety, such as fear from an actual nightmare, your child is trying to avoid the thing that is feared, which in this case is sleep or being alone. Research demonstrates that exposure to the source of anxiety, if we have the tools to manage that anxiety (see below for how to foster this ability), is the best way to *overcome* the anxiety. Which means simply that facing the feared thing is the best way to get over that fear! Thus, much like the case where the night waking is behavioral, to avoid reinforcing the fear or anxiety, you don't want to allow the child to delay or avoid sleep or avoid being alone.

So how do you respond to your child who tells you that they just had a nightmare?

- Go to your child rather than having your child come to you (most of us live in homes that allow us to hear our children when they call out). It is very easy to allow a child to climb into bed with you, as this allows everybody to quickly get back to sleep. What follows, however, is that this is likely to continue happening until you routinely have a mini-bed-mate. In addition, a child getting up and coming to you only further wakes them, making it harder for them to get back to sleep. You getting out of their bed when the time comes to resume independent sleep is easier than kicking them out of yours! This policy also applies when children are sick.

- Provide brief empathy and validation when a child is frightened or struggling to sleep at night. This feels good to both the parent and the child because it does not dismiss feelings and allows the child to feel "heard," which is often necessary to enable them to move on. Nobody wants to listen to someone or trusts what they have to offer unless we feel that the other person understands our perspective. In practice this may be a few words, a hug, a kiss, or a brief back rub.

- Offer reminders of skills or tools they have for managing fears, for example, using belly breathing or thinking about something that feels better (there is more detailed information below about how to teach belly breathing and other calming strategies to your child).

- Remain firm on the rules around sleep in your home.

- Put together, this may look like: Go to your child's room. "I can see that you're feeling really upset—sometimes I feel that way too [empathy]. Having a scary dream doesn't feel very good at all [validation]." (Said while rubbing your child's back.) "Remember, you can tell yourself that dreams aren't real even though they feel like they are [skill reminder]. I love you." Then exit stage left [consistency].

If you believe your child's night waking is largely behavioral, this approach should be both effective and sufficient. If there are underlying fears or anxiety behind the waking, you may want or need to consider focusing on introducing, practicing, and ensuring mastery of strategies to address this before nighttime (rather than during the night). These skills can also be taught to a child who does not seem to have anxiety, as they are generally helpful self-management skills. Some of these anxiety management tools include . . .

Belly breathing (a.k.a. diaphragmatic breathing)
Often, when a person is anxious or upset, one of the things they may notice is that breathing becomes difficult, making it feel that there is not enough air getting in. This forces a person to take faster breaths in an attempt to get enough air in. Belly breathing can help counter this and avoid hyperventilating.

In addition, deep breathing can:

- calm the nervous system
- slow the heart rate
- lower blood pressure
- slow brain waves—"quiet the mind"
- stimulate the immune system
- decrease sweating and lower body temperature
- act as a distraction!

Learning how to correctly use deep breathing to reap the above benefits is more difficult than you may think. To teach your child:

1. Have your child lie flat on the floor, bed, or the couch. Preferably, practice this skill alongside your child. Bedtime can be a great time to practice since your child should already be in bed (and everyone needs to relax to fall asleep anyway!).

2. Tell your child to breathe in through his or her nose slowly.

3. Focus on the stomach, not the chest. Have your child rest one hand on their stomach and the other on their chest—only the stomach should move.

4. Tell your child to pretend to have a balloon in their stomach. (What color is your balloon?) Then inflate the balloon.

5. Their stomach should become big (be careful that they are not using muscles to make this happen), but not so big that the balloon pops!

6. Tell your child to blow out through his or her mouth slowly (prompt that they don't want to let all the air out of the balloon at once and have it fly all over inside their belly!).

7. Imagine exhaling all the air from the balloon.

8. Their stomach should flatten.

9. Repeat five times.

Once your child has mastered this technique when relaxed, encourage using it when they experience anxiety.

Visualization

Visualization is an excellent way to cope with anxiety. Remember, though, for visualization to work, your child must choose something engaging enough that they cannot continue to think about the thing that is making them anxious. Have your child visualize a relaxing scenario (a recent trip to the beach, for example). Encourage him or her to enlist all the senses (what does he or she hear, smell, feel, see?) in a story format. For some children, initially doing this out loud for them, or recording you doing so, may help teach the skill.

Calming self-talk

Encourage positive coping statements such as "Everything is okay," "I'm safe," and "Everything is the same in the dark as in the light—I just can't see it." These thoughts must be accurate and believable for your child, so we can't replace fearful thoughts with "I'm not scared."

It may also be helpful to establish a sticker chart or other positive incentive plan to motivate a child to sleep independently through the night, whether the issue is anxiety or behavioral. When something is difficult or we don't want to do it, a little incentive can go a long way!

Talking to your children about nightmares

If, during the day, your child wants to tell you about the nightmare or fear, they can do so. However, be mindful that children will often tell and retell and retell something! Though there are times when this processing can be helpful, this is generally when the focus is on the positive (such as "I was really scared but then realized I'm safe") versus the negative (such as "It was so scary. I was trying to run and couldn't get away"). You don't want to emphasize the fear by retelling.

After listening to the fear or nightmare, you can educate children about what happens inside their body when a nightmare occurs (the heart beats faster, muscles get tighter, breathing becomes shallow and faster, body temperature increases) as a way to further explain why this experience is unpleasant. Teach them that this is the same thing that happens when they are awake and become frightened (or angry, or embarrassed). Talk about how you can help manage those feelings using the tools discussed earlier. Encourage them to feel power over their nightmares, recognizing that these are created in their mind and, thus, can be altered there too. I may have a child draw a picture of their nightmare and then alter details so it becomes funny.

My son, for example, had a nightmare about a fire-breathing dragon chasing our family, and I had him envision the dragon breathing whipped cream (our family is known for enjoying dessert!).

I am not a fan of "monster spray" or other "magical" strategies to address fear of things that do not exist. I believe that they make that fear more real for children and, in doing so, give that fear power. So my approach is very direct, along the lines of "There is no monster in your closet because there is no such thing as monsters." Then I encourage children to use the strategies outlined above (for example, "Thoughts of monsters are scary even though monsters aren't real. What else can you think about to get your mind off of monsters?"). I use the analogy of TV with older children—if you are watching a channel you don't like, you change the channel. You can do the same in your brain when you are thinking about something scary.

As fears become more rational and realistic, we struggle to help our children because we can't offer the same (simple) promises of safety we offered when they were younger. While you can promise your 3-year-old that a monster will never attack him, you are not able to promise your 6-year-old that the house will never be robbed. As parents, we don't like this because we like to "fix" things for our children. It is unsettling for us when we can't do this. But it's actually good that we stumble into these situations because it forces us to do something even better for our children—teach them coping skills which they will need throughout life!

Sometimes we simply have to sit with, and manage, anxiety or other uncomfortable yet valid feelings. When children hit on these more rational fears around nighttime and darkness (as well as issues unrelated to sleep, such as death or natural disasters), I respond candidly that these are reasonable fears. I am clear that I am not able to promise these events will never occur, but I offer reassurance that we take measures (those within our control tend to decrease anxiety more than highlighting factors outside of our control) to decrease the likelihood that they will occur (for example, "We chose to live in a neighborhood that is very safe. We lock our doors"). Presenting facts that can keep fears at an appropriate level based on the likelihood of them occurring—"Has anyone ever broken into our house? any of your friends' houses?"—can also be helpful.

Once children have learned of these measures, when worries arise in the future I bounce their questions back to them. For example, "I hear that you are worried someone may break into our home. What do we do to prevent that?" The goal is to ultimately transfer the role of "reassurer" to the child so they can independently manage worries. Of course, these strategies are only effective if they are true and support that dangers are unlikely. For some children, fears go beyond what is developmentally typical and these responses do not suffice. If this occurs, it may be time to seek professional help, as you may be looking at an anxiety disorder that will not get better without treatment.

With regard to decreasing general fear of the dark, you can play a "game" from the wonderful book *What to Do When You Dread Your Bed*, by Dawn Huebner, PhD. It is essentially a game of object hide-and-seek (someone hides an object and the child tries to find it). You begin playing this game during the daytime and in one room. Then expand the game to include multiple rooms in the home during the daytime. This encourages children to venture into other rooms without being accompanied by an adult—a prerequisite to feeling okay alone in the dark. Next expand the game to playing at night (starting with all the lights on but gradually, over time, having lights off so the child must turn on a light when entering a room). Finally, the game can be played in the dark with either a flashlight, nightlight, or closet light turned on. To keep the game interesting and fun, you can time how long it takes to find the object and have each family member who did not hide the object try to find it or give clues, like in a treasure hunt. The idea behind this game is graduated exposure, an excellent tool when treating anxiety about being in the dark!

IN SUM, THERE are a lot of creative approaches you can take to address sleep and bedtime issues with older kids. Because your child is older, you've got a lot more options than when they were babies, because now you can talk things through. Feel free to modify the approaches suggested here to match your own parenting style. The keys to sleep issues with older kids are honesty and consistency. The Goddess of Consistency does not play.

The Last Word

~~~~~~~~~~~~~~

(THIS IS PERHAPS the only place I get to have the last word. How exciting! Excuse me while I revel in the moment.)

At the beginning of the book, I promised to share with you everything I wish I had known back when we were in the thick of it. Hoo boy, those were some dark days for us. We felt stuck and helpless. I knew things were terrible, but I figured that was simply our life. Our terrible, terrible life.

But you know what? We weren't helpless. There were loads of things we could do to make things better.

And that's what this book is—a compendium of things *you* can do to make things better. For your child and your whole family.

This is my hope for you—that you feel armed with the knowledge and the confidence to make things better.

Too often I see smart, capable people brought so low by sleep deprivation that their confidence has all but evaporated. They feel that everything is their fault, or that they've messed up things beyond all hope of repair—that they're terrible parents.

But none of us are.

This is tricky stuff, and the path forward is rarely obvious or linear.

But you are an awesome, amazing, loving parent. I know this for a fact. (If you weren't, you wouldn't have read this book.) And now you're going to find a way to help your family sleep better. Because that's what awesome parents do.

It's not always easy but it is *absolutely* worth the effort.

As exhausted as you may be at times, have faith that things will get better—faith in yourself, in your partner, and, most importantly, in your little one. Your child is capable of more than you think! Trust in their ability to figure things out.

I have faith in your child *and in you*.

Tally ho!

ALEXIS

Appendix: Potential Medical Complications for Sleep

THIS IS NOT a medical book, and I am not a doctor. I am in no way qualified to dole out medical advice. This appendix provides just an overview of some of the more common (and generally temporary) medical issues that may negatively affect your child's sleep. If you have a niggling idea that something isn't quite right, you can use this as the background information you need to form the basis for a meaningful discussion with your pediatrician. It is not intended to take the place of that discussion.

A good 95% of the time, the reason your baby isn't sleeping is *because they're a baby*. Babies don't fall asleep easily, don't stay asleep, and resolutely prefer to be held and fed even at the uncivilized hour of 3 a.m. Babies cry a lot, vomit, get constipated, have diarrhea, get horrifying diaper rashes, and are periodically inconsolable for no particular reason—all of which are normal things that perfectly healthy babies do.

So before you go rushing off to visit Dr. Google, remember that the *overwhelmingly likely* explanation for what is happening with your child is "just because." You should assume everything is entirely fine unless there is *compelling* evidence that your baby is among the 5% of infants who may have a relatively minor medical complication that can affect sleep, in which case you're off for that meaningful discussion with the pediatrician.

The two most common (and to be clear, on a relative scale, these issues are quite *un*common) issues that manifest in poor sleep in infants are reflux and food allergies. Although it's probably an under-statement to say "poor sleep." As any parent of a baby who had tummy problems will tell you, when your kiddo has reflux or food allergies, the result is generally unrelenting, inconsolable crying and hardly any sleep. It can feel like an endless parenting gauntlet so grueling, you deserve a medal for having survived. But I digress…

Infant Reflux
. . . .

Babies spit up. Some spit up with such force that it flies across the room. Big spitters will mark every piece of furniture, every carpet, and every piece of clothing you own with baby vomit. The term *spitup* seems too cute for what your baby does. Your baby VOMITS. Often, and with great gusto.

Is this okay?

Probably.

If your baby is content and growing at a pace that keeps your pedi-atrician happy, then regardless of how much the spitup bothers *you*, it's probably not a problem.

But how do you know if your baby is happy? Newborn babies cry… a lot. The average newborn cries 3 hours a day. Does yours cry that much? More?

Let's assume your baby cries so much that you're starting to have concerns about it and you're starting to wonder why he's so unhappy. Could it be reflux?

What Is Reflux?
We all have a valve at the top of the stomach (the lower esophageal sphincter) that lets food go IN but keeps food from coming back OUT. In most newborns, this valve is not fully developed: stomach contents

can sneak back up the esophagus and come out of the baby's mouth. This is called spitup or baby vomit, and it's exceedingly common: 67% of 4-month-olds vomit at least once a day.[1] Over time, this valve matures and the stomach contents stay IN the stomach. It's sort of gross but is totally harmless.

The problem occurs when food in the esophagus leads to irritation, just like in an adult who suffers from heartburn. So the problem is not the spitup—the problem is the resulting discomfort.

A Note on Terminology. Doctors call this normal baby vomit *gastroesophageal reflux*[2] (or *reflux*, for short). This is confusing because parents call it *spitup* or, if you are Australian, *spilling*. Most parents use *reflux* to describe infant heartburn, where doctors would refer to that as *gastroesophageal reflux disease*, or GERD. As I am not a doctor, I'm using *reflux* here to describe "spitup or silent spitting *that is causing problems*," as compared to normal happy-baby spitup.

How Do You Know If Your Baby Has Reflux?

Start with the assumption that your baby is totally fine, because while spitup is common, reflux is rare. Ultimately, whether your baby has reflux is a determination that you and your pediatrician will need to make together—which is enormously challenging, as there are no noninvasive or particularly conclusive medical tests[3] to make a firm diagnosis with. There is also some controversy over whether we are overtreating infants for reflux.[4] And to be clear, we *are* overtreating infants for reflux. Babies spit up and babies cry, so if "spit up + cry" is your diagnostic criteria, you're going to see a lot of cases of reflux … which would explain studies that show that reflux medications don't outperform a placebo in clinical trials[5]—most of the babies we're medicating didn't actually have reflux to begin with.

Observe your baby and listen to your instincts. If your inner voice is screaming at you and your baby has more than a few of the symptoms listed below, it's probably time to make an appointment with your pediatrician:

· Baby cries a lot (substantially more than 3 hours a day).

· Baby may cry excessively after feedings or while or after spitting up.

- Baby is irritable, fussy, or crying due to pain.

- Baby seems to cry even more when placed on their back or in a car seat.

- Baby has frequent hiccups.

- Baby coughs often.

- Baby seems hungry but then refuses breast or bottle after eating very little (but then may want to eat 2 minutes later, just to repeat the same process).

- Baby has chronic ear infections.

- Baby sleeps poorly,[6] especially during the day (although it's not uncommon for refluxing babies to sleep well at night out of sheer exhaustion).

- Baby has chronic wheezing.

- Baby arches their back after feeding.

- Your parenting instinct tells you your baby's tummy hurts.

- Baby is premature (reflux is more common in premature babies).[7]

Managing Reflux

If you strongly suspect or your pediatrician has confirmed that your child has reflux, you can do a lot to improve matters with lifestyle management.

1. Consider cutting out dairy.

Research suggests that up to 50%[8] of refluxing babies also have a dairy intolerance. Further, sometimes the reflux is even caused by milk proteins.[9] If you're nursing, consider cutting out all milk protein in your own diet for at least 2 weeks. No lactose-free milk or cheese: lactose is milk sugar, and lactose-free foods still have milk protein in them. For most babies, the problem isn't the lactose (milk sugar)—it's the milk protein, also known as casein, caseinate, and calcium caseinate. Start reading labels.

If your baby is bottle-fed, talk to your doctor about doing a trial of milk-protein-free formula. When you go to buy these products, you'll notice that most are stupid expensive. As a bonus, they taste yucky and babies hate them.

So you may need to gradually wean your baby onto them. Start by blending the milk-protein-free formula in with your regular formula to get your baby used to the flavor. If you're making an eight-ounce bottle of formula, use three scoops of your regular dairy formula and one scoop of the detestable but potentially medically necessary dairy-free formula. Wait a few days and then use two scoops old formula, two scoops dairy-free formula. Your two-week "dairy-free" trial doesn't officially begin until your baby is drinking 100% dairy-free formula (mixed blend doesn't count).

2. Keep baby upright.

When it comes to aging, gravity is your nemesis. But when it comes to reflux, gravity is your friend. If you want gravity to keep stomach contents out of Baby's esophagus, keep her perpendicular to the floor pretty much all of the time. This is especially true for about 20 to 30 minutes after every feeding.

3. Soothe more, all the time.

Reflux babies need more soothing than non-reflux babies—a lot more. If your child has reflux, you won't want to compare your experience with those of non-refluxing kids. It's too depressing.

During the day, your baby may be fussy as a matter of course. They may cry frequently, and soothing them can be challenging, much in the same way that winning a gold medal at the Olympics can be challenging. Refluxing babies have a hard time falling asleep and an even harder time *staying* asleep. Naps are notoriously short (although remember—many healthy babies have short naps too, so *don't assume* your short napper has reflux).

You're going to want to embrace some if not all of the Sleep Power Tools. Pacifiers are a particularly good candidate: they encourage the production of saliva, which is a natural antacid.[10]

4. Adhere strictly to sleep schedules.

Typically, babies can handle the occasional skipped nap or blown bedtime without incurring the wrath of the Goddess of Consistency. However, for reasons unknown to modern science, the Goddess of Consistency is merciless toward parents of refluxing babies and will rain down furious vengeance upon any family that dares even small disruptions in the sleep schedule.

Unfortunately, this can be very isolating, because most refluxing babies need very specific soothing tools to sleep and are unlikely to just nod off in your lap while you catch up with friends at a café. Parents often ask, "When will I be able to get out of this stupid house?"

April? Never?

Your baby will let you know. One day you'll try, it won't be terrible, and you'll know your child can handle a bit more flexibility.

5. Thicken feeds.

It has long been held that adding rice cereal to formula or expressed breast milk can help with infant reflux. There is some evidence that thickening feeds does reduce the amount babies vomit.[11] It is not clear, however, that it helps reduce the acidity within the esophagus. And it's not the vomit that comes out that causes problems—it's the stomach contents and resulting irritation in the esophagus. So should you add rice cereal to your baby's bottle? The American Academy of Pediatrics suggests that it may be a reasonable strategy to consider for refluxing infants.[12] Ask your pediatrician.

6. Wait.

With each passing month, your infant's digestive tract is maturing and the amount of spitup and resulting discomfort should decrease (if only slightly). If things don't improve, it may be time to look into medications, or possibly an evaluation by a pediatric GI specialist. Most cases of reflux fully subside by Baby's first birthday.[13]

Food Allergy and Intolerance
....

Food allergies are fairly common,[14] occurring in about 5% of children (studies vary on this).[15] However, it's enormously challenging to know if your child has allergies because the symptoms of food allergies occur in most babies who don't have food allergies, including:

- eczema
- diarrhea
- blood or mucus in stool
- constipation
- severe gas pain and/or stomach cramps
- body and facial rashes
- runny nose, congestion, and other cold-like symptoms
- hoarse voice
- vomiting or excessive spitup
- itchy, watery, or red eyes

Some babies have an allergy or intolerance to something in formula or something that passed through breast milk. However, clear diagnosis[16] is challenging, as many of the tests (skin, blood, biopsy) for food issues in infants are not particularly accurate for kids under 1 year.[17] Which is not to say that if you suspect you've got some food allergies on your hands, you shouldn't seek the advice of a qualified pediatrician or allergist—you definitely should. But for infants, your most powerful diagnostic tool is going to be keeping a food diary and looking at symptoms.

Almost 90% of all food allergies are to the "Big 8" foods:[18]

- wheat
- soybeans
- fish
- shellfish
- eggs
- cow's milk
- peanuts and tree nuts

That leaves 10% of food allergies related to "other things," which could literally be anything.

Cow's Milk Protein

For infants, the most common food allergen is dairy,[19] or more specifically, cow's milk protein (CMP). Milk protein is different from lactose (which is a milk sugar) and thus appears in foods even if they're labeled "lactose free."

If you're exclusively nursing and suspect food allergy, you may want to talk to your pediatrician about doing a dairy-free trial. But note that cutting out milk protein is harder than "don't eat cheese." Milk protein shows up in almost all processed foods—you'll need to read the labels of almost everything you eat, and milk protein goes by many names, including *casein* and *caseinate.*

If your baby drinks formula, ask your pediatrician about a trial of hydrolyzed formula with partially broken-down proteins that are easier to digest and contain no cow or soy protein. But be forewarned: these cost a small fortune and taste like dog biscuits, so getting your baby to accept the change will require some finesse (see the previous section, on Reflux, for more on that).

The good news is that babies with milk issues generally respond quickly when milk proteins are removed from their diet, and most babies no longer react to milk protein after their first birthday.

Allergy vs. Intolerance

To further complicate matters, your baby could have a food allergy or it could be an intolerance. A true allergy means that the body has an immune symptom reaction: it responds to the food as harmful and creates antibodies to fight it. Symptoms can range from mildly itchy skin to anaphylaxis (which is super scary but also incredibly rare).[20] A food intolerance often has overlapping symptoms with an allergy but occurs when a certain food irritates the digestive system or can't be easily digested, so the symptoms are more typically digestive (bloating, cramps, diarrhea). If your baby is responding to something they ate, the symptoms of intolerance will generally occur over a longer time and will be gut-related, while an allergic response will happen minutes to hours after consumption and is typically seen as a skin or respiratory problem.

If you suspect your child is reacting to food, start keeping a log of *everything* you eat (get used to reading labels!) and anything you notice in your baby—changes in behavior, rashes, vomiting, etc. If your baby is formula-fed or eating solids, you'll want to keep a food diary for Baby.

Bring your food log to your pediatrician to discuss the possibility of a food allergy or intolerance. I know many of you will be tempted to skip the pediatrician's office and just cut foods out of your diet, but this would be a mistake.

As many as 43% of parents are convinced their child has a food issue when fewer than 5% of children actually do.[21] Thus, hordes of parents unnecessarily cut foods out of their diets, which can negatively affect their own or their child's nutritional intake. Should you eat or feed your child something they react negatively to? Of course not. Should you talk to a medical professional before making dietary decisions? Of course.

Teething

Okay, teething doesn't necessarily qualify as a "medical" issue, but it will happen and it doesn't fall naturally into any other chapter, so let's talk about it here.

As you've probably noticed, your baby was born toothless. That baby will, however, be growing 20 new teeth between 4 months and 3 years of age.[22] That's right—your child will be teething almost continuously for the first 3 years of life!

Every parent since human beings developed the ability to form words has said the following: "My child is teething and we're all miserable!" Parents will tell you horror stories of furious bouts of teething that result in:

- diarrhea
- fever

- severe sleep disruption
- rashes
- runny noses
- extreme fussiness

And yet...

Studies actually show that teething is no big deal,[23] that our perception of how terrible teething is probably has nothing to do with teething and everything to do with the fact that they're babies and teething just happens to coincide with their being babies. Because babies, regardless of tooth eruption, are periodically fussy, sniffly, or rashy, have mushy poop, and wake up more than normal.

However, if you share this fact with a group of 100 parents, 99 will call you a liar and a fraud. Which is why I'm saying it in this book. Because while you may choose to yell at the book, I can't actually hear you.

That said, teething does cause some issues. You'll probably notice periods when your baby:

- is irritable
- drools
- shoves everything possible into their mouths at all times
- sleeps restlessly*
- can't easily fall asleep*
- has visible red bumps

Teething rarely causes any *serious* problems; it's generally more of a nuisance—an unfortunate and common nuisance. The best response is usually to distract your baby from their discomfort: go outside, have a playdate, give Baby cold things to chew on (washcloths, teethers), etc.

Safety note

It's generally best to make things cold in the refrigerator rather than the freezer, as hard or frozen teethers can hurt more than they help.

Also, while it may be tempting to provide your baby with relief with over-the-counter teething gels (containing benzocaine), neither

---

*Hopefully, you've noticed throughout the book that plenty of other sleep-specific issues result in an inability to easily fall and/or stay asleep and are far more likely the culprit than teething.

the AAP[24] nor I recommend you do so. These gels aren't enormously effective, and they only work temporarily, washing off after a few minutes. Further, in rare cases, their use can lead to unintentional overdose. So stick to the cold washcloths and chew toys.

And lastly, I suggest you steer clear of amber beads. Although many people extol their virtues, logic, sadly, doesn't back up their efficacy.[25] And while it is slight, they do present a potential strangulation or choking risk. So from a risk/reward perspective, it's best to steer clear.

WHILE DAYTIME TEETHING is a relatively manageable affair, none of your go-to teething strategies are going to offer much help at night, as they all require your child to be actively holding and/or chewing them to offer any comfort. While you're welcome to rush into your child's room at 2 a.m. offering them a cold washcloth to suck on, this strategy is not conducive to your sleep goals.

If you really feel that your child is suffering acutely from teething (remember: the research says they probably aren't *really* suffering), talk to your pediatrician about the possibility of over-the-counter pain medication to help with tooth-related discomfort during the night.

Sleep Apnea

Sleep apnea is a rare condition (it may impact 2% of children)[26] in which breathing is partially or fully obstructed during sleep. The primary indicators of apnea include:

- snoring routinely
- mouth breathing while sleeping
- extending the neck in sleep to facilitate easier breathing
- observed pauses in regular breathing
- restless or interrupted sleep

The most common thing to be aware of is snoring or mouth breathing while asleep (provided they don't have a cold—babies with stuffy noses often snore and mouth breathe). It is possible to have a baby who snores but doesn't have apnea, but any incidence of snoring is something you want to pursue with your pediatrician. Apnea is typically a mild condition but it can, in some cases, have lasting and significant effects.[27]

If you and your pediatrician feel that apnea is in fact an issue for your baby, you may be referred to a sleep clinic for overnight observation. Treatment generally involves surgically removing the tonsils or adenoids.[28] In rare cases your doctor may recommend a C-PAP (continuous positive airway pressure) device, which is a mask the child wears over her nose to sleep (think Darth Vader without the evil or use of the Force).

Restless Legs Syndrome

Restless legs syndrome (RLS) is a relatively uncommon condition in which children (and adults) express an urge to move their legs, along with having an uncomfortable feeling (like bugs walking on their skin, a buzzing feeling).[29] Movement frequently relieves the feeling, and the urge to move is worse at night or when not moving. RLS can lead to severe sleep deprivation.[30] Diagnosis in young children is challenging, but a recent study found that 2% of children aged 8 to 11 meet the diagnostic criteria for RLS.[31] RLS also has a strong genetic component, so if one or both parents has RLS, the child is at much greater risk. If your toddler or preschooler has significantly disrupted sleep and you have a family history of RLS, it's worth getting a medical evaluation.

Premature Birth

Approximately 1 in 10 babies is born preterm.[32] For the most part, standard sleep strategies apply to preemies. However, there are a few important issues that parents of preemies want to be mindful of:

- Premature babies are at higher risk of SIDS,[33] so parents of preemies need to ensure that their child is always sleeping on their back in a safe sleep environment. Side sleeping and tummy sleep are enormously risky for babies born prematurely.[34]

- Premature or low-birth-weight babies are frequently placed on their side or tummies to sleep.[35] Presumably, this is because parents are modeling sleep positions that are used in the neonatal intensive-care unit. Please do not do this. Your home does not have the monitoring equipment that the medical staff at the NICU does.

- Many parents of premature babies report that their babies struggle to fall asleep and stay asleep.

- Skin-to-skin contact with your baby (while you are awake) is especially helpful.[36]

- Premature babies respond particularly well to swaddling, which has been linked to improved neuromuscular development in extremely low-birth-weight babies.[37]

- When considering "what is normal" for your premature baby, use their adjusted, not their actual, age. Preemies often take a while to catch up to their full-term buddies, but they do get there!

WITH ALL OF the issues presented in this appendix, please start with the assumption that your child is entirely healthy, because overwhelmingly, babies are! It is highly unlikely that anything presented here applies to you. If, however, you have significant concerns, talk to your pediatrician. Pediatricians are amazing people. They're there to help!

Acknowledgments

~~~~~~~~~

THIS BOOK WOULD not exist without the unfailing support of my family, friends, and a chorus of people on the internet who said, "You should write a book." Big hugs to all the beta readers: this was a huge ask and you guys *delivered*! I am also indebted to my stalwart pocket consultants, the Fellowship of the PLS Admins, for their insights on every major book decision and for their humor, wit, and wisdom every. single. day.

It goes without saying (but I'll say it anyway) that I am especially grateful to my husband, who has never once, in the 3+ years that I chipped away at this, questioned my sanity as I flailed about with this book. I love you.

And to everyone who supported me on Kickstarter, THANK YOU. Your unbelievable generosity and support laid the foundation that made this book possible.

Kick A$$ Kickstarter People

Erica Adams

Alex Anonymous

Jill Anonymous

Emily & John Banks

Sandra Bettencourt

Carolyn S. Black

Emily Boer Drake

Erin Brown

Anna Buehler
LuAnn Chai
Emma Clayton
Elizabeth Cooper
Jim, Jen and Julie Cotignola
Lori DeMauro
Michaela Driscoll
Donna "Is Awesome" Earley
Casey Fleischmann
Lidia Frayne
Becky Frazier
Alison Gabriele
Katie Gaide
Diane Gillingham
Kiri Gurd
Leigh Hampton
Emmett Hawkins
Eliza Hyatt
The Ingman Family
Dawn Kirkland
Hadas Korb
Katie Kostis
Jennifer Kumar
Elizabeth Laughlin
Christina and Steve Lecholop
Amber McDonald
Sharon McMillon
Amy Melton
Kelly Milkus
Ashby Mizell
Felicity Montgomery
Shelley Nash
Lindsey Noggle
Brianna O'Hern
Amber O'Leary
Anya Olsen

Jennifer Pfeifer
Aaron Phillips
Sheena Pick
Susan Pierce
Billie Poling
Katherine Price
Kelly Rancourt
Cindy Reeh
Jane Regan
Allana Robinson
Carla Insley Ryan
Amie Scally
Josephine Scoville
Ruchira Shah
Honey Shor-Posner
Kathleen Stompro
Amy Taggart
Julia Talajic
Eric & Alana Torraca
Susan Toth
Ahu Tukel
Brittany Vickers
Warfenhorton Clan
Caroline L. Webster
Stacia Whitaker
Anastacia Whitman
Adrian Winder
Sarah Wineman
May Wong
Matt Zimmerman

Further Resources

The Precious Little Sleep website comprises a wealth of information (case studies, new research, interviews with experts, etc.). If you check out only one of these resources, let it be this one.
http://bit.ly/PLSblog

My newsletter is the best way to stay in the PLS loop. The ~2 emails a month I send out announce new blog posts and podcasts and also include current insights and studies related to parenting and sleep.
http://bit.ly/PLSnewsletter

My Facebook page primarily features posts on parenting, sleep, and anything else that tickles my fancy. Facebook content is different from what's available on the website/podcast and the emphasis is information valuable to parents of young children.
http://bit.ly/PLSfbpage

The Precious Little Sleep Podcast delves into many topics including those not addressed specifically in this book (e.g., going back to work, daycare, etc.). All episodes are available on iTunes or the website.
http://bit.ly/PLSpodcast

And lastly, the Precious Little Sleep Facebook group provides a friendly, judgment-free space where book-readers can connect, ask questions, troubleshoot sleep struggles, share victories, etc. It's been lauded "an absolute lifesaver" and "the best parenting group on Facebook." Join us and see for yourself!
http://bit.ly/PLSgroup

All links/resources are available and accurate as of the date of publication.

References

Chapter 1: Baby Sleep: Essentials

1. P. Lam, H. Hiscock, & M. Wake, "Outcomes of infant sleep problems: A longitudinal study of sleep, behavior, and maternal well-being," *Pediatrics*, 111, no. 3 (2003): E203-7.

2. C. A. Magee, R. Gordon, & P. Caputi, "Distinct developmental trends in sleep duration during early childhood," *Pediatrics*, 133, no. 6 (2014): E1561-67.

3. X. Chen, M. A. Beydoun, & Y. Wang, "Is sleep duration associated with childhood obesity? A systematic review and meta-analysis," *Obesity*, 16, no. 2 (2008): 265-74.

4. J. M. Zeitzer, D. Dijk, R. E. Kronauer, E. N. Brown, & C. A. Czeisler, "Sensitivity of the human circadian pacemaker to nocturnal light: Melatonin phase resetting and suppression," *The Journal of Physiology*, 526, no. 3 (2000): 695-702.

5. D. L. Hoyert & J. Xu, "Deaths: Preliminary data for 2011," *National Vital Statistics Reports* (U. S. Department of Health and Human Services), 61, no. 6 (2012), http://www.cdc.gov/nchs/data/nvsr/nvsr61/nvsr61_06.pdf.

6. AAP TASK FORCE ON SUDDEN INFANT DEATH SYNDROME. SIDS and Other Sleep-Related Infant Deaths: Updated 2016 Recommendations for a Safe Infant Sleeping Environment. Pediatrics. 2016; 138(5): e20162938

7. National Institutes of Health, Eunice Kennedy Shriver National Institute of Child Health and Human Development, Safe to Sleep [public education campaign], http://www.nichd.nih.gov/sts/Pages/default.aspx.

8. A. J. Garcia, J. E. Koschnitzky, & J. Ramirez, "The physiological determinants of sudden infant death syndrome," *Respiratory Physiology & Neurobiology*, 18, no. 2 (2013): 288-300.

9. AAP Task Force, "SIDS and Other Sleep-Related Infant Deaths."

10. E. A. Mitchell, R. P. Ford, A. W. Stewart, B. J. Taylor, D. M. Becroft, J. M. Thompson, . . . & E. M. Allen, "Smoking and sudden infant death syndrome," *Pediatrics*, 91, no. 5 (1993): 893-96.

11. F. R. Hauck, S. M. Herman, M. Donovan, S. Iyasu, C. M. Moore, E. Donoghue, . . . & M. Willinger, "Sleep environment and the risk of sudden infant death syndrome in an urban population: The Chicago Infant Mortality Study," *Pediatrics*, 111, no. 5 (2003): 1207-14.

12. AAP Task Force, "SIDS and Other Sleep-Related Infant Deaths."

13. D. Tappin, R. Ecob, & H. Brooke, "Bedsharing, roomsharing, and sudden infant death syndrome in Scotland: A case-control study," *Journal of Pediatrics*, 147, no. 1 (2005): 32-37.

14. F. R. Hauck, J. M. Thompson, K. O. Tanabe, R. Y. Moon, & M. M. Vennemann, "Breastfeeding and reduced risk of sudden infant death syndrome: A meta-analysis," *Pediatrics*, 128, no. 1 (2011): 103-10.

15. AAP Task Force, "SIDS and Other Sleep-Related Infant Deaths"; R. Carpenter, L. Irgens, P. Blair, P. England, P. Fleming, J. Huber, . . . & P. Schreuder, "Sudden unexplained infant death in 20 regions in Europe: Case control study," *The Lancet*, 363, no. 9404 (2004): 185-91; Tappin et al., "Bedsharing, roomsharing, and sudden infant death syndrome in Scotland"; E. Volkovich, H. Ben-Zion, D. Karny, G. Meiri, & L. Tikotzky, "Sleep patterns of co-sleeping and solitary sleeping infants and mothers: A longitudinal study," *Sleep Medicine*, 16, no. 11 (2015): 1305-12.

16. F. R. Hauck, O. O. Omojokun, & M. S. Siadaty, "Do pacifiers reduce the risk of sudden infant death syndrome? A meta-analysis," *Pediatrics*, 116, no. 5 (2005): e716-23.

17. M. M. Vennemann, M. Höffgen, T. Bajanowski, H. W. Hense, & E. A. Mitchell, "Do immunisations reduce the risk for SIDS? A meta-analysis," *Vaccine*, 25, no. 26 (2007): 4875-79.

18. J. L. Bass & M. Bull, "Oxygen desaturation in term infants in car safety seats," *Pediatrics*, 110, no. 2 (2002): 401-2; A. Côté, A. Bairam, M. Deschenes, & G. Hatzakis, "Sudden infant deaths in sitting devices," *Archives of Disease in Childhood*, 93, no. 5 (2008): 384-89; C. Pollack-Nelson, "Fall and suffocation injuries associated with in-home use of car seats and baby carriers," *Pediatric Emergency Care*, 16, no. 2 (2000): 77-79.

19. U.S. Consumer Product Safety Commission, "Crib safety tips: Use your crib safely," http://www.cpsc.gov/en/Safety-Education/Safety-Guides/Kids-and-Babies/Cribs/Crib-Safety-Tips/.

20. AAP Task Force, "SIDS and Other Sleep-Related Infant Deaths."

21. AAP Task Force, "SIDS and Other Sleep-Related Infant Deaths."

22. S. Latz, A. W. Wolf, & B. Lozoff, "Cosleeping in context: Sleep practices and problems in young children in Japan and the United States," *Archives of Pediatrics & Adolescent Medicine*, 153, no. 4 (1999): 339-46; J. A. Mindell, A. Sadeh, B. Wiegand, T. H. How, & D. Y. Goh, "Cross-cultural differences in infant and toddler sleep," *Sleep Medicine*, 11, no. 3 (2010): 274-80.

23. E. R. Colson, M. Willinger, D. Rybin, T. Heeren, L. A. Smith, G. Lister, & M. J. Corwin, "Trends and factors associated with infant bed sharing, 1993-2010: The National Infant Sleep Position Study," *JAMA Pediatrics*, 167, no. 11 (2013): 1032-37.

24. AAP Task Force, "SIDS and Other Sleep-Related Infant Deaths."

25. R. R. Das, M. J. Sankar, R. Agarwal, & V. K. Paul, "Is 'bed sharing' beneficial and safe during infancy? A systematic review," *International Journal of Pediatrics*, 2014, no. 3 (2014): 1-16.

26. T. Nelson, K. F. To, Y. Y. Wong, J. Dickinson, K. C. Choi, L. M. Yu ... & L. Chen, "Hong Kong case-control study of sudden unexpected infant death," *The New Zealand Medical Journal*, 118, no. 1227 (2005): U1788.

27. Mitchell et al., "Smoking and sudden infant death syndrome."

28. AAP Task Force, "SIDS and Other Sleep-Related Infant Deaths."

29. F. R. Hauck et al., "Sleep environment and the risk of sudden infant death syndrome in an urban population."

30. A. Mao, M. M. Burnham, B. L. Goodlin-Jones, E. E. Gaylor, & T. F. Anders, "A comparison of the sleep-wake patterns of cosleeping and solitary-sleeping infants," *Child Psychiatry and Human Development*, 35, no. 2 (2004): 95-105.

31. O. G. Jenni, H. Z. Fuhrer, L. Molinari, & R. H. Largo, "A longitudinal study of bed sharing and sleep problems among Swiss children in the first 10 years of life," *Pediatrics*, 115, no. 1 (2005): 233-40; S. Li, X. Jin, C. Yan, S. Wu, F. Jiang, & X. Shen, "Bed- and room-sharing in Chinese school-aged children: Prevalence and association with sleep behaviors," *Sleep Medicine*, 9, no. 5 (2008): 555-63.

Chapter 2: The Party That Is Newborn Sleep

1. R. G. Barr, M. S. Kramer, C. Boisjoly, L. McVey-White, & I. B. Pless, "Parental diary of infant cry and fuss behaviour," *Archives of Disease in Childhood*, 63, no. 4 (1988): 380-87.

2. B. C. Galland, B. J. Taylor, D. E. Elder, & P. Herbison, "Normal sleep patterns in infants and children: A systematic review of observational studies," *Sleep Medicine Reviews*, 16, no. 3 (2012): 213-22.

3. T. B. Brazelton, "Crying in infancy," *Pediatrics*, 29, no. 4 (1962): 579-88.

4. I. St. James-Roberts, "Persistent infant crying," *Archives of Diseases in Childhood*, 66, no. 5 (1991): 653-55.

5. M. A. Wessel, J. C. Cobb, E. B. Jackson, G. S. Harris, & A. C. Detwiler, "Paroxysmal fussing in infancy, sometimes called 'colic,'" *Pediatrics*, 14, no. 5 (1954): 421-35.

6. R. G. Barr, "Colic and crying syndromes in infants," *Pediatrics*, 102, suppl. E1 (1998): 1282-86.

7. J. Kirjavainen, T. Kirjavainen, V. Huhtala, L. Lehtonen, H. Korvenranta, & P. Kero, "Infants with colic have a normal sleep structure at 2 and 7 months of age," *The Journal of Pediatrics*, 138, no. 2 (2001): 218-23; B. P. White, M. R. Gunnar, M. C. Larson, B. Donzella, & R. G. Barr, "Behavioral and physiological responsivity, sleep, and patterns of daily cortisol production in infants with and without colic," *Child Development*, 71, no. 4 (2000): 862-77.

8. S. Coons & C. Guilleminault, "Development of consolidated sleep and wakeful periods in relation to the day/night cycle in infancy," *Developmental Medicine & Child Neurology*, 26, no. 2 (1984): 169-76; B. L. Goodlin-Jones, M. M. Burnham, E. E. Gaylor, & T. F. Anders, "Night waking, sleep-wake organization, and self-soothing in the first year of life," *Journal of Developmental & Behavioral Pediatrics*, 22, no. 4 (2001): 226-33.

9. S. A. Rivkees, "Developing circadian rhythmicity in infants," *Pediatrics*, 112, no. 2 (2003): 373-81.

10. J. S. Kemp, B. Unger, D. Wilkins, R. M. Psara, T. L. Ledbetter, M. A. Graham, M. Case, & B. T. Thach, "Unsafe sleep practices and an analysis of bedsharing among infants dying suddenly and unexpectedly: Results of a four-year, population-based, death-scene investigation study of sudden infant death syndrome and related deaths," *Pediatrics*, 106, no. 3 (2000): e41; L. R. Rechtman, J. D. Colvin, P. S. Blair, & R. Y. Moon, "Sofas and infant mortality," *Pediatrics*, 134, no. 5 (2014): e1293-1300; N. J. Scheers, G. W. Rutherford, & J. S. Kemp, "Where should infants sleep? A comparison of risk for suffocation of infants sleeping in cribs, adult beds, and other sleeping locations," *Pediatrics*, 112, no. 4 (2003): 883-89.

11. I. Iglowstein, O. G. Jenni, L. Molinari, & R. H. Largo, "Sleep duration from infancy to adolescence: Reference values and generational trends," *Pediatrics*, 111, no. 2 (2003): 302-7; National Sleep Foundation, "National Sleep Foundation recommends new sleep durations" [press release], February 2, 2015, https://sleepfoundation.org/media-center/press-release/national-sleep-foundation-recommends-new-sleep-times.

12. Iglowstein et al., "Sleep duration from infancy to adolescence."

13. J. A. Mindell, A. Sadeh, B. Wiegand, T. H. How, & D. Y. Goh, "Cross-cultural differences in infant and toddler sleep," *Sleep Medicine*, 11, no. 3 (2010): 274-80.

14. J. A. Owens, "Sleep in children: Cross-cultural perspectives," *Sleep and Biological Rhythms*, 2, no. 3 (2004): 165-73.

15. L. A. Matricciani, T. S. Olds, S. Blunden, G. Rigney, & M. T. Williams, "Never enough sleep: A brief history of sleep recommendations for children," *Pediatrics*, 129, no. 3 (2012): 548-56.

Chapter 3: Bedtime Is the New Happy Hour

1. K. P. Wright, C. A. Lowry, & M. K. Lebourgeois, "Circadian and wakefulness-sleep modulation of cognition in humans," *Frontiers in Molecular Neuroscience*, 5 (2012): 50.

2. J. A. Mindell & L. J. Meltzer, "Sleep and sleep disorders in children and adolescents," *Psychiatric Clinics of North America*, 29, no. 4 (2006): 1059-76, http://www.ncbi.nlm.nih.gov/pubmed/17118282.

3. D. J. Dijk & M. von Schantz, "Timing and consolidation of human sleep, wakefulness, and performance by a symphony of oscillators," *Journal of Biological Rhythms*, 20, no. 4 (2005): 279-90.

4. National Sleep Foundation, "National Sleep Foundation recommends new sleep durations" [press release], February 2, 2015, https://sleepfoundation.org/media-center/press-release/national-sleep-foundation-recommends-new-sleep-times.

5. National Sleep Foundation, 2004 *Sleep in America Poll: Summary of Findings* (Washington, DC: National Sleep Foundation, 2004).

6. P. Lavie, "Ultrashort sleep-waking schedule: III: 'Gates' and 'forbidden zones' for sleep," *Electroencephalography and Clinical Neurophysiology*, 63, no. 5 (1985): 414-25.

7. D. J. Dijk & C. A. Czeisler, "Contribution of the circadian pacemaker and the sleep homeostat to sleep propensity, sleep structure, electroencephalographic slow waves, and sleep spindle activity in humans," *Journal of Neuroscience*, 15, no. 5 (1995): 3526-28.

8. Y. Kelly, J. Kelly, & A. Sacker, "Changes in bedtime schedules and behavioral difficulties in 7 year old children," *Pediatrics*, 132, no. 5 (2013): e1184-93.

Chapter 4: How Babies Sleep

1. T. F. Anders & M. Keener, "Developmental course of nighttime sleep-wake patterns in full-term and premature infants during the first year of life," *Sleep*, 8, no. 3 (1985): 173-92.

2. J. A. Mindell & J. A. Owens, *A Clinical Guide to Pediatric Sleep: Diagnosis and Management of Sleep Problems* (Philadelphia: Lippincott Williams & Wilkins, 2003).

3. Mindell & Owens, *A Clinical Guide to Pediatric Sleep*.

4. "Circadian rhythm," *Wikipedia*, https://en.wikipedia.org/wiki/Circadian_rhythm.

5. S. A. Rivkees, "Developing circadian rhythmicity in infants," *Pediatrics*, 112, no. 2 (2003): 373-81.

6. D. J. Dijk & C. A. Czeisler, "Paradoxical timing of the circadian rhythm of sleep propensity serves to consolidate sleep and wakefulness in humans," *Neuroscience Letters*, 166, no. 1 (1994): 63-68.

7. C. Cajochen, K. Kräuchi, & A. Wirz-Justice, "Role of melatonin in the regulation of human circadian rhythms and sleep," *Journal of Neuroendocrinology*, 15, no. 4 (2003): 432-37.

8. A. A. Borbely & P. Achermann, "Sleep homeostasis and models of sleep regulation," *Journal of Biological Rhythms*, 14, no. 6 (1999): 559-68; "The Drive to Sleep and Our Internal Clock," *Healthy Sleep*, Division of Sleep Medicine, Harvard Medical School, December 18, 2007, http://healthysleep.med.harvard.edu/healthy/science/how/internal-clock.

9. A. B. Dollins, I. V. Zhdanova, R. J. Wurtman, H. J. Lynch & M. H. Deng, "Effect of inducing nocturnal serum melatonin concentrations in daytime on sleep, mood, body temperature, and performance," *Proceedings of the National Academy of Sciences*, 91, no. 5 (1994): 1824-28; M. Nováková, S. Nevšímalová, I. Příhodová, M. Sládek & A. Sumová, "Alteration of the circadian clock in children with Smith-Magenis syndrome," *The Journal of Clinical Endocrinology & Metabolism*, 97, no. 2 (2012): E312-18.

10. "Object permanence," *Wikipedia*, http://en.wikipedia.org/wiki/Object_permanence.

11. R. Baillargeon & J. DeVos, "Object permanence in young infants: Further evidence," *Child Development*, 62, no. 6 (1991): 1227-46.

12. "Hypervigilance," *Wikipedia*, http://en.wikipedia.org/wiki/Hypervigilance.

Chapter 5: Baby Sleep Power Tools

1. Y. Brackbill, "Continuous stimulation and arousal level in infancy: Effects of stimulus intensity and stress," *Child Development*, 46, no. 2 (1975): 364-69.

2. J. A. Spencer, D. J. Moran, A. Lee, & D. Talbert, "White noise and sleep induction," *Archives of Disease in Childhood*, 65, no. 1 (1990): 135-37.

3. H. Karp, *The Happiest Baby Guide to Great Sleep: Simple Solutions for Kids from Birth to 5 Years* (New York: William Morrow, 2012).

4. K. Coleman-Phox, R. Odouli, & D. Li, "Use of a fan during sleep and the risk of sudden infant death syndrome," *Archives of Pediatrics & Adolescent Medicine*, 162, no. 10 (2008): 963.

5. Y. Brackbill, "Continuous stimulation reduces arousal level: Stability of the effect over time," *Child Development*, 44, no. 1 (1973): 43-46.

6. American Hearing Research Foundation, "Noise induced hearing loss," October 2012, http://american-hearing.org/disorders/noise-induced-hearing-loss/.

7. Y. Brackbill, "Acoustic variation and arousal level in infants," *Psychophysiology*, 6, no. 5 (1970): 517-26.

8. "White noise delays auditory organization in the brain," *HHMI News*, Howard Hughes Medical Institute, March 18, 2003, http://www.hhmi.org/news/white-noise-delays-auditory-organization-brain.

9. R. G. Campos, "Soothing pain-elicited distress in infants with swaddling and pacifiers," *Child Development*, 60, no. 4 (1989): 781-92.

10. B. V. Sleuwen, M. L'Hoir, A. Engelberts, W. Busschers, P. Westers, M. Blom, . . . & W. Kuis, "Comparison of behavior modification with and without swaddling as interventions for excessive crying," *The Journal of Pediatrics*, 149, no. 4 (2006): 512-17.

11. C. M. Gerard, K. A. Harris, & B. T. Thach, "Spontaneous arousals in supine infants while swaddled and unswaddled during rapid eye movement and quiet sleep," *Pediatrics*, 110, no. 6 (2002): e70.

12. "Moro reflex," Newborn Nursery Information, Stanford Medicine, http://newborns.stanford.edu/PhotoGallery/MoroReflex2.html; D. I. Zafeiriou, "Primitive reflexes and postural reactions in the neurodevelopmental examination," *Pediatric Neurology*, 31, no. 1 (2004): 1-8.

13. L. E. Meyer & T. Erler, "Swaddling: A traditional care method rediscovered," *World Journal of Pediatrics*, 7, no. 2 (2011): 155-60.

14. A. Ponsonby, T. Dwyer, L. E. Gibbons, J. A. Cochrane, & Y. Wang, "Factors potentiating the risk of sudden infant death syndrome associated with the prone position," *New England Journal of Medicine*, 329, no. 6 (1993): 377-82; C. A. Wilson, B. J. Taylor, R. M. Laing, S. M. Williams, & E. A. Mitchell, "Clothing and bedding and its relevance to sudden infant death syndrome: Further results from the New Zealand Cot Death Study," *Journal of Paediatrics and Child Health*, 30, no. 6 (1994): 506-12.

15. R. P. Oden, C. Powell, A. Sims, J. Weisman, B. L. Joyner, & R. Y. Moon, "Swaddling: Will it get babies onto their backs for sleep?" *Clinical Pediatrics*, 51, no. 3 (2011): 254-59.

16. P. Franco, N. Seret, J. Van Hees, S. Scaillet, J. Groswasser, & A. Kahn, "Influence of swaddling on sleep and arousal characteristics of healthy infants," *Pediatrics*, 115, no. 5 (2005): 1307-11.

17. E. McDonnell, & R. Y. Moon, "Infant deaths and injuries associated with wearable blankets, swaddle wraps, and swaddling," *The Journal of Pediatrics*, 164, no. 5 (2014): 1152-56.

18. B. E. Sleuwen, A. C. Engelberts, M. M. Boere-Boonekamp, W. Kuis, T. W. Schulpen, & M. P. L'Hoir, "Swaddling: A systematic review," *Pediatrics*, 120, no. 4 (2007): e1097-106.

19. Sleuwen et al., "Swaddling: A systematic review."

20. AAP TASK FORCE ON SUDDEN INFANT DEATH SYNDROME. SIDS and Other Sleep-Related Infant Deaths: Updated 2016 Recommendations for a Safe Infant Sleeping Environment. Pediatrics. 2016; 138(5): e20162938

21. Sleuwen et al., "Swaddling: A systematic review."

22. K. Kennedy, "Unwrapping the controversy over swaddling," *AAP News*, May 27, 2013, http://www.aappublications.org/content/34/6/34.full.

23. A. S. Pease, P. J. Fleming, F. R. Hauck, R. Y. Moon, R. S. C. Horne, M. P. Lhoir, A.-L. Ponsonby, and P. S. Blair. "Swaddling and the Risk of Sudden Infant Death Syndrome: A Meta-analysis." Pediatrics 137.6 (2016).

24. International Hip Dysplasia Institute, "Hip-healthy swaddling," http://hipdysplasia.org/developmental-dysplasia-of-the-hip/hip-healthy-swaddling/; C. T. Price & R. M. Schwend,

"Improper swaddling a risk factor for developmental dysplasia of hip," *A A P News*, August 31, 2011, http://www.aappublications.org/content/32/9/11.1.full.

25. A. Dubief, "Everything you ever hoped to know about swaddle blankets," Precious Little Sleep, May 10, 2013, http://www.preciouslittlesleep.com/swaddle-blankets/.

26. National Resource Center for Health and Safety in Child Care and Education, "Safe sleep practices and SIDS/suffocation risk reduction," applicable standards from American Academy of Pediatrics, American Public Health Association, National Resource Center for Health and Safety in Child Care and Early Education, *National Health and Safety Performance Standards: Guidelines for Early Care and Education Programs*, 3rd edition (Elk Grove Village, IL: American Academy of Pediatrics; Washington, DC: American Public Health Association, 2012).

27. F. R. Hauck, O. O. Omojokun, & M. S. Siadaty, "Do pacifiers reduce the risk of sudden infant death syndrome? A meta-analysis," *Pediatrics*, 116, no. 5 (2005): e716–23; D. K. Li, M. Willinger, D. Petitti, R. Odouli, L. Liu, & H. J. Hoffman, "Use of a dummy (pacifier) during sleep and risk of sudden infant death syndrome (SIDS): Population based case-control study," *BMJ*, 332, no. 7532 (2006): 18–22; AAP TASK FORCE ON SUDDEN INFANT DEATH SYNDROME. SIDS and Other Sleep-Related Infant Deaths: Updated 2016 Recommendations for a Safe Infant Sleeping Environment. Pediatrics. 2016; 138(5): e20162938

28. Franco et al., "The influence of a pacifier on infants' arousals from sleep."

29. Campos, "Soothing pain-elicited distress in infants with swaddling and pacifiers."

30. C. R. Howard, F. M. Howard, B. Lanphear, S. Eberly, E. A. Deblieck, D. Oakes, & R. A. Lawrence, "Randomized clinical trial of pacifier use and bottle-feeding or cupfeeding and their effect on breastfeeding," *Pediatrics*, 111, no. 3 (2003): 511–18.

31. S. H. Jaafar, S. Jahanafar, M. Angolkar, & J. M. Ho, "Pacifier use versus no pacifier use in breastfeeding term infants for increasing duration of breastfeeding," *Cochrane Database of Systemic Reviews*, 16, no. 3 (2011); L. R. Kair, D. Kenron, K. Etheredge, A. C. Jaffe, & C. A. Phillipi, "Pacifier restriction and exclusive breastfeeding," *Pediatrics*, 131, no. 4 (2013): e1101–7; M. S. Kramer, R. G. Barr, S. Dagenais, H. Yang, P. Jones, L. Ciofani, & F. Jane, "Pacifier use, early weaning, and cry/fuss behavior: A randomized controlled trial," *JAMA*, 286, no. 3 (2001): 322–26; N. R. O'Connor, K. O. Tanabe, M. S. Siadaty, & F. R. Hauck, "Pacifiers and breastfeeding: A systematic review," *Archives of Pediatrics & Adolescent Medicine*, 163, no. 4 (2009): 378–82; S. Ullah & P. Griffiths, "Does the use of pacifiers shorten breast-feeding duration in infants?" *British Journal of Community Nursing*, 8, no. 10 (2003): 458–63.

32. A. G. Jenik, N. E. Vain, A. N. Gorestein, & N. E. Jacobi, "Does the recommendation to use a pacifier influence the prevalence of breastfeeding?" *The Journal of Pediatrics*, 155, no. 3 (2009): 350–54.

33. P. Ollila, M. Niemelä, U. Uhari, & M. Larmas, "Prolonged pacifier-sucking and use of a nursing bottle at night: Possible risk factors for dental caries in children," *Acta Odontologica Scandinavica*, 56, no. 4 (1998): 233–37.

34. S. Sexton & R. Natale, "Risks and benefits of pacifiers," *American Family Physician*, 79, no. 8 (2009): 681–85.

35. W. Konrad, "How to plan for and handle the cost of braces," *The New York Times*, January 21, 2011, http://www.nytimes.com/2011/01/22/health/22patient.html?_r=0.

36. N. Cox & R. Hinkle, "Infant botulism," *American Family Physician*, 65, no. 7 (2002): 1388–93, http://www.aafp.org/afp/2002/0401/p1388.html; J. L. Hoecker, "How can I protect my baby from infant botulism?" Expert Answers, Infant and Toddler Health, Healthy Lifestyle, Mayo Clinic.

37. R. Leproult & E. Van Cauter, "Role of sleep and sleep loss in hormonal release and metabolism," *Endocrine Development*, 17 (2010): 11–21; K. Spiegel, R. Leproult, M. L'Hermite-Balériaux, G. Copinschi, P. D. Penev, & E. V. Cauter, "Leptin levels are dependent on sleep duration: Relationships with sympathovagal balance, carbohydrate regulation, cortisol, and thyrotropin," *The Journal of Clinical Endocrinology & Metabolism*, 89, no. 11 (2004): 5762–71; K. Spiegel, R. Leproult, & E. Van Cauter, "Impact of sleep debt on physiological rhythms," *Revue Neurologique*, 159, no. 11 suppl. (2003): 6S11–20.

38. J. Owens, "Insufficient sleep in adolescents and young adults: An update on causes and consequences," *Pediatrics*, 134, no. 3 (2014): e921–32.

39. K. McGraw, R. Hoffmann, C. Harker, & J. H. Herman, "The development of circadian rhythms in a human infant," *Sleep*, 22, no. 3 (1999): 303–10; J. M. Zeitzer, D. J. Dijk, R. E. Kronauer, E. N. Brown, & C. A. Czeisler, "Sensitivity of the human circadian pacemaker to nocturnal light: Melatonin phase resetting and suppression," *The Journal of Physiology*, 526, pt. 3 (2000): 695–702.

40. AAP Task Force, "SIDS and Other Sleep-Related Infant Deaths."

Chapter 7: Teaching Baby to Sleep, Part 2: SLIP (Sleep Learning Independence Plan)

1. A. Dubief, "Is sleep training child abuse?" Precious Little Sleep, February 12, 2015, https://www.preciouslittlesleep.com/is-sleep-training-child-abuse/.

2. J. Bowlby, *A Secure Base: Parent–Child Attachment and Healthy Human Development* (New York: Basic Books, 1988).

3. D. W. Beebe, "A brief primer on sleep for pediatric and child clinical neuropsychologists," *Child Neuropsychology*, 18, no. 4 (2012): 313–38; G. Fallone, J. A. Owens, & J. Deane, "Sleepiness in children and adolescents: Clinical implications," *Sleep Medicine Reviews*, 6, no. 4 (2002): 287–306.

4. J. Bowlby, *Attachment and Loss* (Harmondsworth, UK: Penguin, 1969).

5. A. M. Price, M. Wake, O. C. Ukoumunne, & H. Hiscock, "Five-year follow-up of harms and benefits of behavioral infant sleep intervention: Randomized trial," *Pediatrics*, 130, no. 4 (2012): 643–51.

6. K. T. Beuker, N. N. Rommelse, R. Donders, & J. K. Buitelaar, "Development of early communication skills in the first two years of life," *Infant Behavior and Development*, 36, no. 1 (2013): 71–83.

7. R. Ferber, *Solve Your Child's Sleep Problems* (New York: Simon & Schuster/Fireside, 2006).

8. T. I. Morgenthaler, J. Owens, C. Alessi, B. Boehlecke, T. M. Brown, J. Coleman Jr., ... & T. J. Swick, "Practice parameters for behavioral treatment of bedtime problems and night wakings in infants and young children," *Sleep*, 29, no. 10 (2006): 1277–81.

9. B. F. Skinner, *The Behavior of Organisms: An Experimental Analysis* (New York: Appleton-Century, 1938), p. 457.

10. J. Lim & D. F. Dinges, "A meta-analysis of the impact of short-term sleep deprivation on cognitive variables," *Psychological Bulletin*, 136, no. 3 (2010): 375–89.

11. D. C. Lerman & B. A. Iwata, "Prevalence of the extinction burst and its attenuation during treatment," *Journal of Applied Behavior Analysis*, 28, no. 1 (1995): 93–94.

12. D. McRaney, "Extinction burst" [blog post], July 7, 2010, http://youarenotsosmart.com/2010/07/07/extinction-burst/.

Chapter 9: Eating and Not Sleeping

1. J. L. Hoecker, "How much should I expect my baby to grow in the first year?" Expert Answers, Infant and Toddler Health, Healthy Lifestyle, Mayo Clinic, October 10, 2014, http://www.mayoclinic.org/healthy-lifestyle/infant-and-toddler-health/expert-answers/infant-growth/faq-20058037.
2. J. Eaton-Evans & A. E. Dugdale, "Sleep patterns of infants in the first year of life," *Archives of Disease in Childhood*, 63, no. 6 (1988): 647–49.
3. Eaton-Evans & Dugdale, "Sleep patterns of infants in the first year of life"; M. F. Elias, N. A. Nicolson, C. Bora, & J. Johnston, "Sleep/wake patterns of breast-fed infants in the first 2 years of life," *Pediatrics*, 77, no. 3 (1986): 322–29; O. G. Jenni, "A longitudinal study of bed sharing and sleep problems among Swiss children in the first 10 years of life," *Pediatrics*, 115, no. 1 (2005): 233–40; T. Pinilla & L. L. Birch, "Help me make it through the night: Behavioral entrainment of breast-fed infants' sleep patterns," *Pediatrics*, 91, no. 2 (1993): 436–44.
4. J. M. Henderson, K. G. France, J. L. Owens, & N. M. Blampied, "Sleeping through the night: The consolidation of self-regulated sleep across the first year of life," *Pediatrics*, 126, no. 5 (2010): e1081–87.
5. J. C. Kent, L. R. Mitoulas, M. D. Cregan, D. T. Ramsay, D. A. Doherty, & P. E. Hartmann, "Volume and frequency of breastfeedings and fat content of breast milk throughout the day," *Pediatrics*, 117, no. 3 (2006): e387–95.
6. M. Hamosh, "Breastfeeding: Unraveling the mysteries of mother's milk," *Medscape Women's Health*, 1, no. 9 (1996): 4; "How many calories are there in infant formula, ABBOTT NUTRITION, SIMILAC, ALIMENTUM, with iron, ready-to-feed (formerly ROSS)?" A Calorie Counter, http://www.acaloriecounter.com/food/infant-formula-abbott-nutrition-similac-alimentum-with-iron-ready-to-feed-formerly-ross-.
7. Earth's Best, http://www.earthsbest.com/.
8. International Lactation Consultant Association, http://www.ilca.org/home.
9. P. H. Finan, P. J. Quartana, & M. T. Smith, "The effects of sleep continuity disruption on positive mood and sleep architecture in healthy adults," *Sleep*, 38, no. 11 (2015): 1735–42.

Chapter 10: Becoming the Zen Nap Ninja Master

1. S. Coons & C. Guilleminault, "Development of sleep–wake patterns and non-rapid eye movement sleep stages during the first six months of life in normal infants," *Journal of the American Academy of Child Psychiatry*, 69, no. 6 (1982): 593.
2. K. McGraw, C. Harker, & J. H. Herman, "The development of circadian rhythms in a human infant," *Sleep*, 22, no. 3 (1999): 303–10.
3. A. Sadeh, J. A. Mindell, K. Luedtke, & B. Wiegand, "Sleep and sleep ecology in the first 3 years: A web-based study," *Journal of Sleep Research*, 18, no. 1 (2009): 60–73; T. M. Ward, C. Gay, T. F. Anders, A. Alkon, & K. A. Lee, "Sleep and napping patterns in 3-to-5-year old children attending full-day childcare centers," *Journal of Pediatric Psychology*, 33, no. 6 (2007): 666–72; M. Weissbluth, "Naps in children: 6 months–7 years," *Sleep*, 18, no. 2 (1995): 82–87.
4. S. Daan, G. M. Beersma, & A. A. Borbély, "Timing of human sleep: Recovery process gated by a circadian pacemaker," *The American Journal of Physiology*, 246, no. 2, pt. 2 (1984): R161–83.
5. B. S. McEwen, "Sleep deprivation as a neurobiologic and physiologic stressor: Allostasis and allostatic load," *Metabolism*, 55, no. 10, suppl. 2 (2006): S20–23.
6. A. Dubief, "Eat play sleep fail," Precious Little Sleep, April 5, 2013, https://www.preciouslittlesleep.com/eat-play-sleep-fail/.

Chapter 11: Why, When, and How to Wean Off Your Sleep Power Tools

1. M. Niemelä, O. Pihakari, T. Pokka, & M. Uhari, "Pacifier as a risk factor for acute otitis media: A randomized, controlled trial of parental counseling," *Pediatrics*, 106, no. 3 (2000): 483-88.
2. V. S. Nihi, S. M. Maciel, M. E. Jarrus, F. M. Nihi, C. L. Salles, R. C. Pascotto, & M. Fujimaki, "Pacifier-sucking habit duration and frequency on occlusal and myofunctional alterations in preschool children," *Brazilian Oral Research*, 29 (2015): 1-7; S. Sexton & R. Natale, "Risks and benefits of pacifiers," *American Family Physician*, 79, no. 8 (2009): 681-85.
3. P. Ollila, M. Niemelä, M. Uhari, & M. Larmas, "Prolonged pacifier-sucking and use of a nursing bottle at night: Possible risk factors for dental caries in children," *Acta Odontologica Scandinavica*, 56, no. 4 (1998): 233-37.
4. American Association of Pediatrics (AAP), Task Force on Sudden Infant Death Syndrome, "The changing concept of sudden infant death syndrome: Diagnostic coding shifts, controversies regarding the sleeping environment, and new variables to consider in reducing risk," *Pediatrics*, 116, no. 5 (2005): 1245-55.
5. Y. Kelly, J. Kelly, & A. Sacker, "Changes in bedtime schedules and behavioral difficulties in 7 year old children," *Pediatrics*, 132, no. 5 (2013): 1184-93.
6. A. R. Wolfson & M. A. Carskadon, "Sleep schedules and daytime functioning in adolescents," *Child Development*, 69, no. 4 (1998): 875-87.
7. A. K. Pesonen, K. Räikkönen, E. J. Paavonen, K. Heinonen, N. Komsi, J. Lahti, ... & T. Strandberg, "Sleep duration and regularity are associated with behavioral problems in 8-year-old children," *International Journal of Behavioral Medicine*, 17, no. 4 (2009): 298-305.
8. M. A. Short, M. Gradisar, H. Wright, L. C. Lack, H. Dohnt, & M. A. Carskadon, "Time for bed: Parent-set bedtimes associated with improved sleep and daytime functioning in adolescents," *Sleep*, 34, no. 6 (2011): 797-800.

Chapter 12: (Un)Common Sleep Setbacks

1. F. X. Plooij, "The trilogy of mind," pp. 185-206 in *Regression Periods in Human Infancy*, edited by M. Heimann (New York: Routledge, 2003).
2. H. Vanderijt & F. X. Plooij, *The Wonder Weeks: How to Turn Your Baby's 8 Great Fussy Phases into Magical Leaps Forward* (Emmaus, PA: Rodale, 2003).
3. Plooij, "The trilogy of mind."
4. A. Scher & D. Cohen, "Sleep as a mirror of developmental transitions in infancy: The case of crawling," *Monographs of the Society for Research in Child Development*, 80, no. 1 (2015): 70-88.
5. M. D. Ainsworth & S. M. Bell, "Attachment, exploration, and separation: Illustrated by the behavior of one-year-olds in a strange situation," *Child Development*, 41, no. 1 (1970): 49-67; J. Bowlby, "Separation anxiety," *The International Journal of Psychoanalysis*, 41 (1960): 89-113.
6. D. Benoit, C. H. Zeanah, C. Boucher, & K. K. Minde, "Sleep disorders in early childhood: Association with insecure maternal attachment," *Journal of the American Academy of Child & Adolescent Psychiatry*, 31, no. 1 (1992): 86-93; M. S. Moore, "Disturbed attachment in children: A factor in sleep disturbance, altered dream production and immune dysfunction: 1," *Journal of Child Psychotherapy*, 15, no. 1 (1989): 99-111; A. Sadeh & T. F. Anders, "Infant sleep problems: Origins, assessment, interventions," *Infant Mental Health Journal*, 14, no. 1 (1993): 17-34.
7. S. Moturi & K. Avis, "Assessment and treatment of common pediatric sleep disorders," *Psychiatry*, 7, no. 6 (2010): 24-37.

8. C. I. Eastman & H. J. Burgess, "How to travel the world without jet lag," *Sleep Medicine Clinics*, 4, no. 2 (2009): 241–55.

9. D. B. Boivin, J. F. Duffy, R. E. Kronauer, & C. A. Czeisler, "Dose–response relationships for resetting of human circadian clock by light," *Nature*, 379, no. 6565 (1996): 540–42.

10. J. F. Duffy & C. A. Czeisler, "Effect of light on human circadian physiology," *Sleep Medicine Clinics*, 4, no. 2 (2009): 165–77.

11. S. W. Lockley & R. G. Foster, *Sleep: A Very Short Introduction* (Oxford: Oxford University Press, 2012).

12. Duffy & Czeisler, "Effect of light on human circadian physiology"; J. M. Zeitzer, D. J. Dijk, R. E. Kronauer, E. N. Brown & C. A. Czeisler, "Sensitivity of the human circadian pacemaker to nocturnal light: Melatonin phase resetting and suppression," *The Journal of Physiology*, 526, pt. 3 (2000): 695–702.

13. M. A. Bonmati-Carrion, R. Arguelles-Prieto, M. J. Martinez-Madrid, R. Reiter, R. Hardeland, M. A. Rol, & J. A. Madrid, "Protecting the melatonin rhythm through circadian healthy light exposure," *International Journal of Molecular Sciences*, 15, no. 12 (2014): 23448–500.

14. J. C. Pereira Jr. & R. C. Alves, "The 'forbidden zone for sleep' might be caused by the evening thyrotropin surge and its biological purpose is to enhance survival: A hypothesis," *Sleep Medicine*, 12, suppl. 1 (2011): S34.

15. R. Leproult, G. Copinschi, O. Buxton, & E. Van Cauter, "Sleep loss results in an elevation of cortisol levels the next evening," *Journal of Sleep Research & Sleep Medicine*, 20, no. 10 (1997): 865; K. Spiegel, R. Leproult, & E. Van Cauter, "Impact of sleep debt on metabolic and endocrine function," *The Lancet*, 354, no. 9188 (1999): 1435–39.

16. M. Randall, "The physiology of stress: Cortisol and the hypothalamic–pituitary–adrenal axis," *Dartmouth Undergraduate Journal of Science* (2011), http://dujs.dartmouth.edu/2011/02/the-physiology-of-stress-cortisol-and-the-hypothalamic-pituitary-adrenal-axis/#.VxFiWDArKHs.

17. Boivin et al., "Dose–response relationships for resetting of human circadian clock by light."

Chapter 13: Older Kids, Siblings, and Twins

1. National Sleep Foundation (NSF), *2004 Sleep in America Poll: Summary of Findings* (Washington, DC: National Sleep Foundation, 2004), https://sleepfoundation.org/sites/default/files/FINAL SOF 2004.pdf.

2. IgniterMedia, "The Marshmallow Test" [video], September 24, 2009, https://www.youtube.com/watch?v=QX_oy9614HQ.

3. J. A. Mindell & J. A. Owens, *A Clinical Guide to Pediatric Sleep: Diagnosis and Management of Sleep Problems* (Philadelphia: Lippincott Williams & Wilkins, 2003).

4. J. A. Martin, B. E. Hamilton, M. J. Osterman, S. C. Curtin, & R. J. Mathews, "Births: Final data for 2011," *National Vital Statistics Reports*, 62 (2013): 1–69.

5. M. H. Malloy & H. J. Hoffman, "Prematurity, sudden infant death syndrome, and age of death," *Pediatrics*, 96, no. 3 (1995): 464–71.

6. AAP TASK FORCE ON SUDDEN INFANT DEATH SYNDROME. SIDS and Other Sleep-Related Infant Deaths: Updated 2016 Recommendations for a Safe Infant Sleeping Environment. Pediatrics. 2016; 138(5): e20162938

7. NSF, *2004 Sleep in America Poll*.

8. Mindell & Owens, *A Clinical Guide to Pediatric Sleep*.

9. R. Ferber, *Solve Your Child's Sleep Problems* (New York: Simon & Schuster/Fireside, 2006).

10. Mindell & Owens, *A Clinical Guide to Pediatric Sleep*.

Appendix: Potential Medical Complications for Sleep

1. S. P. Nelson, E. H. Chen, G. Svniar, & K. K. Christoffel, "Prevalence of symptoms of gastroesophageal reflux during infancy: A pediatric practice-based survey," *Archives of Pediatric & Adolescent Medicine*, 151, no. 6 (1996): 569–72.

2. A. D. Jung, "Gastroesophageal reflux in infants and children," *American Family Physician*, 64, no. 11 (2001): 1853–61.

3. J. E. Dranove, "Focus on diagnosis," *American Academy of Pediatrics*, 29, no. 9 (2008), 317–20; J. R. Lightdale & D. A. Gremse, "Gastroesophageal reflux: management guidance for the pediatrician," *Pediatrics*, 131, no. 5 (2013): e1684–95; Y. Vandenplas, C. D. Rudolph, C. D. Lorenzo, E. Hassall, G. Liptak, L. Mazur, . . . & T. G. Wenzl, "Pediatric gastroesophageal reflux clinical practice guidelines: Joint recommendations of the North American Society for Pediatric Gastroenterology, Hepatology, and Nutrition (NASPGHAN) and the European Society for Pediatric Gastroenterology, Hepatology, and Nutrition (ESPGHAN)," *Journal of Pediatric Gastroenterology and Nutrition*, 49, no. 4 (2009): 498–547.

4. E. Hassall, "Over-prescription of acid-suppressing medications in infants: How it came about, why it's wrong, and what to do about it," *The Journal of Pediatrics*, 160, no. 2 (2012): 193–98.

5. S. R. Orenstein, E. Hassall, W. Furmaga-Jablonska, S. Atkinson, & M. Raanan, "Multicenter, double-blind, randomized, placebo-controlled trial assessing the efficacy and safety of proton pump inhibitor lansoprazole in infants with symptoms of gastroesophageal reflux disease," *The Journal of Pediatrics*, 154, no. 4 (2009): 514–20.

6. R. Machado, F. W. Woodley, B. Skaggs, C. D. Lorenzo, M. Splaingard, & H. Mousa, "Gastroesophageal reflux causing sleep interruptions in infants," *Journal of Pediatric Gastroenterology and Nutrition*, 56, no. 4 (2013): 431–35.

7. A. S. Dhillon & A. K. Ewer, "Diagnosis and management of gastro-oesophageal reflux in preterm infants in neonatal intensive care units," *Acta Paediatrica*, 93, no. 1 (2004): 88–93.

8. G. Iacono, A. Carroccio, F. Cavataio, G. Montalto, I. Kazmierska, D. Lorello, . . . & A. Notarbartolo, "Gastroesophageal reflux and cow's milk allergy in infants: A prospective study," *Journal of Allergy and Clinical Immunology*, 97, no. 3 (1996): 822–27.

9. S. Salvatore & Y. Vandenplas, "Gastroesophageal reflux and cow milk allergy: Is there a link?" *Pediatrics*, 110, no. 5 (2002): 972–84.

10. J. F. Helm, W. J. Dodds, & W. J. Hogan, "Salivary response to esophageal acid in normal subjects and patients with reflux esophagitis," *Gastroenterology*, 93, no. 6 (1987): 1393–97; A. Shafik, O. El-Sibai, A. A. Shafik, & R. Mostafa, "Effect of topical esophageal acidification on salivary secretion: Identification of the mechanism of action," *Journal of Gastroenterology and Hepatology*, 20, no. 12 (2005): 1935–39.

11. A. Horvath, P. Dziechciarz, & H. Szajewska, "The effect of thickened-feed interventions on gastroesophageal reflux in infants: Systematic review and meta-analysis of randomized, controlled trials," *Pediatrics*, 122, no. 6 (2008): 1268–77.

12. J. R. Lightdale & D. A. Gremse, "Gastroesophageal reflux: Management guidance for the pediatrician," *Pediatrics*, 131, no. 5 (2013): 1684–95.

13. S. P. Nelson, E. H. Chen, G. M. Syniar, & K. K. Christoffel, "Prevalence of symptoms of gastroesophageal reflux during infancy," *Archives of Pediatrics & Adolescent Medicine*, 151, no. 6 (1997): 569–72.

14. R. J. Rona, T. Keil, C. Summers, D. Gislason, L. Zuidmeer, E. Sodergren, . . . & C. Madsen, "The prevalence of food allergy: A meta-analysis," *Journal of Allergy and Clinical Immunology*, 120, no. 3 (2007): 638–46.

15. R. S. Gupta, E. E. Springston, M. R. Warrier, B. Smith, R. Kumar, J. Pongracic, & J. L. Holl, "The prevalence, severity, and distribution of childhood food allergy in the United States," *Pediatrics*, 128, no. 1 (2011): e9-17; K. D. Jackson, L. D. Howie, & L. J. Akinbami, "Trends in allergic conditions among children: United States, 1997-2011," *Data Briefs*, 121 (May 2013), National Center for Health Statistics, Centers for Disease Control and Prevention, http://www.cdc.gov/nchs/data/databriefs/db121.htm.

16. J. J. Schneider, S. J. Newberry, M. A. Riedl, D. M. Bravata, M. Maglione, M. J. Suttorp, . . . & P. G. Shekelle, "Diagnosing and managing common food allergies: A systematic review," *The Journal of the American Medical Association*, 303, no. 18 (2010): 1848-56.

17. H. A. Sampson, "Food allergy: Accurately identifying clinical reactivity," *Allergy*, 60, suppl. 79 (2005): 19-24.

18. S. H. Sicherer & H. A. Sampson, "Food allergy," *The Journal of Allergy and Clinical Immunology*, 125, suppl. 2, no. 2 (2010): S116-25.

19. A. Høst, "Frequency of cow's milk allergy in childhood," *Annals of Allergy, Asthma & Immunology*, 89, no. 6 (2002): 33-37.

20. M. P. Ross, M. Ferguson, D. Street, K. Klontz, T. Schroeder, & S. Luccioli, "Analysis of food-allergic and anaphylactic events in the National Electronic Injury Surveillance System," *Journal of Allergy and Clinical Immunology*, 121, no. 1 (2008): 166-71.

21. S. A. Bock, "Adverse reactions to foods during the first three years of life," *Pediatrics*, 79, no. 5 (1987): 683-88.

22. S. A. Hulland, J. O. Lucas, M. A. Wake, & K. D. Hesketh, "Eruption of the primary dentition in human infants: A prospective descriptive study," *American Academy of Pediatric Dentistry*, 22, no. 5 (1999): 415-21.

23. M. Wake, K. Hesketh, & J. Lucas, "Teething and tooth eruption in infants: A cohort study," *Pediatrics*, 106, no. 6 (2000): 1374-79.

24. American Academy of Pediatrics (AAP), "Teething care & anticipatory guidance," *Protecting All Children's Teeth (PACT): A Pediatric Oral Health Training Program*, Children's Oral Health.

25. J. Snyder, "Amber waves of woo" [blog post], Science-Based Medicine, April 11, 2014, http://www.sciencebasedmedicine.org/amber-waves-of-woo/.

26. American Academy of Pediatrics (AAP), "Clinical practice guideline: Diagnosis and management of childhood obstructive sleep apnea syndrome," *Pediatrics*, 109, no. 4 (2002): 704-12.

27. C. L. Marcus, L. J. Brooks, K. A. Draper, D. Gozal, A. C. Halbower, J. Jones, . . . & R. N. Shiffman, "Diagnosis and management of childhood obstructive sleep apnea syndrome," *Pediatrics*, 130, no. 3 (2012): 576-84.

28. S. L. Garetz, R. B. Mitchell, P. D. Parker, R. H. Moore, C. L. Rosen, B. Giordani, . . . & S. Redline, "Quality of life and obstructive sleep apnea symptoms after pediatric adenotonsillectomy," *Pediatrics*, 135, no. 2 (2015): e477-86.

29. R. P. Allen, D. Picchietti, W. A. Hening, C. Trenkwalder, A. S. Walters, & J. Montplaisi, "Restless legs syndrome: Diagnostic criteria, special considerations, and epidemiology," *Sleep Medicine*, 4, no. 2 (2003): 101-19.

30. K. Ekbom & J. Ulfberg, "Restless legs syndrome," *Journal of Internal Medicine*, 266, no. 5 (2009): 419-31.

31. D. Picchietti, R. P. Allen, A. S. Walters, J. E. Davidson, A. Myers, & L. Ferini-Strambi, "Restless legs syndrome: Prevalence and impact in children and adolescents: The Peds REST Study," *Pediatrics*, 120, no. 2 (2007): 253-66.

32. National Center for Health Statistics, Centers for Disease Control and Prevention, "Births and natality," last updated February 25, 2016, http://www.cdc.gov/nchs/fastats/births.htm.

33. M. H. Malloy & H. J. Hoffman, "Prematurity, sudden infant death syndrome, and age of death," *Pediatrics*, 96, no. 3 (1995): 464-71; E. A. Mitchell, R. Scragg, A. W. Stewart, D. M. Becroft, B. J. Taylor, R. P. Ford, . . . & A. P. Roberts, "Results from the first year of the New Zealand Cot Death Study," *New Zealand Medical Journal*, 104, no. 906 (1991): 71-76; B. Sowter, L. W. Doyle, C. J. Morley, A. Altmann, & J. Halliday, "Is sudden infant death syndrome still more common in very low birthweight infants in the 1990s?" *Medical Journal of Australia*, 171, no. 8 (1999): 411-13.

34. N. Oyen, T. Markestad, L. M. Irgens, K. Helweg-Larsen, B. Alm, G. Norvenius, . . . & R. Skjaerven, "Combined effects of sleeping position and prenatal risk factors in sudden infant death syndrome: The Nordic Epidemiological SIDS Study," *Pediatrics*, 100, no. 4 (1997): 613-21.

35. L. Vernacchio, M. J. Corwin, S. M. Lesko, R. M. Vezina, C. E. Hunt, H. J. Hoffman, . . . & A. A. Mitchell, "Sleep position of low birth weight infants," *Pediatrics*, 111, no. 3 (2003): 633-40.

36. R. Feldman, A. Weller, L. Sirota, & A. I. Eidelman, "Skin-to-skin contact (kangaroo care) promotes self-regulation in premature infants: Sleep-wake cyclicity, arousal modulation, and sustained exploration," *Developmental Psychology*, 38, no. 2 (2002): 194-207.

37. M. A. Short, J. A. Brooks-Brunn, D. S. Reeves, J. Yeager, & J. A. Thorpe, "The effects of swaddling versus standard positioning on neuromuscular development in very low birth weight infants," *Neonatal Network*, 15, no. 4 (1996): 25-31.

Index

About the Author

ALEXIS DUBIEF gave birth to her first child in 2006 and quickly realized that sleep—or a lack thereof—was suddenly the bane of her existence. Yet no book, website, or community seemed to have ready answers. Figuring that "this shouldn't be so hard," she spent the next five years researching and analyzing infant and child sleep. Combining scientific evidence with insights gleaned from working with thousands of families, she founded the *Precious Little Sleep* blog/podcast in 2011. In just a few short years, this passion project meant to demystify baby sleep blossomed into a popular online destination for sleep-starved parents from all over the world, garnering millions of hits annually and inspiring a loyal following. Dubief holds a Master of Finance and an MBA from the University of Colorado. A trail runner and Spartan racer, she writes and rabble rouses near Burlington, VT, with her husband and their two boys who are growing up faster than she would like.

Made in the USA
Coppell, TX
07 December 2020